The Metamorphoses of the City of God

The Metamorphoses of the City of God

Étienne Gilson

Translated by James G. Colbert

FOREWORD BY RÉMI BRAGUE

THE CATHOLIC UNIVERSITY
OF AMERICA PRESS
Washington, D.C.

Originally published as *Les Métamorphoses de la cité de Dieu*

http://www.vrin.fr

The paper used in this publication meets the minimum
requirements of American National Standards for Information
Science—Permanence of Paper for Printed Library Materials,
ANSI Z39.48-1984.
∞

Cataloging-in-Publication Data available
from the Library of Congress
ISBN 978-0-8132-3325-3

CONTENTS

FOREWORD

RÉMI BRAGUE

As a Frenchman who cares for the United States, I cannot help feeling some vicarious embarrassment whenever, while browsing in the "cultural studies" section of some academic bookshop, I stumble upon the kind of intellectual wares that my country exports, especially what is commonly known as "French theory." As a Catholic, my pains are alleviated when I think of some French thinkers who made their careers, or part of them, on the Western shores of the pond. Taking up the task of the French missionaries who evangelized Louisiana (before and after the purchase of 1803) and newly conquered southern states, they contributed to raise the level of consciousness and learning of many students.[1] And at the same time, they greatly benefited from the experience of a living democracy at peace with the Churches that embody the deep intellectual and spiritual roots of democratic life, in a country in which Catholics sided with the poor and were eager to help them. Alongside many Jewish scholars and scientists, like the Russian-born philosopher Alexandre Koyré or the mathematician André Weil (Simone Weil's brother), the first Catholic names that spring to the mind are Jacques Maritain, who spent the years of the last World War in New York, and of his disciple Yves Simon. More recently, René Girard spent his whole career in Maryland and later in California, where he died. Nowadays, Jean-Luc Marion (a friend of more than fifty years) has been spending some months at the University of Chicago for more than twenty-five years.

Among those Catholic great minds, Étienne Gilson (1884–

1. See Earl Boyea, *Gabriel Richard: Servant of God* (Ann Arbor, Mich.: University Litho, 2000), and the wonderful 1927 novel by Willa Cather, *Death Comes for the Archbishop*.

1978) may deserve pride of place. On this giant of French intellectual life, we possess two biographies, which happily complement each other. Laurence Shook has produced a careful chronicle of Gilson's life and achievements.[2] Recently, Florian Michel has written a thoroughly researched intellectual and political biography, crammed with unpublished material: private letters, articles found in little-known places (even in newspapers), etc.[3]

Gilson would cross the ocean once or twice a year in order to teach, first at Harvard, then in Toronto, where he founded the Pontifical Institute of Mediaeval Studies.[4] Fluent in English, he wrote several books directly in this language. Some partially overlap works in his native French, like *L'Être et l'essence* (1948, later 1962), summarized in *Being and Some Philosophers* (1949). Some broach original topics in a way that has no equivalent in French, like the extraordinary (in my opinion) *The Unity of Philosophical Experience* (1937). Those books are being translated into Gilson's native language by some monks of Fontgombault, who wish to remain anonymous—which enables me to say that they are doing a superb job without my jeopardizing their humility.

The lectures that the present work reproduces were given in May 1952. This date is not insignificant, for it constitutes the context. The pope is Pius XII. Harry Truman is president of the United States, Konrad Adenauer, premier of Western Germany. In France, the president—then a merely symbolic figure—is Vincent Auriol and the premier, Antoine Pinay. Stalin is at the peak of his power: the Soviet Union has atomic weapons, and the countries of Eastern and Central Europe are under his sway. Mao Zedong, who seized power in China in 1949, is still Stalin's faithful ally. So-called Marxism-Leninism, together with its secular arm, the Red Army, are clear and present dangers.

2. L. Shook, *Étienne Gilson* (Toronto: PIMS, 1985).

3. F. Michel, *Étienne Gilson: Une biographie intellectuelle et politique* (Paris: Vrin, 2018).

4. Ibid., chap. 3.

Two long-run movements are playing the lead in the cultural atmosphere of the postwar world. First, as Gilson observes right at the outset, there takes place an overall movement toward what we now call "globalization." It had already set in, perhaps for centuries or even millennia, but its speed kept increasing in the wake of science and technology. Parallel to the improvement of knowledge, power, and communication, Gilson feels that a "universal human society" is in the pangs of childbirth (3). The founding of the United Nations (1945) may be a sign of this.

The second fact, at a smaller scale, is that the European countries (at least the Western half of the continent) are groping for some sort of union. Gilson did not remain a simple onlooker, but actively took part in those attempts. As a member of the French delegation, he played an important, albeit discreet, role in the wording of the UNESCO Charter.[5] In 1948, he took part in the Congress of United Europe in The Hague, where he gave a lecture and listened to one given by Winston Churchill, a fact that he mentions in the present work (172n3). He objects to a federal solution, which would perpetuate division instead of fostering unity (189).

Little wonder that Gilson should have chosen a topic whose actuality he deeply felt, although one of its monikers, "Christendom," had been at the center of his attention for many years. We possess a letter of 1921 to another philosopher, Xavier Léon, in which Gilson sketches what would become, thirty years later, the present work.[6] The book consists of a series of short monographs that follow "the high road that descends from St. Augustine towards us across the centuries" (189). It begins with an analysis of *The City of God*, which Gilson sees, most revealingly, as a later parallel to the *Letter to Diognetus*, an early anonymous work of apologetics that he

5. Ibid., 175–87.

6. Ibid., 131; in addition, 125–41 sheds much light on the intellectual context of the work.

quotes three times (37, 77, 233).[7] This parallel, if properly understood, would be enough to reestablish the real genealogy of Augustine's masterpiece, thereby staving off the long series of misunderstandings, all of which tried to force the heavenly citizenship to fit into an earthly polity, with a full-fledged system of policy—and police. Little wonder that the emperor of the West, hailed as "Father of Europe" *(pater Europae)*, Charlemagne, liked the work to be read aloud for him.[8] Yet, the real meaning of Augustine's *civitas* is Paul's πολιτευμα as a "way of life," a "citizenship" whose abode is "in heavens" (Phil 3:20) rather than a political entity. Augustine's real intellectual forebears are the apologists of the second century.

The chapters deal, in chronological order, with various attempts at conceiving (more than building) a unity of humankind.[9] This unity can hardly limit itself to mere commercial links, military treatises of alliance, or simple coexistence in the same space. It must tally with the definition of a *civitas* by Augustine that Gilson puts at the very beginning of his work, like its motto: "A people is a multitude of rational beings joined together by common agreement on the objects of their love."[10] There must be a common good that each member of the *civitas* strives to reach. But whenever this common good is not God, any attempt at building such a society is doomed to failure.

Each of these attempts is something like a caricature of the Christian Church. Roger Bacon has the conversion of non-Christian nations depend on other principles than faith (65). Some, like Nicholas of Cusa, water down the Christian dogma by simply silently dropping some of its elements and by replacing faith with

7. The last reference alludes to a particular passage: *A Diognète*, ed. H.-I. Marrou, Sources Chrétiennes 33 (Paris: Cerf, 1965), 64.

8. Einhard, *Vita Karoli Magni / Das Leben Karls des Großen*, ed. E. S. Firchow (Stuttgart: Reclam, 1981), 46.

9. This rule allows a single, slight exception: chapter 7 focuses on the Abbé de Saint-Pierre (1658–1743) and Rousseau (1712–78), while chapter 8 focuses on Leibniz (1646–1716).

10. Augustine, *De civitate Dei* XIX.24; ed. C. J. Perl (Paderborn: Schöningh, 1979), 2:508.

intelligence of faith (134, 149). After Campanella, charity could be replaced by law, and faith replaced by natural reason and metaphysics (168). Others, with Leibniz, translate faith into a philosophical worldview and empty it of its religious content (191). With his positivist *Catechism*, his new calendar with "great men" as saints, etc., Auguste Comte bluntly apes Christianity, or more precisely the Catholic Church, by replacing faith with "Science." His attitude toward God is, more than plain atheism, an "anti-theism" (213n15).[11] His work is "the final metamorphosis of the City of God into an earthly city" (216).

Or perhaps only the last but one, its last *intellectual* metamorphosis, for the Soviet empire may have represented the last stage of an attempt at its *concrete* enactment. Gilson, who could speak Russian, had been in Ukraine in 1922 for the French equivalent of the Hoover Relief Mission and had seen the horrors wrought by the new regime,[12] and he never flirted with communism like so many French "intellectuals" of his time. Indeed, he hardly pulls his punches against it (see 219n1, 231n10, 232n11).

Now, the lesson Gilson draws from those attempts is the need for clarification. He dispels the common confusion of identifying Europe and Christendom. This confusion already loomed in the Abbé de Saint-Pierre; it was theorized from the time of Novalis's half ironical speech by this title,[13] and it is still rampant in some circles, which lump together Christendom and "the West." Gilson qualifies the famous statement, without his naming its author: "The Faith is Europe and Europe is the Faith."[14] Whereas he wholeheartedly accepts the second sentence, he rejects the first

11. On Comte, see the detailed analysis by H. de Lubac, *Le Drame de l'humanisme athée*, second part: *Auguste Comte et le christianisme* (Paris: Cerf, 1998), 141–278.

12. Michel, *Étienne Gilson*, 108–14.

13. Novalis (Friedrich von Hardenberg), *Die Christenheit oder Europa* (1799), in *Schriften*, vol. 1: *Das philosophisch-theoretische Werk*, ed. H.-J. Mähl (Darmstadt: Wissenschaftliche Buchgesellschaft, 1999), 732–50.

14. Introduction to Hilaire Belloc, *Europe and the Faith* (London: Constable, 1920).

one (178). According to him, Europe, or for that matter the West, may *belong to* Christendom without *being* Christendom. Christendom is the Christian Gospel as received and produced by the local worldview, with effects that remain partial. A Christendom that would fully deserve the name would coincide with the Church. The City of God is the Church, and nothing else. Every attempt at aping it in the form of an earthly kingdom begets monsters.

Interestingly, Gilson quotes as an already hackneyed idea the avowal according to which Europe will be a body that badly needs a soul and is looking for it (189). Now, his and my fellow countryman Jacques Delors (1925–)—a Catholic, by the way, albeit a discreet one[15]—once chairman of the European Commission (1985–94), made a buzz in the early nineties by asking for "a soul for Europe." This was forty years after Gilson's sober and sobering observation: "when Europe attempts to reflect on itself and formulate its own essence, it tends to be dissolved in a broader society than itself, for which in fact it recognizes no other limits than those of the globe" (177). Defining the European man is an impossible enterprise that can even lead to contradictory statements (182n12).[16] A European "soul" would, if it were really a soul, be broader than Europe and include the whole world (96, 177).

Gilson rounds up his reflections with a bold, albeit traditional, thesis, theological in nature: grace does not abolish nature, but brings it to perfection (*gratia non tollit naturam, sed perficit eam*). This could be understood as meaning that grace builds upon the level of nature and adds a higher story to this foundation. Gilson interprets the formula as meaning that grace lifts up nature (another meaning of *tollere*!) to itself and enables it thereby to become what it had to be. Unaided, nature cannot reach its own fulfillment by its own exertions. Nature depends on grace for it to be able fully

15. See Joseph H. H. Weiler, *Ein christliches Europa: Erkundungsgänge* (München: Pustet, 2004), 21–22.

16. A clear allusion to Denis de Rougemont's September 1946 speech, *Les maladies de l'Europe*, in *L'Esprit européen* (Neuchâtel: La Baconnière, 1947), 155.

to unfold its own naturalness (123n39). "Nature is only more perfectly nature by being informed by grace" (125). In another work, Gilson claimed that, in the same way, theology alone can free philosophy of its own limitations: "Seeing philosophy in the light of the divine revelation, sacred science descries in it possibilities of which natural theology itself is unaware."[17] By this token, Christianity as such, not as "Christian civilization," not as "Christian values," or leprechauns of all ilks, but as Christian *faith*, has a maieutic function toward human experience in its whole.

The cultural backdrop against which works like the *Letter to Diognetus* and Augustine's *The City of God* were written resembles very much the one against which we have to live again in the present day. Hence the extraordinary actuality of Augustine's and Gilson's reflections. The latter points this out elsewhere in an extremely far-reaching sentence, which sketches our present predicament: "For the first time since the end of the ancient era, the Western world has begun not only to reject Christian faith, but to refuse to live on the moral and intellectual capital that Christianity had hoarded up for it."[18] Modern Western culture is parasitic in nature, a fact that had already been observed by people like Charles Péguy and G. K. Chesterton.[19] If the modern Western mistletoe finally succeeds in killing the Christian oak whose sap it has been draining but not renewing for now a matter of two or three centuries, it will not be able to survive much longer.

17. Étienne Gilson, *Elements of Christian Philosophy* (Garden City: Doubleday and Co., 1960), 34.

18. Étienne Gilson, *Pour un ordre catholique* (1934), chap. 4, §24 (Paris: Parole et Silence, 2013), 162. The book, although it refers to concrete problems of French Catholicism of the prewar period, and especially problems of the Catholic school system, deserves translation.

19. C. Péguy, *De la situation faite au parti intellectuel dans le monde moderne devant les accidents de la gloire temporelle* (1907), in *Œuvres en prose*, ed. R. Burac (Paris: Gallimard, 1988), 2:725; G. K. Chesterton, "Is Humanism a Religion?," in *The Thing* (London: Sheed and Ward, 1929), 16. Gilson admired Chesterton and quotes him twice in the present work, 168 and 233, from *Orthodoxy* (1908) (San Francisco, Calif.: Ignatius Press, 1995), 24 and 35.

To end on a positive note, I am happy that the Catholic University of America Press and Professor James Colbert had the good idea of translating this book. I hope that other new translations of Gilson will follow. In any case, I wish this one full success.

TRANSLATOR'S NOTE

Étienne Gilson delivered the lectures that constitute the "substance" of the *Metamorphoses of the City of God* as the European Union was being born, or perhaps better, was still in gestation. In 2020, the EU seems to be in something of a crisis. It certainly does not conceive of itself as a metamorphosis of the City of God. This may be an auspicious moment to revisit the visions offered by Gilson's thinkers, from Augustine to Auguste Comte. At the very least, we could ask whether any such overarching vision is possible today and, if not, what that means. Here, I think, Gilson has something to tell us.

A few practical observations: Gilson's decisions about capitalization occasionally seem to this translator idiosyncratic and not entirely consistent. I have tried to establish consistency in the use of capital letters and to conform to something like recognizable practice in English. So, since City of God is capitalized, City of Man is as well. As Supreme Pontiff and Church are capitalized, so are Emperor and Empire when, as happens in Dante, we are talking about the real or even ideal temporal society parallel to the universal Church. I have also capitalized State when it refers to the political arrangement, as opposed to some natural or psychic phase.

I have sought the English originals of quoted works and English translations, where available, of material Gilson had translated into French. I have checked Gilson's footnotes for some of the primary sources, notably St. Augustine, *De Civitate Dei*, and Roger Bacon, *Opus Tertium* and *Compendium Philosophiae*.

A word may be in order about the numbering of psalms. Gilson followed the enumeration of the Septuagint (and the Vulgate). The Hebrew text has a slightly different numeration, to which Protestants returned at the time of the Reformation and which has become universal in the past few decades. Both enumerations have a total of 150 psalms. St. Augustine follows the Septuagint. Translations of Augustine's works sometimes correct his enumeration of the psalms (making the English different from the Latin).

To avoid confusion, below is a helpful table that I have adapted from *A Catholic Commentary on Holy Scripture*, edited by Bernard Orchard et al. (London: Thomas Nelson and Sons, 1953), section 335d:

Hebrew and contemporary numbering	Septuagint and Vulgate numbering
1 through 8	1 through 8
9 and 10	9
11 through 113	10 through 112
114 and 115	113
116	114 and 115
117 through 146	116 through 145
147	146 and 147
148 through 150	148 through 150

—*James G. Colbert*

The Metamorphoses of the City of God

Preface

THIS BOOK contains the substance of the Cardinal Mercier Chair inaugural course delivered at the University of Louvain in May 1952. We gladly accepted the invitation to publish this text. The lectures are found here as they were delivered. None of them has any interest outside of the sequence that they constitute. Some notes or references, fewer or more numerous according to different chapters, have been added with a view to publication, but they cannot transform this course into a scholarly endeavor. Here, history is only the raw material for philosophical reflection, and incidentally the occasion for a layman to pose a question to theologians. We are not aware of any explicit theological treatment of Christendom. We would like to know whether this notion must be regarded as strictly identical to that of "Church," or if it is distinguished and how. The remarks scattered throughout the book, especially at its close, do not express an intention to dogmatize about a problem that escapes the competence of a historian of philosophy. Their only object is to gather some of its data and to clarify the meaning of the question.

The disparate views of history from which we take the occasion to raise the problem of the City of God mark the steps of a development that we do not regard as progress. We hope this will be seen clearly, but perhaps some confusion will arise about the subject matter of our reflections. Here, we are not directly dealing with the concept of the Church, nor even with the relations of the temporal and the spiritual, but only with a concept that still remains extremely confused, the notion of the people formed by Christians dispersed throughout all the nations of the earth, whose temporal relations are, or should be, affected by their shared membership in the Church. This explains the absence of illustrious names like

St. Bonaventure, St. Thomas Aquinas, or Duns Scotus. It is precisely why the problem ought to be proposed. Does the *Respublica Fidelium* of which Roger Bacon speaks so well, which we ordinarily call *Christendom*, stem from an error of perspective to which laymen are especially exposed by the fact that their involvement in the temporal realm makes them exaggerate its importance? Or, on the contrary, do we reach a point where the reality of Christendom must be acknowledged, described, defined, and integrated into its place in the concept of Church? If the theologians, for whom it is easy to understand that the problem is less urgent than for the laity, judge that the problem is meaningful, we can expect its solution from them alone.

History itself is one reason that leads us to believe in the reality of the problem of the City of God. These lectures sum up all too briefly the principal stages of that history. Even if the theologians were to conclude that there exists no genuine Christendom, we can assure them that there are many false ones. The history of our own time abounds in parodies of the City of God. As was to be feared, members of the Earthly City have tried to temporalize the City of God. The long-range preparation by the Church of a temporal organization of the Christian people and of its temporal integration into the City of God would doubtless do much to avoid or limit the repetition of costly experiments, whose cost is inevitably borne by both the temporal and spiritual orders. It will be apparent in our conclusions that no strengthening of scholarship would have changed their nature. We are inside the puzzle, and the very reality of the problem is at issue.

We take this opportunity to thank the University of Louvain for having offered us the opportunity to publish reflections that would probably never have been made public without its gracious hospitality. We hope we have made no serious errors. If any are found in this book, they must be considered strictly our own. Let it be clear that we have no intention to hold on to them. The truth alone matters.

ONE

Origins of the Problem

HOWEVER FUTURE historians judge our epoch, at least we who live in it cannot put in doubt the profound meaning of its travails, its weaknesses, and of so many convulsions of which we are causes or victims. The contemporary world suffers the pains of childbirth. With enormous turmoil a universal human society is being born. It will stand to contemporary States as they stood to the formerly divided peoples who comprise them, and as those peoples still earlier seem to have stood to families, clans, and tribes, whose unity they came to assure. How was this ideal born? These lectures will address the problem of how it might be fulfilled outside of the spiritual climate in which it was born.

What characterizes the events we witness, what distinguishes them from everything that preceded them since the beginnings of history is their world character, as they say, or planetary character, as perhaps it might be more exactly put. There is no longer local history. There is no longer exclusively national history whose events concern a particular people and it alone, in the sense that this people alone is the cause or will undergo the effects of those events. Planetary unity has been achieved. Economic, industrial, and technical reasons in general, all of which we can view as tied to practical applications of the natural sciences, have established a *de facto* solidarity among peoples of the earth. Consequently, their vicissitudes are combined in a universal history of which they are particular aspects. Whatever the different peoples of the world may think about it, they have become parts of a humanity that is more natural than social. Henceforth, they must become aware of that humanity in order to will it instead of just undergoing it, and in order to think about it with a view to organizing it.

History may have a role here. Certainly, by its own nature, it can only report the past. It cannot resolve any problem, least of all the one whose solution contemporary peoples must create. Yet no problem is absolutely new. There is hardly any problem that will not be clarified by a reflection upon its data. The only service that we can ask of history is to seek the first traces of this universal human society whose future is a certainty. Perhaps this brief investigation will be the occasion for general conclusions, but they must follow from the investigation. They cannot precede it in any sense.

Christianity was born in the Roman Empire, which itself was only a vast enlargement of the city of Rome. Or, if the expression seems imprudent, the Empire took from Rome its laws, its order, and what unity it had. But, first of all, what was Rome? Different explanations of Rome's origin have been proposed. As the specialists have not yet found a solution that is acceptable to everyone, it would be somewhat rash to choose for them and more rash still to build on any one of their hypotheses.[1] However, no one doubts that like Athens, Rome was one of the ancient cities, each of which was a State or the center of a State. We can admit that people united by common descent initially inhabited these cities.[2] In 451 B.C. under Pericles, it was again decreed that only children of a legitimately married Athenian father and mother could be citizens of Athens. The division of the cities into phratries and lines, which is also found in the Roman *familia* and *gens*, thoroughly confirms this hypothesis.

1. André Piganiol, *Essai sur les origines de Rome* (Paris: E. de Boccard, 1917).

2. Ulrich von Wilamowitz-Mollendorf and B. Niese, *Staat und Gesellschaft der Greichen und Römer* (Berlin: B. G. Teubner, 1910), 42–51, 97, 100; Ernest Barker, *Greek Political Theory: Plato and His Predecessors* (London: Methuen, 1917). This is a completely revised version of the author's 1906 *The Political Thought of Plato and Aristotle* (New York: Putnam's Sons). Note the interesting remark in the preface: "The Laws are the most modern or medieval of all Plato's writings" (viii).

That in no way excludes the profound perspectives developed by Fustel de Coulanges in his book *The Ancient City*, a classic from its first appearance, because the family already presented itself in the ancient city as tied to religious belief and sacred rites from which it was inseparable. This is exactly the reverse of historical materialism. Fustel de Coulanges professed what might be called "historical spiritualism." According to him, if humans are not governed today as they were twenty-five centuries ago, it is because we do not think as humans thought then.[3] From that comes his fundamental thesis: "History does not study material facts and institutions alone. Its true object of study is the human mind; it should aspire to know what this mind has believed, thought, and felt in the different ages of the life of the human race."[4]

From this standpoint, it is religion that most profoundly dominates the ancient family in the city. Founded on the religious cult of the hearth, that is, upon the real domestic fire and not a mere metaphor, each family initially constituted a closed society. It was separated from others by its own cult:

> Religion did not say to a man, showing him another man, "That is thy brother." It said to him, "That is a stranger; he cannot participate in the acts of thy hearth; he cannot approach the tomb of thy family; he has other gods than thine, and cannot unite with thee in a common prayer. Thy gods reject his adoration and regard him as an enemy. He is thy foe also."[5]

3. Numa Denis Fustel de Coulanges, *La Cité Antique*, 28th ed. (Paris: Hachette, 1924), 1:2–3 [*The Ancient City*, trans. Willard Small (Garden City: Doubleday Anchor Books, 1956), 12]. Haunted by the harm done to France by the imitators of ancient democracy during the revolution of 1879, Fustel wants above all to prove that ancient democracy cannot be imitated.

4. Ibid., II.103–4 [94].

5. Ibid., II.104 [95]. This is doubtless why love plays a secondary role in the ancient family; see II.40 [42]: "The members of the ancient family were united by something more powerful than birth, affection, or physical strength. This was the religion of the sacred fire and dead ancestors." To guarantee the cult of the dead, marriage was necessary in order to have children to perpetuate the cult. From this comes the sacramental formula pronounced in the act of marriage: "ducere uxorum liberorum quaerendorum causa" (II.52 [51]); "Everything in the family was divine" (II.109 [99]). See also: "Then a

It was first necessary to overcome the separation of families in order to establish broader social groups.

Let us suppose that the families are grouped in *gentes* or lines, the *gentes* in tribes, and the tribes in cities. There again we will find a cult, the cult of another group of divinities like Zeus or Herakles. The origin of these cults is uncertain, but we know that the latter cult was superimposed upon the cult of the domestic gods, without eliminating it. Therefore, only the acknowledgment of gods common to several families permitted the birth of the city. "Society developed only as fast as religion enlarged its sphere. We cannot indeed say that religious progress brought social progress; but what is certain is that they were both produced at the same time and in remarkable accord."[6]

This is why, even when the ancient city expands into an empire, it cannot change character. Such an empire can be conceived in two different ways, by a philosopher or by a politician. Philosophically speaking, the idea that the universe is one and that, in a certain sense, it constitutes a single City is not new. When we speak today of "one world" we regress within the history of philosophy, because we merely understand that the earth is one, instead of that the universe is one, as the Stoics already thought. How could it be other than one? The acceptance of the cosmic order and with it all that does not depend on us becomes the first rule of wisdom. With this acceptance the sage sees himself as a participant in an infinitely more vast order than the particular political society in which he was born. Marcus Aurelius writes: "Everything is right for me, O Universe, which is right for you Nothing for me is too early or too late, which comes in due time for you. Everything is fruit to me, which your seasons bring, O Nature. From you are all

man loved his house as he now loves his Church" (ibid.). Even slaves were integrated into the family through a religious ceremony analogous to the marriage ceremony, and they participated in the cult of the hearth. Slaves were interred in the burial place of the family whose *lares* had been their gods (II.127 [114–15]).

6. Ibid., III.147–48 [131].

things; in you are all things, to you all things return. The poet says, 'Dear city of Cecrops,' and will you not say, 'Dear city of Zeus'?"[7] In this sense, it is true to say that a citizen of the universe is "a citizen of that loftiest city, to which all other cities are as families."[8]

Are we really dealing with a city here? When Marcus Aurelius says, "My city and country, so far as I am Antoninus, is Rome, and so far as I am a man, is the world," he pens a noble phrase, but does he take the word *fatherland* in the same sense both times?[9] That can be doubted. Rome is a society of humans. The world is an order of things. The Stoic sage is a cosmopolitan, but, on the one hand, the totality of the universe is much more vast than a society would be, even a society that extended to the ends of the earth. On the other hand, one cannot really be a citizen of the cosmos, because the cosmos is not a society. To fit into a physical order whose laws one accepts and within which one is in sympathy is perhaps to perform an act of wisdom, but it is not to perform an act of citizenship. The Stoics do not seem to have conceived the ideal of a universal society coextensive with our planet, capable of uniting all humans.

Still, it is possible that their cosmopolitanism indirectly contributed to the birth of this idea,[10] because they conceived the universe as unified and bound by a force of "harmony" or "empathy" (*homonoia*) that could inspire the desire to unite all humans by one single law. If we believe the testimony of Eratosthenes,[11] Alexander the Great let himself be persuaded to divide humans only into good and bad, in opposition to those who divided them

7. Marcus Aurelius, *Meditations* IV.23 [*Marcus Aurelius and His Times*, trans. George Long (New York: Walter J. Black, 1945), 37–38].

8. *Meditations* III.11 [31]. Seneca, *De Tranquillitate Animi* III.9: "Ideo magis animo nos non unius urbis moenibus clausimus, sed in totius orbis commercium emisimus patriamque nobis mundum professi sumus, ut liceret laborem virtuti campum dare." See Seneca, *Consolatio ad Helviam Matrem* XI.1 and IX.7.

9. *Meditations* VI.44 [65].

10. W. W. Tarn, "Alexander and the Unity of Mankind," *Proceedings of the British Academy* 19, n.d.: 16–17 and 28; published separately in London: Milford, 1933.

11. Strabo, *Strabonis Geographica: Graece cum versione refecta*, ed. C. Müller and F. Dübner (Paris: Firmin Didot, 1853), 1:55.

into Greeks and barbarians, counseling Alexander to treat the first as friends and the second as enemies. With more insistence yet, Plutarch specifies[12] that Alexander undertook an immense task, not only as conqueror but as global citizen, by introducing everywhere, along with Greek religion and philosophy, the common order that respect for their laws imposed. To conquer in order to civilize, to civilize in order to unite, was his ideal. Evidently, it would be imprudent to grant solid historical value to this testimony, but even if we admit that Plutarch lends his own Stoicism to a warrior whose ambition would explain his undertakings equally well, the fact remains that the gradual conquest of the Greek city-states and the Oriental peoples, followed by their absorption into the unity of a single empire, could resemble the genesis of a universal society. This prodigious enlargement of the Greek city by force of arms necessarily implied a corresponding religious conquest or at least an attempt to achieve it. While assuring his political domination, Alexander did not fail to introduce the Hellenistic gods into the conquered countries, and we are not surprised that he even wished to complete this work by requiring the Macedonians and Greeks to acknowledge his own divinity. Aristotle's nephew, the philosopher

12. Plutarch, *De Alexandri Magni Fortuna sive Virtute*, in *Plutarchi Chaeronensis Scripta Moralia Graece et Latine*, ed. Jean-Fédéric Dübner (Paris: Firmin-Didot, 1839–41), 1:303–4. On the strength of this and one or two other bits of evidence, several historians honor Alexander for "a great intellectual revolution, the necessary prelude to the future imperial system of the West. Besides W. W. Tarn, whom we have already cited, see Ernest Barker, *Church, State, and Study* (London: Methuen, 1930) [reprinted in Westport, Conn.: Greenwood Press, 1974], 3. Without claiming to plumb Alexander's heart from this distance in time, we at least must say that his friendship was a little too conquering, and that the ideal attributed to him on Plutarch's authority was certainly less clear in Alexander's mind than in that of his historians. Supposing—what is not certain—that Alexander invented the political notion of empire and that he colored it with a humanitarian ideology, something still less certain, we can in no way assimilate Alexander to St. Paul's teaching as Ernest Barker does in *Church, State, and Study*, 4. Only a completely equivocal term lets two essentially different cases be assimilated. All these general interpretations are disputable, including our own, against which an antidote is found in Robert Warrand Carlyle and Alexander James Carlyle, *History of Medieval Political Theory in the West* (London: W. Blackwood and Sons, 1903) [New York: Barnes and Noble, 1964], 1:8.

Callisthenes, staunchly opposed this, and on this account was put to death in 327 B.C.

A similar development took place in the history of Rome, where Seneca's Latin Stoicism adapted very well to a single homeland, the single world City, common to humans and gods, embracing all reality, which it binds by the necessity of its laws. The universe is truly the homeland of the Stoic sage, if he has a homeland.[13] But here again the field that Seneca opens to the exercise of virtue is more a "cosmos" than a genuine society. Even if the Roman Empire, the successor to Alexander, whose effigy graces the seal of Augustus, is acknowledged to have nurtured Seneca's dream, we still must specify that the acknowledgment of world unity is incommensurate with the political unity that emerges from conquest. The Roman law imposed by Augustus is not of the same nature as the cosmic order to which the Stoic submits himself. Lastly, even supposing that Stoic dialectic permits us to reduce one to the other, the fact remains that the consent of the peoples of the earth to the domination of a State, and ultimately of a man, does not yet constitute the ardently desired and voluntarily preserved union that every society worthy of the name supposes. Here, as in the case of his Macedonian predecessor, the emperor's divinity expresses no more than a necessity linked to the very nature of the ancient city,[14] and it is a misunderstanding to make Augustus the pioneer of a political revolution with worldwide signif-

13. Seneca, *Ad Marciam* 18.1 and *De Tranquillitate Animi* 4.4; see Barker, *Church, State, and Study*, 6–11. The point here is not to deny or minimize Stoic texts where all humans are invited to consider themselves of one society (Barker, *Church, State and Society*, 8), but to specify thoroughly how much the unity of this society looks to the unity of the cosmos of which it is just a facet. What is true is that Stoicism had effects of de-nationalization similar to what we observe in certain Christians, but there is a great difference between accepting oneself as a citizen of the world and wanting oneself to be the citizen of a universal human society that, even if it is not based on the rejection of the world, professes to have nothing to do with it.

14. Gaston Boissier, *La religion romaine d'Auguste aux Antonins* (Paris: Hachette, 1874), 1:173–77. These facts are noted by Barker, *Church, State, and Study*, 4–6 (esp. 5n2) and 11–20.

icance, or Alexander the apostle of human fraternity and the unity of humankind. The executioner of Callisthenes has no right to this honor. From the sacred character of the law, Augustus sought a simple justification of force.

The sense of these reservations itself calls for clarifications. It is not debatable that all these events and doctrines are symptoms of a more or less confused desire to unite all human beings in a universal society. The empires of Alexander and Augustus broke down national barriers and probably favored the dawning of more openly communitarian sentiments than those that ordinarily accompany local political or even religious loyalties. That Alexander and especially Augustus may have colored their imperialisms with more or less vague ideological justifications is certainly not impossible. However much we may suspect the ancients who make this claim of romanticizing history, they cannot have invented everything, and their modern successors are right if they desire to follow them. Stoicism is a still more significant symptom, first because it was a revolution in the spiritual and not political realm, but also because it did much to free citizens from the limited framework of the ancient city by integrating them directly into the universe. However, when all is said and done, the problem remains untouched. What we must do is discover where and when the *idea* of a universal human society appeared. Now, even supposing that a conqueror managed to dominate the world, the idea of such an empire would still not be the idea of a society. What such a monarch would want would be union of all in common submission, not union of all in agreement of wills. As for Stoicism, if it conceives the universe itself as a society, it does not think of a society of men broader than the city, a society which, without being confused with the cosmos or even equaling it in extension, would gather together within the cosmos all humans of the world. In these undertakings and reflections we see no glimmer of the idea of a universal social body that would be to particular cities what the city itself is to families and through them to individuals, in short a human society worthy of the name. Without denying that we ought to see these accounts and ideas as signs that announce a new idea, without disputing that they favored the dawning and spread of that idea, we must specify that the events and ideas are not yet that new idea. In the particular form attributed to it here, the idea does not stem from a reflection about the cosmos or from an empire, even Alexander's. History attributes to Alexander the noble ambition of uniting all humans in one stroke of love. This kind of stroke is very familiar. Emperors offer them, and they are primarily quite bloody.

However, it is in the Roman Empire and even under the rule of Augustus that the peaceful founder of a genuine universal "society" appears. But the origins of this decisive event in the history of the world are mixed with the history of the Jewish people. From Abraham's times this people was other and more than a simple race, because one could join it by a rite, circumcision.[15] But also from then on Abraham's whole posterity was blessed in the person of its ancestor and chosen by Yahweh as his own people in whom all the nations of the earth would be blessed.[16] The mysterious promise renewed to Isaac was never made again, but the people of Israel could not yet foresee how it would be kept one day. The history of the people of Israel, as its priests told it, is indeed dominated by a pact with God, whose terms were defined by Yahweh himself, in short: "If therefore you will hear my voice, and keep my covenant, you shall be my peculiar possession above all people: for the earth is mine. And you shall be to me a priestly kingdom, and a holy na-

15. Quotations from scripture are taken from A. Crampon, *La Sainte Bible*, ed. members of the Society of Jesus with the cooperation of professors of Saint Sulpice (Paris: Societé de S. Jean l'Evangeliste, Desclée, 1939). [Translator: English translations are taken from Douay-Confraternity version, contemporary to the one Gilson uses.] Gn 17:27: "And all the men of his [Abraham's] house, as well they that were born in his house, as the bought servants and strangers were circumcised with him"; see also Gn 17:12–14.

16. Gn 17:3–6; 18:18; 22:15–18. See Gn 26:4–5 for the promise renewed to Isaac.

tion." Still more simply: "And I will take you to myself for my people, I will be your God."[17]

We can have no doubt about the meaning of such a treaty. In exchange for the exclusive worship that the people of Israel would render him, Yahweh assured it of his exclusive protection against all other peoples of the earth:

> This day the Lord thy God hath commanded thee to do these commandments and judgments: and to keep and fulfill them with all thy heart, and with all thy soul. Thou hast chosen the Lord this day to be thy God, and to walk in his ways and keep his ceremonies, and precepts, and judgments, and obey his command. And the Lord hath chosen thee this day, to be his peculiar people, as he hath spoken to thee, and to keep all his commandments: And to make thee higher than all nations which he hath created, to his own praise, and name, and glory: that thou mayst be a holy people of the Lord thy God, as he hath spoken.[18]

A more perfect formulation of more complete religious nationalism cannot be imagined. Yahweh, the creator of the universe, is also the creator of peoples. Like the universe itself they are his. Why, therefore, will he not freely choose one of them to make it his own people among the others? Why will he not separate it from them, freely making an alliance with it against them?[19] Indeed, this is what happened. But, however the Jewish people itself understood this treaty, Yahweh alone possessed the deep meaning of its terms and remained the master of its interpretation.[20] If there

17. Ex 6:7 and 19:5–6.

18. Dt 26:16–19; see Lv 26.

19. Lv 20:26. Also Dt 10:14–15 and 28:2, 7, 13. This alliance between Yahweh and his people against the other peoples does not exclude the duties of justice and humanity toward strangers with whom Israel maintains peaceful relations; see Lv 19:30–34 and Dt 29:19. By contrast, in ancient Israel before the prophets, it is very difficult to find a clear reference to the possibility of a religious society separated from the context of a nation. Some even doubt that Yahweh's promises to Abraham (Gn 12:13) ought to be interpreted in this sense. On this point see Antonin Causse, *Israel et la vision de l'humanité* (Strasbourg: Librairie Istra, 1924), 16n2. However, it seems difficult to us, instructed by the developments of history to understand it otherwise.

20. This alliance supposes that the Jewish people was not yet free of polytheism

really exists only one God, sole creator and sovereign of all peoples, why would he only make an alliance with one people? This is what the prophets of Israel ultimately asked, not all of them, nor with equally clear awareness of the ultimate implications of the problem, but sometimes in terms such that they irresistibly evoke the vision of a world where all people are finally united in adoration of the same God. However, even in the well-known texts in which, through Isaiah's voice, Yahweh calls all the people of the earth to him, their salvation still remains linked to the glory of Israel.[21] Set up as the light of nations for salvation to reach the ends of the earth,[22] Israel sometimes rebels like the prophet Jonah against the mission entrusted to it by God,[23] and even those who

during this period. If Israel continually fell back into the cult of idols, the fact is that it considered the gods of other nations as *their* own gods, just as Yahweh was *its* own God. Jgs 11:24: "Are not those things which thy God Chamos possesseth, due to thee by right? But what the Lord our God hath obtained by conquest, shall be our possession." Adolphe Lods, *Israël des origines au milieu du VIIIe siècle* (Paris: Renaissance du livre, 1932), 526–29 [reprinted in Paris: A. Michel, 1969; translated as *Israel from Its Beginnings to the Middle of the Eighth Century* by S. H. Hooke (London: Routledge and Kegan Paul, 1948)], which effectively delineates monotheistic tendencies that were already very powerful in ancient Israel. Let us add that the very notion of Yahweh conceived as He who Is, however it was initially understood, necessarily had to lead Israel to strict monotheism. Étienne Gilson, *L'esprit de la philosophie médiévale* (Paris: J. Vrin, 1932), 1:53 [*The Spirit of Medieval Philosophy*, trans. A. C. H. Downes (London: Sheed and Ward, 1936)].

21. Causse, *Israël et la vision*, 26: "Judaism will develop between these two poles without ever being able to overcome the contradiction between its original nationalism and the ethical aspirations at work within the soul of Israel." Perhaps these aspirations might more aptly be called *religious*, because the prophets are at a level different from moralism, but the expression is essentially true (Is 45:20–25).

22. Is 49:6: "And he said: It is a small thing that thou shouldst be my servant to raise up the tribes of Jacob, and to convert the dregs of Israel. Behold, I have given thee to be the light of the Gentiles, that thou mayst be my salvation even to the farthest part of the earth."

23. Jonah's prophecy is directed against the religious nationalism of some Jews. Having received the order from Yahweh to go to Nineveh in order to preach repentance, Jonah flees to Tarshish, out of fear that if he converts the inhabitants of Nineveh, Yahweh may not pardon them and Nineveh may not be saved. In fact, what happens is this. Brought to Nineveh by Yahweh, Jonah fulfills his mission, saves Nineveh, but feels such resentment that he asks Yahweh to make him die. The whole last part of the book, as beautiful as it is instructive, vigorously brings out the idea of a God as creator of all things and full of solicitude for all humans; in short, Yahweh is not God of the Jews only (Jon 4:10–11). This lesson, which many Jews must have found unpleasant, testifies to the deep feeling that some

accept it continue to imagine a planet whose center was the earthly Jerusalem. Jewish nationalism was never completely overcome, so that religious universalism, of which monotheism was the seed, might completely triumph over its religious imperialism. The peace to which Israel aspired and that its prophets expected from the religious unification of the earth always remained the peace of the city of Jerusalem: the "vision of peace."

Jesus' preaching was the liberation in Israel, by Israel and, however little Israel consented to it, first of all for Israel—liberation from the contradiction in which Israel was entangled. By bringing the good news of salvation to all human beings, the Gospel revealed to them before all else that they were all children of the same heavenly Father as brothers of the Son of God, made man to save them. This is why, from that moment, faith in the word and person of Christ became the bond of a religious society to which neither race nor place can impose limits. Purely spiritual in its essence, the family of the children of God can still require of its members the sensible sign of a rite, but it will be quite different from circumcision. The issue is no longer to join a foreigner to a race or even just to a people but to include a new member in a spiritual society by purifying him from sin. "He who believes and is baptized shall be saved."[24] From that moment evangelization of the whole world became a necessary task because from now on the spread of salvation becomes identified with the spread of the faith that saves. "Go, therefore, and make disciples of all nations, baptizing them in the name of the Father, and of the Son, and of the Holy Spirit, teaching them to observe all that I have commanded you; and behold I am with you all days, even unto the consummation of the world."[25]

among them had of the necessarily universal character of the worship of Yahweh. The story of a Jewish prophet compelled by God to save Nineveh and this time not Jerusalem wonderfully defines the problem that Judaism needed to solve and Christianity solved.

24. Mk 16:16.

25. Mt 28:19–20; Mk 16:15.

However, we know that after the death of Christ, there was hesitation even at the core of the fledgling Church,[26] so that for some time two Churches were distinguished, that of the synagogue and that of the gentiles, but the message of St. Paul finally won acceptance by all. Paul's peculiar mission was precisely to lead all gentiles into obedience of faith in the name of Jesus Christ, those of Rome as those of Jerusalem, and by those of Rome, those of the whole world.

This time we certainly are dealing with a society, because the Church founded by Christ[27] united members among themselves, not to the universe that surrounded them. It was certainly a society open to everyone because, "the gospel . . . is the power of God unto salvation to everyone who believes, to Jews first and then to Greeks. For in it, the justice of God is revealed, from faith unto faith, as it is written, *He who is just lives by faith*."[28] Here, everything suggests that the society we are talking about transcends the limits of time and space, because it only invokes the spirit. True circumcision is circumcision of the heart.[29] To be sure, the Jewish people are still privileged, because God first confided his word to them, but the conditions for salvation are now the same for all humans. Pushing on with incredible boldness to the very heart of the mystery, the apostle assures that it is not by the Jewish law but by the justice of faith that the inheritance of this world was promised in former times to Abraham and his posterity.[30]

If ever the word *revelation* is appropriate, it is certainly here. Through an extraordinary metamorphosis, the Judaic perspective is suddenly transformed into the Christian perspective at the exact moment when, in the apostle Paul's teaching, the message of Jesus finally reveals its peculiar meaning. It embraces as much the past

26. Gal 2:1–9.
27. Mt 16:18.
28. Rom 1:16–17.
29. Rom 2:25–29.
30. Rom 4:13–17 and 9:6–13.

as the future. Everything that Abraham's posterity had believed true according to the flesh now appeared true according to the spirit, and this is why, hereafter, it will be true to say: "For there is no distinction between Jew and Greek for there is the same Lord of all, rich toward all who call upon him."[31] Paul has the peculiar mission of announcing exactly this, and it is the very mystery of Christ: "that the Gentiles are joint heirs, and fellow members of the same body and joint partakers of the promise in Christ Jesus through the gospel."[32] At the call of the universal vocation, all barriers are lowered and all distinctions abolished, at least in the sense that, if they subsist in themselves and in their order, they cease to prohibit the universal union of human beings in a single body whose soul is faith itself. The true authentic sons of Abraham are now all those who live from faith: "For you are all children of God through faith in Christ Jesus. For all of you have been baptized into Christ, have put on Christ. There is neither Jew nor Greek; there is neither slave nor freeman; there is neither male nor female. For you are all one in Christ Jesus. And if you are Christ's, then you are the offspring of Abraham, heirs according to promise."[33]

Obstacles cannot be denied more magnificently, but it is important to note immediately that the issue is less to abolish than to transcend them. The immense entanglement of things temporal remains under the spiritual unity announced in the apostle's message. There are always men and women. There are still slaves and freemen, Jews and Greeks, Caesar who demands taxes, and authorities of this world whom God himself makes it a duty to obey.[34] How long will all that be there? Not long, no doubt,[35] but

31. Rom 10:12 and Gal 3:1–18.

32. Eph 3:6.

33. Gal 3:26–29. Remembering texts like these, Auguste Comte will hold that St. Paul, not Jesus Christ, is the true founder of Catholicism. After him, some politicians will recommend a distinction between *Catholicism* and Christianity itself, from which Catholicism is born.

34. Rom 13:1–7.

35. Rom 13:11–14.

ultimately, as long as things last, the entanglement certainly must be accepted. If there are no longer Jews or Greeks, it is not that by ceasing to be national the Church becomes international. If there are no longer slaves or freemen, it is not that by freeing humans from the law through grace, the Church carries out some economic or social revolution. The Church annuls these distinctions, as it annuls those between the sexes, neither more nor less. To speak the truth, the Church ignores them because her kingdom is not of this world, and even while the Christian lives on earth, his life as a Christian is spent in a *city* that is not earth but heaven.[36]

This doctrine still creates two formidable difficulties for Christianity even today. The first difficulty concerns the universality of the society that is to be founded. It affects at the same time its basis and its extension. It affects its basis because, if this society rests upon the common acceptance of a belief that transcends reason, it only becomes universal through faith. Now, the content of faith is not knowledge that can be rationally universalized. Doubtless, Christian apologetics devotes its energies to put reason on the side of faith. We will even see it maintain that, all things taken into account, Christian faith is still the most reasonable thing in the world, but it remains no less true that the act of faith in the word of God is always irreducibly distinguished from the simple assent to a rational proposition's evidence. How then do we universalize what of itself is not rationally universalizable? It may in fact be that faith alone is authentically universalizable, but it will take humans so long to perceive it that perhaps they have not yet perceived it. While we wait, we ought to keep in mind how this problem, which we already see is at the very heart of the matter, is posed.

A second difficulty directly involves the possible relation of a Christian society to the temporal order. As Christ's faithful, we should say with St. Paul that a Christian does not live on earth but in heaven. A new problem arises from that because, if the Chris-

36. Phil 3:20.

tian's faith is such, the more intense it is, the more it will detach him from the love of this world and, in the first place, from the love of the City. Consequently, it is not surprising that one of the most notable effects produced by Christianity has been denationalization. At a distance from this event and with the scant documentation that we possess to discuss it, it is difficult to measure its intensity or to appreciate its extent. We can still note it because it remains one of the problem's constant data, something that has certainly occurred in our time, in any case. The *Letter to Diognetus* already describes with truly surprising acuteness the double life that their religion imposes on Christians. From the outside, Christians are not distinguished in any way from others whose cities, language, and customs they share. So they do not lack a homeland, but they are still not national like others, "because they live in homelands that belong to them, but as foreigners would dwell. They participate in everything as citizens, and they hold back like foreigners. Every foreign land is theirs, and every land is foreign to them." How could it be otherwise, if, even while they are on earth, the home they have chosen is in heaven? Tertullian's strange declaration is to be understood in the same sense: "Nothing is more foreign to us than the State. One State we have, of which all are citizens—the universe.[37] The Stoic flavor of the expression is undeniable, though as a historian justly remarks, this paradoxically different position is "cosmopolitanism founded upon cosmism."[38] In truth, as we will observe by examining St. Augustine's thought on this point, to define the Christian position now would be to resolve it immediately, because it is quite

37. Tertullian, *Apologeticus*, chap. 36, trans. T. R. Glover in *Tertullian, Minucius Felix*, Loeb Classical Library 250 (Cambridge, Mass.: Harvard University Press, 1940), 172–73: "Nobis . . . nec ulla magis res aliena est quam publica. Unam omnium rem publicam agnoscimus, mundum."

38. Heinrich Scholz, *Glaube und Unglaube in der Weltgeschichte: Ein Kommentar zu Augustinus' De Civitate Dei, mit einem Exkurs: Fruitio Dei, ein Beitrag zur Geschichte der Theologie in der Mystik* (Leipzig: J. C. Hinrichs, 1911), 95. Scholz quotes other similar texts. See also Gustave Combès, *La doctrine politique de saint Augustin* (Paris: Plon, 1927), 217–18.

true that the Christian is no longer a member of the cosmos conceived in the Stoic manner. Therefore, he is no longer a cosmopolitan in the Stoic sense of the term. But we can ask whether Christianity has not transformed the very idea of cosmos to the point of making it into genuine society, in which case the idea of Christian cosmopolitanism would admit a precise definition.

Whatever the case may be on this point, the effect that their integration into a society other than their earthly homeland produced on certain Christians seems to be difficult to dispute. How often have they been reproached for it! Not only did they refuse the gods of the Empire the worship that was their due, but, like Tertullian, they detached themselves from it to the point of considering themselves as foreigners, Adolf von Harnack insisted with vigor and truth on this sense of Celsus's *True Discourse*: Do not situate yourself outside the Empire, Celsus told Christians, and we will try to put up with you.[39] Now, in our turn, we must insist on the moment when the problem is posed for the first time. We can ask whether the very essence of Christianity did not make it inevitable. From his own point of view, Celsus was right to force the Christians to choose between the two Cities, one of which they used without loving it, serving only the other with love, while they remain in the first.

Reason wants there to be a choice between the two sides. If Christians refuse to perform the usual sacrifices and to honor those who preside over them, then they should not be allowed to be emancipated, marry, raise children, or fulfill any obligation in public life. It only remains for them to go far away and leave no posterity behind. In this way such scum will be completely eradicated from the earth. But if they marry, if they have children, if they enjoy the fruits of the earth, if they share the joys of life

39. Adolf von Harnack, *Mission und Ausbreitung des Christentums*, 3rd ed., 1:474, quoted in Pierre de Labriolle, *La réaction paiênne: Essai sur la polémique antichrétienne du Ier au VIe siècle* (Paris: L'artisan du livre, 1934), 122. Labriolle thinks that this concern is less profound or sincere in Celsus than Harnack says. That may be, but Harnack bases his judgment on more than Celsus's texts, and his facts are undoubtedly right. However, Labriolle admits that himself (169).

along with the inevitable misfortunes, then they must pay a just tribute to those who watch over these things, discharge the duties that life imposes until they are freed of earthly bonds. Otherwise they have the appearance of ingrates, since it would be an injustice to enjoy the goods by which they benefit without any return.[40]

Assuredly, the Christians had some responsibility. They could protest their fidelity to the Empire except to its worship and gods, but besides the emperor's divinity being argued against them as inseparable from the Empire, it could be observed that, if their own City was not of this world, they had the duty to leave the Empire. The Desert Fathers were Christians after Celsus's heart. In a sense they gave him satisfaction almost to the point of proving him right. In a slightly different sense, Origen himself did the same thing when he replied to Celsus that the Christians were not without a homeland, because they had one in their churches. That was to answer the question with the same question, which, let us remember, is at the very heart of the history whose outlines we are retracing. We do not say that Christianity put people in an impossible situation. Rather the opposite is true, as whatever else they thought of the situation, Christians certainly had to accommodate themselves to it, but Christianity clearly provoked a conflict of tendencies among those who, being completely devoted to their earthly homeland,[41] conceived nothing beyond it, and those

40. Celsus, *The True Discourse* VIII.55, in de Labriolle, *La réaction*, 121. [Translator: *The True Discourse* or *True Doctrine* is a lost work of Celsus largely known from Origen's *Contra Celsum*.]

41. Let us recall that this State totalitarianism is also inherent in every pagan conception of the City. It is clearly affirmed in Aristotle's doctrine, *Politics* VIII.1 [The *Basic Works of Aristotle*, ed. Richard McKeon (New York: Random House, 1941), 1305]: "Neither must we suppose that any one of the citizens belongs to himself, for they all belong to the State, and are each of them a part of the State, and the care of each part is inseparable from the care of the whole." This is why the education of children is carried out by and for the city. It must be *public* in the strong sense. See Thomas Aquinas, *In I Ethicorum*, Book 1, l. 2, a. 9, nos. 11–27 [*In Decem Libros Ethicorum Aristotelis ad Nichomachum Expositio*, ed. Angelo M. Pirotta, OP (Turin: Marietti, 1934)]. Besides Fustel de Coulanges, on the Greek concept of the State, see Ernest Barker, *Greek Political Theory*, chap. 1.

who, being citizens of the Heavenly City before all else, more or less tend to lose interest in their homeland here below. Such was Tertullian, and such also that Origen, who without denying that Christianity might improve morality in benefit of the State, is still described to us as only feeling "modest interest" in the State and living above this world in a metaphysical, or perhaps more exactly religious, dream. If he certainly suggests that every cultivated Christian reserve his activity "for the service of the churches, the authentic body of the homeland [*systema patridos*] that are established in every town,"[42] let us agree that a pagan like Celsus might be excused for holding Christianity to be, if not a sedition, at least a secession from the body politic. Certain early Christians found and practiced one of the possible answers to the new question posed by Christianity: to renounce the world is to renounce the City.

There are other answers and the very spread of the good news could not help suggesting a totally different, even opposite one: instead of renouncing the City, to Christianize it, and by Christianizing it, to take it over. Nothing proves that this was the idea of Constantine, whose secret escapes history like almost everything that relates to individual psychology. Whatever the motives that recommended the conversion of a Roman emperor to Christianity, it still remains a fundamentally important historical fact, less perhaps for its aftermath than for the actual situation to which it bears witness and which itself had provoked it.[43] The least that can be said is that thereby the Empire entered into combination with the Church, or in other words, the Empire agreed to let itself be Christianized.

42. Labriolle, *La reaction paiënne*, 168–69.

43. Norman Baynes, "Constantine the Great and the Christian Church," *Proceedings of the British Academy* 15 (1929), attributes to Constantine the feeling that the God of the Christians had entrusted him with a mission. This is not impossible. Christopher Dawson, *The Making of Europe* (London: Macmillan, 1932), 34–45, would not go nearly that far, but he at least has no doubt at all of the sincerity of Constantine's conversion.

A completely new situation for Christians arose from that. Henceforth, loyalty without reservations could be granted to the Empire, that is to say, one could serve the emperor without betraying God. Formerly members of a persecuted minority or, in the most favorable circumstances, one that confined itself to the margins of the State, Christians were now subjects of a leader who acknowledged that he was subject to the same supreme leader as his own subjects. Thus, the "Christian citizen" became the normal case instead of being an anomaly, and the day seemed to be dawning when the status of member of the Church would be combined in practice with that of member of the State.[44] Even more, as has been rightly noted, henceforth it was impossible that members of the ecclesiastical hierarchy should not sooner or later become members of the hierarchy that directed the State under the emperor. The religious authority that the emperor now recognized in them even confirmed a moral authority on them that, before long, would be exercised in the guise of remonstrances or even reprimands. Eusebius of Caesarea in the East and St. Ambrose in the West did not hesitate to use it publicly to the degree that it is possible to see in the first interpretations of "the ideal of a Christian State."[45] Even if we admit that the notion was not yet very clear when in 390 Ambrose severely reprimanded Emperor Theodosius for the massacre at Salonika, it seems unquestionable that from that point it began to achieve self-awareness, at least in the form of a possibility whose principle was already grasped. In a very recent yet vanished past, one could not have served at once and with one heart God and Empire. Hereafter, it was completely the contrary, because Ambrose assures the Emperor Gratian that when his subjects betray God, they betray the Empire.[46] The dogmatic sedition

44. Dawson, *Making of Europe*, 35: "The Citizenship of the future lay in the membership of the Church."

45. Ibid., 44; see 43–44 for an excellent description of the new feeling that a Christian must have experienced toward the State from that time forward.

46. St. Ambrose, *De Fide* II.16.139, in Patrologiae Cursus Completus: Series Latina,

of Arianism is manifest proof: the Empire's unity is not tied to the unity of faith.

In this way, the holy people whose history the Old Testament had told was reconstituted in the light of the New Testament. It was the same history, because at bottom it was the same people, although now spread over the known world and virtually master of what remained to be discovered or conquered. Submitted to a holy emperor, this people had the same treaty of alliance with God, from which it hoped for union, peace, and prosperity in this world, while awaiting glory in the other. Furthermore, what is wiser and more reasonable? The Empire was Christian, so why would not the Church guarantee the Empire? Even more, did it not seem rather that God himself in his providence willed the Roman Empire of Augustus in order to prepare for his Church an already unified and pacified world? Would it not be enough for the Church to baptize that world to make it at least the center of a universal Christian society to which one would belong by the mere fact of being a Christian?

At least certain Christians thought so, and none said it better than the poet Prudentius, writing against the pagan Symmachus between 385 and 388. To Prudentius the Roman Empire appeared, with evidence that is still arresting to us, to be the providential preparation of a universal society for human beings united by the bonds of Christianity. From that point, Christian patriotism, that is to say, love of Rome justified by Christianity itself, became

ed. J.-P. Migne (Paris: Garnier Frères, 1958) [hereafter, PL], 16:612: "Nec ambiguum, sancte imperator, quod qui perfidiae alienae pugnam excepimus, fidei catholicae in te vigentis habituri simus auxilium. Evidens etenim antehac divinae indignationis causa praecessit, ut ibi primum fides romano imperio frangeretur, ubi fracta est Deo." See PL 16, *Epistola* 11.4, col. 986, where the heretic is presented as a danger for the whole political body. Let us note in this regard that Ambrose, like the future Gregorians, is already an anti-dialectician, certain of whose themes anticipate those of Peter Damian. See *De Fide* I.5.41–42, col. 559; I.13.84–85, cols. 570–71; IV.8.78, col. 658; see also *De Incarnatione* IX.89, col. 876. As he says himself: "Non lex ecclesiam congregavit, sed fides Dei" (*Epistola* 21.24, col. 1057).

something conceivable and even natural,[47] because the history of Rome was already integrated by that into the universal history whose center is the incarnation of Christ and which will be the only intelligible history for so many Christian thinkers:

We live in countries with the most diverse like fellow-citizens of the same blood dwelling within the single ramparts of their native city, and all united in an ancestral home. Regions far apart, shores separated by the sea, now meet together in appearing before one common court of law, in the way of trade in the products of their crafts they gather to one thronged market, by the way of wedlock they unite in legal marriage with a spouse of another country; for a single progeny is produced from the mixed blood of two different races. Such is the result of the great successes and triumphs of the Roman power. For the time of Christ's coming, be assured, was the way prepared which the general good will of peace among us had just built under the rule of Rome. For what room could there have been for God in a savage world and in human hearts at variance, each according to its different interest maintaining its own claims, as once things were? Where sentiments are thus disordered in man's breast, agreement upset, and faction in the soul, neither pure wisdom visits nor God enters. But if a supremacy in the soul, having gained authority to rule, checks the impulse of refractory appetite and rebellious flesh and controls all its passions under a single order, the constitution of life becomes stable and a settled way of thought draws on God in the heart and subject itself to one Lord. Come thee, Almighty; here is a world in harmony; do Thou enter it. An earth receives Thee now, O Christ, which peace and Rome hold in a bond of union.[48]

47. G. Boissier, *La fin du paganisme: Étude sur les dernières luttes religieuses en Occident au quatrième siècle*, 2nd ed. (Paris: Hachette, 1894), 2:153 [reprinted in New York: G. Olms, 1987].

48. Prudentius, *Contra Symmachum* II.609–36 [*Contra Orationem Symmachi*, trans. H. J. Thompson, Loeb Classical Library 398 (Cambridge, Mass.: Harvard University Press, 1979)]. Gilson cites Gaston Boissier's translation in *La fin du paganisme,* 2:136–37, for the first third of the passage. See also Dawson, *The Making of Europe*, 23. Boissier, *La fin du paganisme*, 2:137 cites similar evidence from Claudianus, *In Secundum Consulatum Stilichonis*, 150, and Rutilius Namatianus, *De Reditu Suo*, ed. J. Vessereau and F. Préchac (Paris: Belles-Lettres, 1933), 61–66. When Rutilius, writing after the fall of Rome, tells Rome: "You formed one same homeland for the most distant nations . . . by offering a share in

The hope was beautiful, but the Roman Empire was to perish at the exact moment when the Christians intended to utilize it.

On August 24, 410, Alaric entered Rome and, although a Christian, he handed it over to be pillaged for three days. When his troops finally withdrew on the fourth day they took an immense booty and left behind mounds of corpses and ruins. So the Empire foundered for the first time at the very moment when the Church was forming the hope of being supported by it. That was not to be the last experience of its kind. However, in a sense, it would remain the most striking, because in the first moment it seemed that the ruin of Rome would entail that of the Church, whereas of the armed political colossus and the people united only by faith, the second alone has survived.

A lesson like this could not be lost. The capture of Rome by the barbarians had a deep impact on the Empire. The polemics between Christians and pagans, which had never ceased,[49] only became more violent and bitter. To analyze the opposing arguments put forth by the two sides would be long, intricate, and to tell the truth would end only with the polemic itself. On the pagan side, the two principal arguments are simple and directly or indirectly engender all the others. First, Christian doctrine teaches renunciation of the world. It turns the citizen away from service to the State, whose neglect prepares ruin. Next, the destiny of Rome has always been linked to the cult of its gods. Since the Christian religion began to spread, pagans had announced terrible punishments with which the gods would not fail to strike the Empire, but they

---

your own laws to the captives. You made a city out of what was formerly the universe" (5), he does not draw a Christian conclusion. To him the gods seem to have worked for Rome, not Rome for the gods: "sollicitos habuit Roma futura deos" (36). Christian thinkers will often take up the idea that God willed the Roman Empire as a providential preparation for the Church. We meet it again in Dante.

49. See especially the affair of the altar of victory in Boissier, *La fin du paganisme*, 2:231–91. On the violent reaction of certain Christians against the empire see Henri Leclercq, "Église et État," 4:2255–2556 in *Dictionnaire d'archéologie et de liturgie*, ed. Fernand Cabrol and Henri Leclercq (Paris: Delouzey et Ané, 1907–53).

went unheard, and now events finally justified the prophecies with such brilliance that nobody could refuse to take notice. The empire had become Christian and under the reign of a Christian emperor Rome had just been conquered and sacked for the first time since the remote origins of its history. How could one not understand the meaning of such a tragically evident lesson?

These objections are formulated with all desirable clarity in a letter from the Christian Marcellinus to the bishop of Hippo. The pagan Volusianus had addressed them to Marcellinus in 412, and Marcellinus immediately turned to Augustine to request him to respond. Volusianus, Marcellinus says, objects that Christian doctrine and preaching are completely unsuitable to the practices of national life (*reipublicae moribus*). Among other things, is it not said that Christianity teaches that evil never be returned for evil (Rom 12:17)? Or, if we are struck on one cheek to turn the other? Or again, if someone summons us to court to get our tunic, to also relinquish our cloak, and if someone wants to oblige us to go a mile, to go two miles with him (Mt 5:39–42)? It seems clear that a country could not put such customs into effect without being brought to ruin. Who, therefore, will bear it without reaction when an enemy seizes his property and will thereafter refuse to punish according to the rules of war those who devastate a Roman province? These arguments are familiar enough. For example, they are constantly renewed by "conscientious objectors," who refer to some of the deepest demands of Christian conscience whose force cannot be ignored. However, it is remarkable that it is not the pagan Volusianus, but the Christian Marcellinus who adds the last and strongest objection: "It is manifest . . . that the very greatest calamities have befallen the commonwealth under the government of emperors observing, for the most part, the Christian religion."[50]

50. St. Augustine, Letter 136, in PL 33:515 [In Nicene and Post-Nicene Fathers, First Series (hereafter, NPNF-I), ed. Philip Schaff (Grand Rapids, Mich.: Christian Literature Publishing, 1974), 1:473].

The objection was urgent, and Augustine does not delay his answer. He is first asked how to live as a Christian in a State or how a State composed of Christians could live, insofar as the practice of Christian virtues would infallibly entail the ruin of the State. Augustine counters with the unexpected answer that the pagans have already preached the same virtues that Christianity is reproached for recommending. There is no need to recall this to a cultured person like Volusianus. Does not Sallust praise the Romans for having preferred to forget injuries to violence? Does not Cicero praise Caesar for never having forgotten anything except the wrongs that had been done to him?[51] If we judge by Roman history, observance of these precepts does not turn out too badly for Rome. Furthermore, let us understand the Gospel teaching. Such commandments do not prescribe that Christian soldiers drop their weapons or refuse to serve. In fact, they forbid no one to devote himself generously to State service. Quite the opposite! Let them rather show us husbands and wives, parents and children, masters and slaves, leaders, judges, tax collectors, and payers comparable to those whom Christian doctrine requires, and it will certainly be obvious whether this doctrine is harmful to the State. The best thing that can happen to the Empire is that Christian teachings be faithfully observed.[52]

How then should we explain that the Empire's misfortune came through Christian emperors? Simply by denying the fact! It is not the Christianity of the emperors that harmed the Empire; it is its own vices, the inundation that nothing would now stop if God himself had not finally planted the cross in the Empire. Read Sallust and Juvenal, and see what grade of immorality the Roman Empire had achieved.[53] For what nascent Christianity is reproached,

51. Sallust, *Catalina*, chap. V; Cicero, *Pro Quinto Ligario* XII.35. St. Augustine, *De Civitate Dei* II.18.2, in PL 41:63 [*City of God*, trans. William Babcock (Hyde Park, N.Y.: New City Press, 2012–13), 1:52–54].

52. St. Augustine, Letter 138 (PL 33:531–32 [NPNF-I, 1:486]).

53. St. Augustine, *De Civitate Dei* II.19 (PL 41:64 [1:54–55]).

therefore, we must rather accuse dying paganism, because Christian revelation took on two objectives: to save human society, then to construct one that would be completely divine. It is not clear what the State can fear in this dual effort, rather it is clear what it can gain, because Christianity will achieve the first by pursuing the second.

The first thing is to save natural, human, political society from the inevitable disappearance to which its corruption inevitably leads. What puts Roman society in danger is that it is ignorant of the virtues required to assure its happiness and prosperity. Its members know well to what they are obliged by the purely natural love of this Empire, whose past virtues made all its greatness, but they lack the courage to put it into practice. The God of Christians requires them to do for love of him what they lack the strength to do for love of their country. Thus, amid the universal shipwreck of morality and civic virtue, divine authority intervenes to impose frugality, continence, friendship, justice, and harmony among citizens, so much so that anyone who professes Christian doctrine and observes its precepts will be found to do for the love of God everything that the mere interest of his fatherland would require that he do for it.[54] Augustine already posits as the great principle that justifies the Church's insertion in any human city of any time and any place whatever: have good Christians, and good citizens will be given you in addition. Certainly, this will never satisfy the requirements of Gospel fundamentalism. Yet, otherwise, the demands of the world where the Gospel purists ultimately accede to live will never be satisfied, a world that is theirs despite all the difficulty of using it without ever rendering to it some of what they do not cease to receive from it. Supposing that Christ himself had not expressly reserved a portion for Caesar, there would still be a problem of moral equity, about whose correct solution we could not doubt.

54. St. Augustine, Letter 138 (PL 33:533 [NPNF-I, 1:486–87]).

So, let us admit that Christian virtues are useful to the commonwealth's good order and prosperity; it remains no less true that this order and prosperity do not constitute their own end. A clear indication of this is that as long as the State assures the exercise of natural moral virtues, it suffices to assure its prosperity. This was outstandingly the case of early Rome, whose virtues Augustine does not hesitate to praise, following the tradition of Latin historians. Did not ancient Rome owe its triumphs precisely to its frugality, its fortitude, and the purity of its customs? Did not Rome itself date the origin of its decay from the decadence of its customs, so frequently denounced by its historians and poets? Far from feeling embarrassed by the memory of a prosperous though pagan Rome, Augustine sees the marks of providential destiny in that. If God willed temporal greatness obtained by purely civic virtues, it was so no one could be misled about the peculiar end of Christian virtues. As the world can prosper without them, they are not present with a view to the world: "For, in the most opulent and illustrious Empire of Rome, God has shown how great is the influence of even civic virtues without true religion, in order that it might be understood that, when this is added to such virtues, men are made citizens of another commonwealth of which the king is Truth, the law is Love, and the duration is Eternity."[55] This sufficiency of political virtues in their order testifies to the supernatural nature of Christian virtues in their essence and end.

Accordingly, from now on two Cities are present in Augustine's thought, and we immediately see that. For him, relieving the Church of any responsibility for the misfortunes of Rome was not at all a crafty lawyer's plea in an unsound case. The causes and the existence of the Roman Empire's decadence were prior to the advent of Christianity, which could not be judged responsible for them.

However, the disaster of 410 was there, and the pagans did not

55. Ibid. [1:487].

cease to exploit the argument, which, it will be agreed, appearances favored. This is why Augustine endeavors to mount a response in 413.

> Meanwhile Rome was overthrown by the eruption of the Goths acting under King Alaric and by the impact of a great defeat. The devotees of the multitude of false gods, whom we usually call Pagans, trying to relate Rome's overthrow to the Christian religion, began to blaspheme against the true God more harshly and bitterly than usual. Whence I, burning with zeal for the house of God [Ps 68:10], began to write the books of *The City of God* against their blasphemies and errors.... This great work about *The City of God* ultimately finished with twenty-two books.... The first four of the twelve following books [i.e., of the second half] contain the birth of two cities, one of which is of God, the other of this world.... Thus all twenty-two books, since they are written about both cities, take their title from the better one, so that they are called rather *The City of God*.[56]

If the work is entitled *The City of God*, it is because Augustine takes the title from the better city, but he certainly narrates the history of both.[57] Augustine is not deceived about his work's real objective. Undertaken under the pressure of circumstances, perhaps suggested by the question posed by the same Marcellinus to whom he dedicates it, the work proposes much more than to justify the Church from a circumstantial accusation. The drama, whose twists and turns Augustine wants to narrate and whose meaning he was to extract has literally cosmic dimensions, because it is identified with world history. The message that the bishop of Hippo thus presents us is, indeed, that the whole world from start to finish has the single end of constituting a holy society in function of which everything, the universe itself, has been made. Perhaps never in the history of human speculation has the concept of society undergone a metamorphosis that is comparable in depth or that, by

56. St. Augustine, *Retractationes* II.43.1–2 (PL 32:648) [Translator: my rendering from the Latin on 801–3, *Obras Completas de San Agustín*, *Escritos Varios 2*, *Retractationes* (Madrid: BAC, 1995), 643–826].

57. St. Augustine, *De Civitate Dei* II.19, preface (PL 41:13).

being metamorphosed, led to such amplification of perspective. Here the City does more than extend to the limits of the earth or the world; it includes it and explains it, to the point of justifying its very existence. Everything that is, except God alone whose work the City is, exists only for it, has meaning only through it, and if we can have faith in the ultimate intelligibility of the smallest occurrence or the most humble being, the City of God holds its secret.

TWO

The City of God

WHAT IS A CITY, not in the material but in the social sense of the term? Within the world that is *The City of God*, we would seek in vain for a general, abstract discussion of the problem, as philosophers envisage it when they try to define the nature of the social bond in itself. Through a thousand twists and detours, Augustine pursues his own enterprise, which it would not be unfair to call apologetic,[1] but which still engages him in some discussions where philosophy as such is judged from a Christian standpoint. This is precisely the case of the concept of *city*. He does not discuss it as a philosopher indifferent to Christianity or as a Christian indifferent to philosophy, but a Christian who judges philosophy and, if necessary, reforms its notions in the light of faith.

When he speaks of a human city, Augustine thinks of Rome and its history first of all as the Latin writers had taught it to him.[2] If he was able to refute the reproach that the Church had caused the ruin of Rome, it is because Sallust himself, as we have seen, held that Rome's own vices had ruined it before the birth of Christ. When he wonders at what moment of its history Rome deserved the name *city*, Augustine still appeals to a pagan definition of *city*. Thus, in

1. Heinrich Scholz, *Glaube und Unglaube in der Weltgeschichte: ein Kommentar zu Augustins De Civitate Dei, mit einem Exkurs, Fruitio Dei, ein Beitrag zur Geschichte der Theologie und der Mystik* (Leipzig: J. C. Hinrichs, 1911). Scholz opposes those who see a "philosophy of history" in *The City of God*. He is right in this, which does not exclude that a philosophy of history indeed issued from it centuries later. According to Scholz, this work's dominant theme would be "the struggle of faith and infidelity" (2), which is very reasonable. The simplest thing is to admit that *The City of God*'s dominant theme is precisely the City of God.

2. *De Civitate Dei* XV.8.2, col. 447 [2:149–50]: *city* means society, "civitas, quae nihil aliud est quam hominum multitudo aliquo societatis vinculo colligata."

judging pagan society in the name of norms it had posited itself, Augustine is inspired by rules that pagan society could not reject.

To Augustine the notion of justice seems to dominate the pagan concept of *city*, which is both a political and social body. As Cicero, for example, conceived it, every society would be similar to a musical concert where agreement or harmony finally emerge from different sounds from instruments or voices. What the musician calls harmony, the politician calls concord. Without concord there is no city, but without justice there is no concord. Therefore, justice is the first condition required for the existence of the city. That is why Augustine believes that he can conclude, despite all contrary appearances, that when a historian affirms that Rome had lost all justice at a certain moment of its history, Rome had ceased to exist from that moment. It is not enough to say with Sallust that Roman society was corrupted then. We must go so far as to say with Cicero that it had totally ceased to exist as a society: *iam tunc prorsus periisse et nullam omnino remanisse rempublicam*.[3]

Is it enough to say even this? If we refer to the thesis that republican Rome prospered because of its virtues, similarly maintained by Augustine,[4] it certainly seems that we can admit a pagan society worthy of the name. God, Augustine wrote to Marcellinus in 412, wanted to manifest the supernatural end of Christian virtues by permitting ancient Rome to prosper without them. This acknowledged a certain temporal efficacy in pagan civic virtues, and even the character of an authentic society in Rome itself. Indeed, Augustine will never deny it. For whatever divine or human reason it may be, ancient Rome was truly a society in its fashion. It was administered better by the ancient Romans than by their successors, but ultimately it was one, *pro suo modo*. Except that, in the very place where Augustine concedes this,[5] he adds that there

3. Ibid., II.21, cols. 65–67 [1:56].

4. See chapter 1 in this book.

5. *De Civitate Dei* II.21.4, col. 68 [1:59]: "nunquam illam fuisse rempublicam quia

never was a society, and that he will prove it later basing himself on the definitions of social body proposed by Cicero himself. There never was a true Roman society because true justice never reigned. Obviously, we are confronted here with a problem that cannot be resolved by a simple *yes* or *no*. In one sense, there was a Roman *commonwealth*, where, particularly in its beginnings, a sort of justice prevailed that itself engendered a sort of society. However, as this justice was not *true justice*, this society was not a true society. Here, yielding to the temptations of dialectic, we might say that there never was a Roman society because not to be a true society is not to be one. It is not to be a society at all.

Taken strictly, this thesis signifies that there exists and can exist only one society worthy of the name, that which observes true justice, in short, the City whose chief is Christ. No doubt there must be at least a second that is constituted by all those whose chief is not Christ. But the latter is hardly more than the refuse from the first, and it is even because of the first city that it exists. There would be no city of injustice if there were not one of justice. Every society worthy of the name is, therefore, either the City of God or defined in relation to the City of God.

We cannot doubt that this is Augustine's absolute position, and we have several proofs of it. Still, we also cannot doubt that Roman virtues and the civic grandeur of the Roman order posed a problem

---

nunquam in ea fuit vera justitia. Secundum probabiliores autem definitiones, pro suo modo quodam respublica fuit: et melius ab antiquioribus Romanis, quam a posterioribus administrata est. Vera autem justitia non est, nisi in republica, cujus conditor rectorque Christus est; si et ipsam rempublicam placet dicere, quoniam eam rem populi esse negare non possumus. Si autem hoc nomen, quod alibi aliterque vulgatum est, ab uso nostro locutionis est forte remotius, in ea certe civitate est vera justitia, de qua Scriptura sancta dicit: *Gloriosa dicta sunt de te, Civitas Dei*, Ps. 86, 3." This very rich text resolves several points: the totality of human beings subject to Christ form a people. We could call it the *respublica* of Christians. As the term *respublica* was already adapted to Rome, we could at least call the Christian people a *civitas*. The term "Civitas Dei" is taken from scripture, its source. This does not keep us from also admitting with Scholz, *Glaube und Unglaube*, 78, that Ticonius suggested to Augustine the notion of the two opposed cities: "Ecce duas civitates, unam Dei et unam diaboli."

to which, to put the best face on the matter, Augustine had to accommodate himself as best he could. The ambiguity of the concept of justice was the cause; because, if the idea of true justice is clear, that of false justice is not, and as we then no longer know whether we now are talking about justice that is still justice, and neither do we know any longer whether the society it grounds is still a society. Doubtless, this is why, when Augustine later resumes the examination of the problem, he is led to a new definition of the social bond, in which, although the notion of justice is not eliminated, it recedes into the background. This has been lamented,[6] but it is no less certain that it occurs with good reason, and that in any case, it is good to understand why Augustine is led to do so. To identify the social bond with justice produces two difficulties, first the one constituted by Rome, which we just saw Augustine dodge; then that of the City that is not of God, about which we see that, if the social bond is true justice, Augustine absolutely cannot escape an objection. How could there be two Cities in a doctrine where, because every city is founded on justice, there can only be one City of Christ founded on the justice of Christ?

This dialectical movement effected by Augustine parts from the definition of a people as Cicero proposed it in his now-lost dialogue *De Republica*, speaking through Scipio: "For he [Scipio] defined *a people* as a multitude joined together by *a common sense of what is right and by a community of interest*."[7] To submit to right (*jus*) is to submit to justice, because where there is no *jus*, how could there be *justitia*? What is done *quite rightly* is done *justly*, and we cannot give the label of *right* to iniquitous decisions taken by any persons whatsoever in contempt of all justice. From the principle posited by Scipio and Cicero it follows that a multitude that justice

6. A. J. Carlyle, "St. Augustine and the City of God," in F. J. C. Hearnshaw (ed.), *The Social and Political Ideas of Some Great Medieval Thinkers* (London: G. G. Harraph, 1923), 42–52.

7. *De Civitate Dei* XIX.21.1, col. 648: "Populum esse definit coetum multitudinis juris consensu et utilitatis communione sociatum" [2:378].

does not unite, does not constitute a people. But where there is no people, there is no longer the *people's thing*, the *public thing*, or as they say, *republic* [translator: *res publica*]. Now what is justice but the virtue that gives each one what is due to him? What is human justice that snatches men from God to submit them to demons? Is that to render to each what is due to him? Yet the Roman gods were nothing but the demons themselves, and under the guise of innumerable idols, it was certainly impure spirits that made themselves adored.[8] Therefore, it is necessary to give up saying that the Romans were ever a people, which would be rather awkward, or to define a people other than in relation to justice, which St. Augustine finally decides to do.[9]

After having recalled once more that, if the Ciceronian definition is true, there cannot be a people where there is no justice,[10] Augustine proposes this completely different definition: "A peo-

8. St. Augustine, *De Civitate Dei* XIX.21.1–2, cols. 648–50 [2:378–79].

9. Speaking of the new definition that we are going to examine, A. J. Carlyle, "St. Augustine and the City of God," 50, says that he is unable to determine whether it is a firm definition in Augustine, or whether it amounts to an accidental, isolated judgment within his work. Carlyle says that if the first hypothesis were true, it would be a very serious matter, because it would mean that the greatest Christian doctor wanted to eliminate the notion of justice from the definition of a people. He concludes: "I am myself, therefore, not at all certain whether St. Augustine did deliberately attempt to change the conception of the State. If he did, I cannot but feel that it was a deplorable error for a great Christian teacher. Happily the matter is not important, for, if indeed he did make this mistake, it had no significance in the history of Christian ideas. It is a notable fact that this passage of St. Augustine is hardly ever quoted at all in later Christian writers." The last point seems true to us, but not what precedes it. Augustine eliminated the notion of justice from the definition of peoples, because there can be a people without there being justice (for the same reason he deliberately changed the Ciceronian definition of people), but he never claimed to free any people from respect for justice. As for saying that the new Augustinian definition of people remained without influence in the history of ideas, this is a point that the present work intends to offer many reasons to doubt.

10. This would amount to saying that there can only be one people, that of the City of God; see *De Civitate Dei* XIX.23.5, col. 665 [2:385]: "Quapropter ubi non est ista justitia, ut secundum suam gratiam civitas obedienti Deus imperet unus et summus . . . profecto non est coetus hominum juris consensu et utilitatis communione sociatus. Quod si non est, utique populus non est, si vera est haec populi definitio: Ergo nec respublica est: quia res populi non est, ubi ipse populus non est."

ple is a multitude of rational beings joined together by common agreement on the objects of their love."[11] It is not difficult to see what society Augustine was thinking about when he defined all societies. If the issue is to discover what association of rational beings above all is founded on this common love of the same thing, then about which will we think but the *Ecclesia Christi*? Assuredly, the Church is established on divine authority that legitimates its teaching, but the faith on which it is founded is not separated from charity, which is its bond. Love is present from the Church's very origin, and it is what holds together the whole people in the common love for good of which its faith assures it. Jesus himself enjoined Christians to love God and love each other as he loved them and they loved him. By his teaching, these two commandments of the Law became the "great commandments," and thereby attained completely new force, because henceforth they sum up the whole law and all the prophets. Jesus certainly address a new people, when he speaks thus to his disciples, because the mutual love he prescribes and that he gives them is precisely the sign in which the world will recognize Christians.[12] Is it necessary to recall here Jesus' prayer to his Father, not only for his disciples but also for the disciples of his disciples unto the consummation of the ages?

Yet not for these only do I pray but for those also who through their word are to believe in me, that all may be one, even as thou, Father, in me and I in thee; that they also may be one in us, that the world may believe that thou hast sent me. And the glory that those hast given me, I have given to them, that the may be one, even as we are one: I in them and thou in me; that the world may know that thou hast sent me, and that thou hast loved them even as thou hast loved me. Father, I will that where I am they also whom thou hast given me may be with me; in order that they may

11. *De Civitate Dei* XIX.24, col. 665: "Populus est coetus multitudinis rationalis, rerum quas diligit concordi ratione sociatus" [2:385; the BAC Latin has *communione* instead of *ratione*].

12. Mt 5:43–48, 19:19, 22:34–40; Mk 12:29–31; Lk 6:27–36.

behold my glory, which thou hast given me, because thou hast loved me before the creation of the world. Just Father, the world has not known thee, but I have known thee, and these have known that thou hast sent me. And I have made known to them thy name, and will make it known, in order that the love with which thou hast loved me may be in them, and I in them.[13]

Thus is born a new family of those predestined to be adopted children of the Father in Jesus Christ,[14] where we already said, "there is not 'Gentile and Jew,' 'circumcised and uncircumcised.' 'Barbarian and Scythians,' 'slave and freemen,' but Christ is all things and in all."[15] That ultimately is why Christians are members of a single body whose head is Christ,[16] and where all share in mutual charity "to preserve the unity of the Spirit in the bond of peace."[17]

We seek in vain in scripture for an abstract definition of a people, but the New Testament lets us see one being born, and it is that same one whose essence Augustine has just defined: persons united by their communion in love for the same good. A definition of a purely religious and even mystical society, as we will see, this formula does not immediately reveal itself to be applicable to every society, whatever it may be and first of all to the Roman people. The question of knowing whether a given society is good or bad is no longer confused with this other one: is a certain human group a people or not? Interpreted by a Christian, Cicero's expression leaves room for only one people, the Christian people, who possess the only true justice, that of Christ. By contrast, the new expression allows us to recognize a people worthy of the name, even though they are unjust:

No matter what it loves, however, if it is an assembled multitude, not of animals but of rational creatures, and is joined together by common

13. Jn 17:20–26.
14. Eph 1:5.
15. Col 3:11.
16. 1 Cor 12:27; Eph 1:22 and 4:15; Col 2:19; Rom 12:4.
17. Eph 4:3, 1:2–3.

> agreement on the objects of its love, it is not absurd to call it a people, and it is clear that, the better the objects of its love, the better the people, and the worse the objects of its love, the worse the people. According this definition of ours, the Roman people is a people, and its common good is without doubt a republic.[18]

Thus, despite Rome's political decadence, whose cause was the decadence of its morality, we cannot refuse it the name *people*, as long as there subsists any assembly of rational beings united in the unanimous communion of all its members in the things they love. Now, adds Augustine, what I say about this people and this *republic* is to be understood of the Greeks, Egyptians, Assyrians, about ancient Babylon, and generally speaking, about any great or small people, once it is a people. Therefore, if there exists a city of the impious, it assuredly does not possess justice, but it is no less a city, one that is not the city of peace.

Only two of the innumerable cities scattered throughout the world hold St. Augustine's attention, that is to say "two human societies,"[19] and because the individual is to the city what letters are to words, the origin of the two societies into which humans are divided must be sought in the nature of their elements itself. There was a moment when the unity of humankind was effectively achieved: when it was still composed of just a single man. Indeed, it is precisely to assure that unity that God first created a single man, from whom all others descend. This was not necessary in itself. The earth might have been populated by descendants of several humans simultaneously created at the beginning of time, each of whom founded a line. Even if it were thus, the unification of humankind would remain desirable and possible, but through the single ancestor from whom humankind was born, its unity is not only an achievable ideal, it is a fact. It is a physical fact, because all humans are relatives. It is also a moral fact, because instead

18. *De Civitate Dei* XIX.24, col. 655 [2:385].
19. *De Civitate Dei* XV.1.1, col. 437 [2:139]. See also 37n2, above.

of feeling connected only by a bond of nature, they are linked by properly familial feeling. That all humans, however they differ in terms of race, skin color, or even in the form of their bodily parts, take their origin from the first man formed by God and that the first man was a single individual cannot be doubted by any of the Christian faithful.[20] "God started the human race from a single individual for the express purpose of showing men how much he prizes unity among many,"[21] in order that this unity should really be that of a family.[22] Augustine has no doubt at all. Thus, as faith assures us, humans are naturally brothers in Adam, even before being brothers supernaturally in Jesus Christ.[23]

However, since the very origin of human history two species of men appear: Abel and Cain. Rational beings, born to the same father, indeed to the person from whom their mother had been drawn, they are identically human. Yet, having two radically dif-

20. Augustine's anti-racism extends to all humans, whoever they are, including Pygmies and even the Skiopods, if they exist, about which he is not sure. (The Skiopods protect themselves from the sun in the shadow of their foot.) He includes the headless humans and the Cynocephali or dog-headed. *De Civitate Dei* XVI.8.1, col. 485 [2:195–96]: "Sed omnia genera hominum quae dicuntur esse, credere non est necesse. Verum quisquis uspiam nascitur homo, id est animal rationale mortale, quamliber nostris inusitatam sensibus gerat corporis formam seu colorem sive motum sive sonum sive qualibet vi, qualibet parte, qualibet qualitate naturam: ex illo uno protoplasto originem ducere nullus fidelium dubitaverit. Aparet tamen quid in pluribus natura obtinuerit et quid sit ipsa raritate mirabile." Note the expression *nullus fidelium*.

21. Ibid., XII.22, col. 373 [2:63].

22. Ibid., XII.21, col. 372 [2:62]: "Hominem vero . . . unum ac singulum creavit, non utique solum sine humana societate deserendum, sed ut eo modo vehementius ei commendaretur ipsius societatis unitas vinculumque concordiae, si non tantum inter se naturae similitudine, verum etiam cognationis affectu homines necterentur; quando nec ipsam quidem feminam copulandam viro, sicut ipsum creare illi placuit, sed ex ipso, ut omne ex homine uno diffunderetur genus humanum."

23. Ibid., XII.22, col. 373 [2:62–63]. The very fact that there is natural unity of humankind is known only by faith, because Christians believe that God created a single man from whom he drew the first woman and that all others are born from the first couple. The creator could have done otherwise. If he acted as he did, it is precisely so that the people of the elect would be prepared to conceive itself as one. The unity of humankind is a sketch and prefiguration of the unity of the holy people called to adoption in Jesus Christ. This whole perspective on nature is taken from faith.

ferent wills, each represent the possibility at least of a radically distinct society. According to whether they follow one or the other example, humans are divided between two peoples, that which loves good and that which loves evil. Abel is the founder of the first, Cain of the second.[24] From this origin, the history of the two peoples is confused with universal history, or rather it just is that history.[25] Augustine traced that history's basic outline; after him others have taken it up or prolonged it. We have only to ask ourselves how Augustine himself conceived the two societies of which he spoke. Their very nature is what we have to define.

We were saying that there are as many societies as there are loves shared in common. When Augustine himself speaks of a City, it is therefore in the figurative or even *mystical* sense, as he calls it, that the term must be understood. On the one hand, there is the society or City of all humans who, by loving God in Christ, are predestined to reign eternally with him; and, on the other hand, there is the City of all humans who, by not loving God, are predestined to suffer eternal punishment with the devils. Therefore, Augustine never conceived the idea of a single universal society, but of two, which are universal at least in the sense that every human, whoever he is, is necessarily a citizen of one or the other, even predestined to one or the other.[26] In this sense it is true to say that two loves made two Cities, one where the love of God unites all members; and the other where all citizens, whatever the time or country in which they live, are united by their common love of the world. Au-

24. *Ennarationes in Psalmos* 142.3 (PL 37:1846): "Antiqua ergo ista civitas Dei, semper tolerans terram, sperans coelum quae etiam Jerusalem vocatur et Sion." See *De Civitate Dei* XV.1.2, col. 437 [2:139]: "Natus est igitur prior Cain ex illis duobus generis humani parentibus pertinens ad hominum civitatem; posterior Abel, ad civitatem Dei." Here again, note that *city of men* does not mean State or nation, but the people whose end is not God. This is evident because, as a man, Abel is not distinguished from Cain in any way.

25. There is indeed only one humankind, divided into two peoples. St. Augustine, *De Vera Religione* 50 (PL 34:144): "Universum genus humanum, cujus tanquam unius hominis vita est ab Adam usque ad finem hujus saeculi, ita sub divinae providentiae legibus administrantur, ut in duo genera distributum appareat."

26. *De Civitate Dei* XV.1.1, col. 457 [2:139–40]. See 44n32, below.

gustine distinguished their principles in several ways: love of God or love of the world, love of God to the point of contempt of self or love of self pushed to contempt for God; love of the flesh or love of the spirit; in any case they are certainly distinguished by the love from which each springs as from its very root. By whatever name we distinguish them, it remains true to say: *duas civitates faciunt duos amores*, or *fecerunt civitates suas amores duo*.[27]

Even before Augustine wrote the history, and when *The City of God* was still only a project, he conceived the Cities in that way. After distinguishing between the perverse love of self and holy charity, he immediately added:

> These two loves of which one is holy, the other impure; one social, the other private; one seeking the good of all with a mind to the society above, the other in a spirit of domineering arrogance reducing what belongs to all to its own power; one submitted to God, the other in rivalry with him; one tranquil, the other turbulent; one peaceful, the other seditious; one preferring truth to deceitful praise, the other avid for praise whatever it is worth; one friendly, the other jealous; one who wants for others what he wants for himself, the other that wants to subject his fellows; one who directs his neighbor in his neighbor's interest, the other who directs him in his own interest. These are the two loves, one of which is affirmed first of all among the good angels; the other among the bad angels, they found the division of humankind into two cities, according to God's admirable and ineffable providence that ordains and administers all his creatures. Two cities, one of the just, the other of the wicked, which remain mixed throughout time until the last judgment separates them, when one is rejoined to the good angels under their king and obtains eternal life, the other is rejoined to the bad angels under their king and is delivered into eternal fire.[28]

This summary of the history of the two loves, therefore, also contains the summary of universal history including the ultimate root

27. *Enarrationes in Psalmos* 64.2 (PL 36:773) [NPNF-I, 8:268]. See also *De Civitate Dei* XIV.1, col. 403; XIV.28, col. 436; XV.1.1, col. 437 [2:98, 136, 138–39].

28. St. Augustine, *De Genesi ad Litteram* XI.15.20 (PL 34:437).

of its intelligibility. Tell me what a people loves, and I will tell you what it is.[29]

Exactly what are the two Cities? As we have said, they are two peoples whose nature is defined. The word *city* already designates them in symbolic fashion, but we can give them still more symbolic names: *Jerusalem* (vision of peace) and *Babylon* (Babel, confusion).[30] Whatever name we give them, we are always dealing with the same thing, namely, two *human societies*.[31] To grasp their notion better, the surest method is to define the elements of which they are composed, but, on this point, Augustine expressed himself in so many different ways that we may certainly excuse his readers for hesitating and even some of his interpreters for becoming lost. Still, a connecting thread allows us to situate ourselves confidently in the maze of the texts. It is the principle posited by Augustine several times that the two Cities recruit their

29. *De Civitate Dei* XIX.24, col. 655 [2:385]: "Profecto ut videatur qualis quisque populus sit, illa sunt intuenda quae diliget."

30. All kinds of human societies, however numerous and varied they may be, are therefore reduced to two. Augustine labels these *genera humanae societatis* as *civitates*, inspiring himself in the language of scripture; see *De Civitate Dei* XIV.1, col. 403 [2:99]. Augustine does not specify his scriptural sources here, but he already did so in *De Civitate Dei* XI.1, col. 317 [2:1–2], where he first offers: "Gloriosa dicta sunt de te civitas Dei" (Ps 86:3), as well as Ps 47:2, 3, 9, and 45:5–6. Scholz, *Glaube und Unglaube*, remits to other New Testament passages (the last reference is to be corrected, Rv 21:2). It would be beneficial to discuss the prehistory of the Augustinian notion; see Scholz, *Glaube und Unglaube*, 71–81. The passages taken from Ticonius (ibid., 78–81), are particularly important. Ticonius had already spoken about Babylon, the impious city, and Jerusalem, church of the living God. Let us recall, furthermore, that the meaning of these names is *visio pacis* for Jerusalem, and *confusio*, for Babylon (and for Babel); see *De Civitate Dei* XVI.4, col. 492 [2:182], for Babylon, and *De Civitate Dei* XIX.11 [2:364–65] for Jerusalem. [Translator: Gilson's note has XIX.9, where Jerusalem is not mentioned. For Babylon, Gilson also cites XVIII.2, but there, Babylon is mentioned as the place of Abraham's origins, not of confusion.]

31. *De Civitate Dei* XV.18, col. 461, and XV.20.1, col. 463 [2:165–68]. Therefore, Augustine remains faithful to the Greco-Roman tradition of the city-people. Augustine himself distinguishes only three organic forms of social life (*vita socialis*): the family, the city (*civitas vel urbs*), and the planet, in *De Civitate Dei* XIX.7, col. 633 [2:361]: "Post civitatem vel urbem sequitur orbis terrae, in quo tertium gradum ponunt societatis humane, incipientes a domo, atque inde ad urbem, deinde ad orbem progrediendo venientes." Scholz, *Glaube und Unglaube*, 85–86, correctly observes that it is usually inexact and often dangerous to translate *civitas* by State, although it may be licit in relatively rare cases.

citizens solely according to the law of divine predestination. All humans are part of one or the other, because all humans are predestined to happiness with God or misery with the Devil.[32]

As no other alternative is conceivable, we can affirm without fear of error that the quality of being a citizen of one or the other City in the last analysis depends on divine predestination of which each human is object. So, it is in this sense that the different expressions Augustine uses must be interpreted. Certain of them cause no difficulty, for example "the City of God and the City of the Devil,"[33] or, what amounts to the same thing, "the City of Christ and the City of the Devil." Likewise, we find "the family of those who love from faith and those who do not love from faith," "the people of the faithful and the people of the unfaithful," or "the society of the pious and the society of the impious," that is to say those whom the love of God unites and those whom love of self unites.[34] On the other hand, we may hesitate when Augustine contrasts "Earthly City and Heavenly City," "temporal city and eternal city," or even "mortal city and immortal city,"[35] because, ultimately, the two Cities are immortal; the predestined who live in them are still members of one of the Cities and on this earth can already be a member of the Heavenly City by the fact of being predestined.[36] Thus, Augustine sometimes uses precise expressions

32. *De Civitate Dei* XV.1.1, col. 457 [2:139]: "Quas etiam mystice appelamus civitates duas, hoc est duas societates hominum; quarum est una quae praedestinata est in aeternum regnare cum Deo; altera, aeternum supplicium subire cum diabolo."

33. Ibid., XXI.1, col. 709 [2:448]: "Civitates quarum una est Dei, altera Diaboli." See also XVII.20.2, col. 556 [2:274]: "quod pertinet ad civitates duas: una, diaboli, altera Christi." Augustine adds "et earum reges diabolum et Christum" and further on calls the City of God "liberam."

34. Ibid., XIX.17, col. 645 [2:374–75]. See also XIV.13.1, col. 421 [2:120]: "una scilicet societas piorum hominum, altera impiorum, singula quae cum angelis ad se pertinentibus in quibus praecessit hac amor Dei, hac amor sui."

35. Ibid., XI.1, col. 317 [2:1–2]. Observe here, "quamdam civitatem Dei, cujus cives esse concupiscimus illo amore, quem nobis illius Conditor inspiravit" (V.18.3, col. 165, and XXI.11, col. 726 [1:170–71 and 2:466–67]).

36. Augustine himself says so in appropriate language, first of all in the passages where he presents the two cities as "mixed" with each other in this life; next and especially in the

and sometimes he does not. In case of doubt, the former must serve as the rules of interpretation for the latter: whatever name it is given, every City reduces either to the one where God is king or to the one where the Devil rules, and their different denominations never mean anything different.

Therefore, we will avoid the unfortunately rather frequent misunderstanding of confusing the City of the Devil with political societies as such, or, as is sometimes said, the State. The two may coincide in fact, in determined historic circumstances, but they are always distinguished in principle. The genuine definition of the Earthly City is completely different.[37] The question is not to know whether we live or fail to live in one of the societies that presently share the earth. This is inevitable. The question is whether we ourselves situate our ultimate end on earth or in heaven. In the first case we are citizens of the Earthly City, in the second we are citizens of the Heavenly City. The problem does not change its character when it no longer deals with individuals but with the societies themselves: those who are organized exclusively with a view to happiness of the world are thereby incorporated into the Earthly City, which is that of the Devil. Those who are organized with a view to divine beatitude are by that very thing incorporated into the Heavenly City, which is none other than the City of God.

For example, Roman society in the period of decadence, with all the vices reproached by her poets, historians, and moralists, is found to have been exactly a fragment of the Devil's City, traveling on earth toward the nefarious end that awaits it. In the measure in which such a society lives on after Christ's coming, what can be done but to tolerate it patiently while foretelling its fate?

---

passages where he writes: "Civitas autem coelestis, vel potius pars ejus, quae in hac mortalitate peregrinatur et vivit, ex fide." See also ibid., XIX.17, cols. 645–46 (2:374–75): "Haec ergo coelestis civitas dum peregrinatur in terra." See ibid., XXII.6, col. 758 (2:503–6).

37. On this point see the sound observations by Scholz, *Glaube und Unglaube*, 87–89, and Otto Schilling, *Die Staats- und Soziallehre des hl. Augustinus* (Freiburg im Breisgau: Herder, 1910), 54.

Christ's servants—whether they be kings or princes or judges, whether soldiers or provincials, rich or poor, free or slave, men and women alike—are told to endure, if need be, the worst and most depraved republic and, by their endurance, to win for themselves a place of glory in the most holy and majestic senate of the angels, so to speak in the heavenly republic, whose law is the will of God.[38]

There can be no doubt. The earthly republic that Augustine condemns is certainly Rome and the one he opposes to it is the City of God, the only one where true justice rules, because its founder and ruler is Christ.[39] Furthermore, speaking of those who are "citizens of the earthly republic,"[40] Augustine certainly thinks of members of a people or a State. However, in all these cases, neither a people nor a State are condemned as such, but because in placing their end on earth they join the City of the Devil whose law they accept. They are only bad insofar as they want to be exclusively earthly, which suffices to exclude them from the City of God.

The precise meaning of *Civitas Terrena*, therefore is *city of the children of earth*, which is to say, of the societies whose members are linked by the exclusive or preponderant love for earthly things and consider earth as their only or their true city. But whether it is earth or heaven, what end do the *cities* seek? When Augustine develops his thinking on the point completely, he demonstrates that every social group proposes to achieve peace. Two different sorts of peace can be conceived. Nothing prohibits humans from desiring both at once, but a radical difference separates those who pursue earthly peace exclusively from those who further desire the peace of heaven. Through this we return to the distinction of societies in function of their dominant wills: all the wills that tend toward the peace of God form the people of the City of God. All the wills that tend toward the peace of this world, as if toward their

38. *De Civitate Dei* II.19, col. 65 [1:55].
39. Ibid., II.21.4, cols. 68–69 [1:59].
40. Ibid., XXII.6, col. 759 [2:504].

ultimate goal, form the people of the Earthly City. The first people unites all those who use the world to enjoy God. The second people unites all those who, whether they acknowledge one God or many gods, intend to use them to enjoy the world.[41] As the love, so the people, we say. If a certain people can be legitimately identified with the Earthly City, it is only in the measure in which that people itself is incorporated into it by its dominant will, and it is not incorporated into it by the fact that it sojourns in time, as its condition of creatureliness imposes, but by its refusal to use time with a view to enjoying eternity.

Just as human society as such is not identified with the Earthly City, the Church is not identified with the City of God. Let us remember that the latter includes all those predestined to heavenly beatitude and them alone. That is not the case of the Church. However strictly the Church is conceived, there may be persons who one day will enjoy the vision of God who do not yet belong to the Church. St. Paul before his conversion is a typical case. He was not yet in the Church of Christ, but he was already a predestined citizen of the City of God. Conversely, there are Christians in the Church who are not destined to celestial beatitude. Therefore, they are members of the Church, but they are not citizens of the City of God. Still, just as certain people are incorporated into the Earthly City by the fact of their dominant will, the Church incarnates in fact and, by its essential will, even in principle the City of God. This is why St. Augustine expresses himself with precision by saying that here below the two Cities are *perplexae*, that is to say, still mixed one with the other. The expression must be understood in the strong sense, because if their ideas are irreducibly distinct to the point of excluding each other mutually, their cities are not always distinct, as long as they journey in time, where they must be. When St. Paul persecuted Christians, this predestined member

41. Ibid., XV.7.1, col. 444 [2:146]; IV.34, col. 140; XV.11, col. 456; and XIX.17, col. 645 [1:141–42 and 2:160, 374–75].

of the City of God was still mixed within the people of the Earthly City. Therefore, the City of God counts future citizens even among its enemies. "By the same token, so long as it is on a pilgrimage in this world, the City of God has with it [*habet secum*], joined to it by participation in the sacraments, some from the number of its enemies who will not be with it in the eternal destiny of the saints."[42] Mixed together now, the last judgment will separate them, but the members of the Church who will not enjoy heavenly beatitude are those within the Church who do not live according to the Church. That is why the confusion between their numbers that may exist in time does not alter the purity of their ideas. Even if they are inside the Church, those whose love aspires to the goods of the earth are citizens of the earthly cities, while the Church herself unceasingly aspires to the goods of the Heavenly City. In this capacity, insofar as she is the Church, she is already identified with the City of God,[43] because, just as those who live in the world according to the world are already members of the Earthly City, those who live in the Church, according to the Church, already reign with Christ in the heavenly kingdom.

The City of God thus conceived has frontiers that, however spiritual they may be, are unshakable, because they coincide with the limits set by faith. Because the City of God is Christ's kingdom, faith in Christ animates it from within. The City lives on faith and is coextensive with the totality of human beings who themselves live on faith, because Christ reigns everywhere that faith reigns, and where Christ reigns, there also is the kingdom of Christ. This is an extremely important point. A new society is constituted by the agreement of wills united in love of the same good, which is

42. Ibid., I.35, cols. 45–46 [1:35].

43. Ibid., VIII.24.2, col. 251: "Aedificantur enim domus Domino civitas Dei, quae est sancta ecclesia, in omni terra"; XIII.16, col. 387: "Sed philosophi, contra quorum calumnias defendimus civitatem Dei, hoc est ecclesiam"; XVI.2.3, col. 479: "neque nisi ad Christum et ejus Ecclesiam, quae Civitas Dei est"; XX.9.3: "Ecclesia quae nunc etiam est regnum Christi"; XX.9.3, col. 674: "de regno ejus, quod est Ecclesia" [1:24, 2:80, 187, 408].

proposed to them by the same faith. The agreement of hearts presupposes here the agreement of minds, and this is also why at the same time that the good of a holy society is a love, it is also a doctrine. Its love is of a truth and of a truth that can only be one thing, the truth of Christ. Augustine feels this so vividly that from here he has deduced a doctrine on the essential difference that distinguishes the attitude of the world and that of the Church toward the truth.[44]

Philosophies promise human happiness. They even trace the path that leads to it, but no two philosophies of any importance agree on what happiness is, or on the road that we must take to achieve it. There are many reasons for this disagreement: for example, vanity that pushes philosophers to desire originality at any cost or to exceed others in wisdom. The primary reason is deeper: being humans these philosophers have sought happiness as humans, with human feeling and human reasoning. What they lacked in order to find truth and agree about it was to be supported by a divine revelation that was at once certain and common to all. The sacred authors proceed in a completely different way. Few in number, they all say the same thing, and this unity of sentiment makes them obtain credit from a great multitude. Thus, on the one hand, there are many different philosophers, each of whom has only a few disciples. On the other hand, there are a few sacred writers who are all in agreement and carry behind them an immense crowd of disciples.

This fundamental difference explains why the attitude of States toward philosophy is not the same as the Church's attitude. For a pagan people, the State remains indifferent to doctrines taught by professors of wisdom. Historical experience is conclusive on this point: in the Earthly City, the State has never become the patron

44. Here, the human beings themselves are the city and the kingdom. Regarding those whose conversation is already in heaven (Phil 3:20), we can say with ibid., XX.9.1, col. 673 [2:406]: "eo modo sunt in regno ejus, ut sint etiam ipsi regnun ejus [*scilicet*, Christi]"; see also XX.9.3, col. 674 [2:407–8].

of any philosophical doctrine so resolutely as to condemn all other doctrines: "But is there any author from any philosophical sect who is so fully accepted in this demon-worshipping city, that all the others, who hold different and contrary views, are rejected?"[45] Writing these lines, Augustine thinks particularly of the history of Athens, where we see—simultaneously taught—both Epicureanism, which denies divine providence, and Stoicism, which affirms it. Yet, it would have mattered to human happiness to know who was right and who was wrong. Antisthenes places the highest good in pleasure, Aristippus in virtue. One says that the wise man must shun public affairs, the other that he must seek power. Let us consider other no less important points of doctrine: whether the soul is mortal or immortal, whether there is or is not transmigration of souls; we come up against contradictions everywhere. Did the State intervene to establish harmony? Never.

> In the face of all these disagreements among the philosophers, and almost innumerable others, has any people or senate or public authority or high office in the Ungodly City ever shown any interest in deciding among them, approving and accepting some, condemning and rejecting others? Instead, has not that city held in its lap—at random, in utter confusion, and without passing judgment—all these controversies among men whose differences are not about fields or houses or any financial matter but about the very things that determine whether our lives will be miserable or happy?[46]

In fact, the pagan city is a Babylon, because it is a city of confusion, even the worst confusion, that which by authorizing all errors takes no interest in truth. Furthermore, we might anticipate that,

45. Ibid., XVIII.41.2, col. 60 [2:324]; see XVIII.41–43, cols. 600–603. Against this might be objected the divergences that translators may introduce into the teaching of scripture. But Augustine feels no qualms on this point. For him, even the discrepancies of translators are inspired by God, so much so that in these cases and after their fashion those translators were prophets (XVIII.43, cols. 603–4 [2:326–28]). If we think about what fruitful doctrine Augustine himself drew from clearly preposterous translations, we might be inclined to agree with him.

46. Ibid., XVIII.41.2 [2:324–25].

because the Earthly City is where the Devil is king, and what does it matter to him, to this king, that the most varied errors oppose or are in combat with each others? As diverse as they may be, their whole business is impieties, and it is enough for them to be false to assure the Devil's power.

We see that Augustine has not anticipated the official philosophy of a Marxist State, but the Marxist State itself perhaps only represents the late awareness of an intrinsic necessity within the conception of a universal society. From the moment at which the Earthly City aspires to the universality that is initially attributed to the City of God, it must in its turn promulgate a single dogma, assign to all humans a single and even very earthly good, the love of which will make them into a single people, a single city. Between the pagan State of antiquity and the pagan State of our days, there is the Catholic Church, whose spiritual authority the contemporary State demands and usurps. Even insofar as it is atheist, the modern State is completely totalitarian in principle.

The intellectual regime of the City of God, which is completely contrary to that of the ancient city, is also different from that of the modern city. This is very apparent if we compare the people of Israel from its origins with Greek city. Certainly this *republic* has never known such indifference. In it, true prophets are immediately distinguished from false prophets, and the perfect agreement of sacred authors among themselves has always been regarded as a sure sign of truth. "These [the prophets] were their philosophers, that is, their lovers of wisdom, these were their wise men, their theologians, their prophets, their teachers of integrity and piety. Anyone who thought and lived as they did thought and lived not according to men, but according to God, who spoke through them."[47] Accordingly, what gives such teaching its coherence and force is that it rests upon God's authority. The authority of human reason has demonstrated its weakness by its very failure. Not only

47. Ibid., XVIII.41.3 [2:325].

does Augustine seem to fail to foresee the appearance of peoples where the State, by making itself a teacher, will in its turn decree a truth of State, but he visibly doubts that any society whose sole truth belongs to this world could be interested in such matters. It is not that philosophy might not lack some truths accessible to reason among many errors. Even so long after the first enthusiasm that reading Plato had inspired, Augustine still did not forget the partial truth that philosophers had spoken about God, author and providence of the world, about the excellence of virtue, the love of country, and confidence in friendship. The philosophers, indeed, knew and taught all these truths and many others in addition, but mixed with numberless errors, without knowing what goal to relate them to, or how to relate them to it. At the same time, the prophets were teaching these same truths to the people of God, but free from any error and with an authority that way irrefutable and definitive. The people of God owed its own unity to the unity of this sacred doctrine.

As the City of God's incarnation, the Church only maintains the tradition of the Jewish people of which it is the heir and whose sacred deposit the Church has enriched by adding the New Testament to the Old. Its catholicity, which is to say its universality, only obliges it to preserve this doctrinal unity more strictly. Moreover, the care the Church employs in discharging this duty has given birth to heresy, a phenomenon unknown to the ancients. Socrates was put to death for impiety toward the gods of the city, not for having committed some doctrinal error about the nature of the gods in general. Provided that one said nothing against the ancient city's gods, it could tolerate all theologies. By contrast, the City of God can tolerate only one, whose common acceptance assures the City's very existence along with its unity. He who breaks the doctrine breaks the bond of the City. That is precisely what the heretic does. By choosing his own truth, the heretic acts as a destructive force provoked by the Devil to shake the City of God from within at the exact moment when it begins to triumph by the grace of God over its enemies without. From that comes the compelling duty of doctrinal absolutism for the Church, which later will take on the form of a properly civic and social intolerance in the periods in which the City of God would, so to speak, absorb States, but which in its own essence is required only within the Heavenly City. Nothing is more evident than that it is required there. It is a question of life or death for the Heavenly City. The Church cannot tolerate with indifference and without intervening that those who speak in its name should maintain what pleases them. The City of God whose existence is attached to the unity of faith cannot grant its doctors the right of combating and contradicting each other that the City of Confusion indifferently grants to its philosophers. The only thing it can do in such cases is to intervene with authority to reestablish unity by calling back the deviant. A person who is mistaken is not a heretic, but if he who is mistaken becomes a heretic by preferring his own sense to the doctrine by which the Church lives, he can only be excluded from the body that he works to destroy.[48] To tell the truth, the Church does not exclude him. It takes notice that he has excluded himself.

Through this we see the conflicting attitudes of the two Cities on the subject of doctrine: indifference on the one hand, dogmatism on the other. This Augustinian approach to the problem simultaneously defines one of its constant ingredients and the organ of innumerable difficulties, some of which captured Augustine's own attention, but many of which, and by far the most serious, were to arise later in the course of history. Because the City of God is not of this world, it has no duty of intolerance toward things of this world, and as long as it does not oblige the Earthly City to re-

48. Ibid., XVIII.51.1–2, cols. 613–14 [2:337–38]. Regarding the problems that Augustine's eventual recourse to the secular arm posed to Augustine himself, see Jean Félix Nourisson, *La philosophie de Saint Augustine* (Paris: Didier, 1869), 2:65–73. Gustave Combès studied thoroughly the evolution of Augustine's thought on this point; see *La doctrine politique de saint Augustin* (Paris: Plon, 1927), 352–409.

nounce its peculiar mission, the City of God bothers no individual or State. Let Christians think and live as they please, what does it matter as long as they do not oblige others to think like them? Still, the City of God cannot approve the Earthly City. It is bound rather to reproach it, to condemn it, and if it can, even to reform it. What are the means by which the City of God judges itself entitled to intervene in the Earthly City? This is the whole problem, and the solution can vary by time or place. However, if we hold the Augustinian position, nothing can prevent the City of God from intervening to order that temporal freedom of which it is the very essence of the temporal city to avail itself according to Augustine's own description. When their "mystical" opposition is carried to the temporal realm, it inevitably degenerates into conflicts. Although Augustine never seems to have foreseen it, it is no longer impossible to imagine the temporal city becoming unified in its turn in the image of the Heavenly City and becoming like a counter-Church, with its own doctrinal truth, this time imposed by force, excluding all discussion and intolerant of any contradiction.

When the bishop of Hippo wrote *The City of God*, nothing yet presaged that anything of the sort was possible. Among the Greeks, a total of 288 different ethical sects offered themselves to the public. Even if we reduce the definitions of the highest good to three, as Varro proposed, there remains a choice of answers, none of which unfortunately can satisfy the Christian. If the Christian wants to know what the highest good consists of, he directs himself to revelation. He learns from revelation what eternal life is, and he accepts it on faith.[49] Henceforth, faith directs everything in the same way for all who accept it. For Christians, the present life, into which they are plunged by birth, is only a time of trial that awaits them at each of the three levels of the social order in which they must be involved. Their family is full of worries. Their country is full of injustices. Ultimately, the whole earth is full of

49. *De Civitate Dei* XIX.4.1, cols. 627–28 [2:354].

every kind of confusions that cause wars between States, first of all even by mere diversity of languages. Someone prefers to live with his dog rather than with a stranger whose language he does not understand.[50] *Domus*, *urbs*, *orbis*—where can we find a society worthy of the name to give us peace? By uniting the earth under a single empire?

But the experiment has been carried out, and its failure is evident. It is somewhat naive to believe that world unification would suppress wars. Within the Roman Empire and because of its very extension, how many internal wars were there? International conflicts have been replaced by civil or social war, which is difficult to regard as progress.[51] In whatever direction we look the earth offers no refuge for peace except the Christian hope for a peace that it does not expect on this earth but in eternal happiness.[52] Moreover, this is why already in this life, Christians dwell in the other. They already participate in its peace, but they can only do so by participating in its order from which all peace derives. This order itself presupposes knowledge of the truth, which one day will give the vision of God fully that already faith alone sufficiently assures in this life. This is what St. Augustine says in one of those passages that sums up his whole doctrine: "But, because in his very eagerness for knowledge, he [a human] may fall into some deadly error due to the weakness of the mind, he has need of divine guidance, which he may obey with certainty, and divine help, so that he may obey it freely."[53] For grace does not suppress freedom; it gives it a foundation. Thus, in this journey in life where the mortal human body hides the sight of God from us, faith is the only guide. Because the whole human race is only one man on a journey toward God, just as faith alone assures the unity of peace in the heart of every human being, every family, every people, and every empire,

50. Ibid., XIX.5–6, cols. 631–33 [2:359–61].
51. Ibid., XIX.7, cols. 633–34 [2:361–62].
52. Ibid., XIX.11, col. 637 [2:364–65].
53. Ibid., XIX.14, col. 642 [2:371]; see 2 Cor 5:6–7.

so also and still more evidently, our faith alone assures the peace of the City of God. "The peace of the heavenly city is perfectly ordered and wholly concordant fellowship in the enjoyment of God, and of each other in God."[54] But the Heavenly City owes this order and harmony to the submission that makes her accept the eternal law that she receives here below by faith.[55]

It is impossible to read St. Augustine without experiencing the impression of his doctrine's huge importance or without hesitating frequently about how to interpret it. So much stems from it that one is afraid of attributing to Augustine's doctrine what the doctrine prepared through it did not contain, and inversely of denying what it certainly must contain at least in embryo insofar as it gave birth to it. We would like to distinguish those consequences of Augustine's principles of which he himself was conscious from those he did not foresee and no doubt could not foresee. How can we achieve that? Augustine himself hesitated, varied in the application of his ideas to changing circumstances. The circumstances he knew are few in comparison with the enormous sequence of those he did not know, because they occurred after his time in the course of an experience that is now fifteen centuries old. It is not always easy to know how Augustine himself applied his principles to diverse and varied conditions in his time. Knowing how he would have applied them to others is impossible, but we can at least note how his successors understood them.

The two Cities are equally constituted in a single universe, whose head is God himself, its creator. However, against the Stoics, Augustine does not conceive of the universe as a "city." He never speaks of the cosmos as the City of God in the sense in which a Stoic could speak of it as the City of Zeus. For him a society can only exist among beings endowed with reason. This is why we have seen him posit the universe as the scenario where the history of

54. Ibid., XIX.13.1, col. 640 [2:368].
55. Ibid., XIX.14, col. 642 [2:370–71].

societies unfolds, and if the universe is affected by that history in some way, it is not exactly its own history. In this sense Augustine is profoundly different from the Stoics. When he talks about "city," he intends to talk about a genuine society, not about an order of things.

If we consider the totality of rational beings with him, including the angels, all appear to be answerable for a single history that is prepared from all eternity in the secret of divine predestination and begins with the creation of the world and time, and that will finish only with the end of the world and the consummation of time. Accordingly, Augustine really undertook to write a discourse on universal history, and if he was not to be the last to attempt this undertaking, he certainly seems to have been the first. In what particularly regards human nature, this project implies the prior acknowledgment of the unity of humankind and, consequently, the unity of its history. He said this in passing when he proposed to consider all humans as a single individual whose history unfolds without interruption from the beginning to the end of time. Despite the absence of the actual expression, the idea of universal history is clearly implied in St. Augustine's work.

Is it the same as another idea, that of "philosophy of history"? This time it seems difficult to answer simply yes or no, because the answer implies a certain concept of philosophy. The presence of a Christian wisdom of history is indisputable in Augustine. We can already wonder whether, according to him, simple universal history would be possible without revelation, which alone unveils the origin and end of history. Still, even divorced from everything that universal history owes to revelation for Augustine, the concept of universal history would remain possible, because it is not contradictory to admit that all humans could be considered a collective being whose single history unfolds in time. The limits and method of its history would then be at issue, but not its possibility.

The problem is more complex if we are talking about a philosophy of history, because we then must ask whether from the viewpoint of Augustine himself, history would have admitted a purely rational and nevertheless true overall interpretation without the light of revelation. It is certain that Augustine himself did not attempt this undertaking. His explanation of universal history is essentially religious in the sense that it derives its light from the light of revelation. Therefore, in fact, Augustine was a theologian of history. The interpretation he proposes falls less under what we call *philosophy* today, than what he himself labeled *Wisdom*, understanding by that the wisdom that is not only Christ's but is Christ. If he had been questioned on this point, which would have surprised him very much and which nobody dreamt of doing, would he have admitted that reason alone can extract meaning from universal history that is both intelligible and true within its own boundaries? As that did not happen, this question no longer belongs to history, and if there are serious reasons to think that such an endeavor would have seemed disastrous to Augustine, it cannot be proved.

Does it follow that Augustine has nothing to do with the birth of a philosophy of history? This is a third question different from the other two. For, if he did not think about it, because it had not been thought about, this is not a reason to say that Augustine's work is not the origin of the philosophy of history. On the contrary, everything leads us to believe that the different philosophies of history that developed after Augustine have been so many attempts to resolve, by the light of natural reason alone, a problem that initially was only posed by faith and that perhaps cannot be resolved without it. In this sense the first theologian of history[56]

56. *Theology* here has the sense of speculative doctrine, because the Old Testament, with its interpretation by the New Testament, was in fact already a universal history of known societies treated from the standpoint of revelation. The history of the people of God was a history of God's plan for all peoples. We even find an overall sketch of this history in Wis 10–19, which tells how Wisdom has led peoples since Adam's creation. It is already a "discourse on universal history." For the sense in which we can speak of historical

would be the father of all philosophies of history. This does not mean that Augustine wanted philosophies of history, and perhaps those philosophies do not recognize themselves as the rubble from a more grand edifice in which alone they might find full justification of their own truth, in an authentic sense of which they themselves are not aware.

When we admit that Augustine proposed his theology and provoked the emergence of this philosophy, it remains to be seen whether his doctrine implied a precise notion of a single temporal society. It does not, but it suggested one. We have already observed that Augustine never spoke of one society but of two, between which all humankind is divided. In this sense the doctrine is both broader and narrower than that of a universal political society. It is broader not only because it includes angels as well as humans, but also because it rests on revelation that transcends the scheme of empirical history in the past as in the future, grounding what humans know and Christians believe about their history in a total explanation. It is narrower because its very unifying principle forbids it to join all humans in only one society. In principle, this single and truly universal society would have been possible: it would be enough for all rational beings to be united in the same love for the same Good. In fact, the rupture occurred immediately, and because every society is the union of a group of rational beings in the communion of the same love, the society of those who do not love God is irremediably divided from the society of those who love him. Whether a universal earthly society is possible in the world or not, an absolutely universal Heavenly City of all humans seems impossible unless the distinction that is fundamental in Augustine (between the City of the Devil and the City of God) is erased.

Consequently, there we have the first obstacle, which seems insurmountable, to translating directly the Augustinian notion of

progress in Augustine's doctrine, see Theodore Mommsen's essay, "St. Augustine and the Christian Idea of Progress," *Journal of the History of Ideas* 12 (1951): 346–74.

the Heavenly City into terms of temporal unity. To unite humans with a view to the other life, the Church only disposes of faith. It does not suffice for the cross of Christ to be placed in the middle of the world. It is still necessary for humans to consent to look upon it, and for those who have done so once not to close their eyes to avoid seeing it again. Even if humans carry the cross on their shoulders, they do not always recognize that it is what God has given them to carry after having borne it himself. So, in order to think only about the future from now on, what means does the Church, which is only the City of Christ in pilgrimage toward God, dispose of to assemble all its sheep in a single fold under a single shepherd? In other words, what means does the Church dispose of to make all humans accept the faith deposited in her and that her love proposes to them?

Love is not imposed by force. Jesus Christ possessed force and willed that it should be left to Caesar. But could Caesar, perhaps, be converted? Through Caesar, who legitimately possesses force, could the temporal city be reformed in the image of the City of God? It is not necessary for that which is in this world to be of the world, for the earthly to wish to be of the earth, or for the temporal to always refuse to conceive itself as a stage toward the eternal. Faith, which transcends reason, can conquer and give understanding. The Church transcends people of every race, country, language, and condition. If those people were all united by faith in the love of Christ, as the Church herself invites them to be, could not the Church give them a completely terrestrial unity and peace that they might enjoy immediately on earth? At the same time, Augustine's doctrine establishes faith as the boundary of its universal society, and it would suggest an unceasing effort to push that frontier out to the limits of the earth. Despite its misfortunes, Rome had already had Christian emperors, and it was still Rome. If Augustine perhaps has not clearly conceived of a single world united and pacified under a single Christian emperor who would find in Christian faith itself the basis of a kind of temporal peace on earth while awaiting the perfect peace of heaven, he made no bones about showing earthly sovereigns that the fate of their empires was henceforth tied to that of the Church. To inspire princes with the desire to organize the earth in a single society made in its image and likeness, it was enough for the City of God to exist.

Everything is clear in St. Augustine himself. The City of God and the Earthly City are two mystical Cities, to the point that citizens are distributed among them by divine predestination. It would be impossible to be further from any kind of politics in the temporal sense of the term. In Augustine's successors a dual, complementary tendency was gradually affirmed. On the one hand, forgetting the great apocalyptic vision of the heavenly Jerusalem, the City of God was reduced to the Church, which in the genuine Augustinian perspective was only its pilgrim part, laboring in time to recruit citizens for the City of God for eternity. On the other hand, more and more, Augustine's Earthly City—the mystical city of perdition—tended to be confused with the temporal, political city. From that moment, the problem of these two Cities became the problem of two powers, one spiritual, that of the popes, and the other temporal, that of the States or the princes. But because even the spiritual is present in the temporal through the Church, the conflict of the two Cities descended from eternity into time. With one stroke, the universal human society descended from heaven to earth, and because the same society cannot have two heads, the problem was posed of knowing which of the two powers exercised supreme jurisdiction. The history of this problem would be one of permanent conflict between priesthood and empire in the Middle Ages. Today we still suffer from the same conflict, but it does not date from today, and it is enormously naïve to suppose that the Middle Ages were a golden age when princes followed the crook of the Roman shepherd of nations like lambs. By itself, the ignominious slap at Anagni should be enough to dissipate that illusion. But bound up though it is with this problem of conflict, our problem is different. It is exactly to find out how, once established in time, the universal human society knew its own nature. We must get through many centuries to encounter the genius who clearly grasped the new elements of the problem. We will find them gathered in the *respublica fidelium* of the English Franciscan Roger Bacon.

THREE

The Christian Commonwealth

Among the incredibly diverse figures that populate the thirteenth century, none is more original than Roger Bacon. We cannot read him without loving him, though sometimes we wonder if we love him more dead than we would have loved him alive. This Franciscan friar spent long years in trouble with members of his order, perhaps a little through their fault, doubtless through his own, but what do we know exactly? We only know him by his writings, which reveal one of those apostles consecrated to the mission God entrusts to them, incapable of talking about anything else, a bit comic at first, then boring to their contemporaries, ultimately frankly unbearable. But perhaps we are mistaken and this Englishman was rather a taciturn fellow whose agitation was carried out exclusively in his books. Nothing is less interesting than to invent history. The only absolutely certain thing is that the spirit of this friar was obsessed by an incomparably noble dream, because it was his gift to conceive, in the fullness of its implications and requirements, the idea of a universal people whose citizenship would be open to all persons of good will united by their common profession of Christian faith.

Assuredly, the ideal of Roger Bacon recalls that of St. Augustine, but the Republic of the Faithful about which Bacon thinks is very different from the City of God. It is a Republic, if not of this world, at least in this world. It is not the City of God, or even exactly the Church. Although the Republic must grow up in the light of the Church and prepare the advent of the City of God in its manner, it is a true temporal people under the direction of human wisdom engaged in the search for the goods than mankind can enjoy in time. To imagine that this Republic was even merely possible, it is necessary to have that peculiar genius that reveals to certain persons the clear expression of confused aspirations of their own time. They know and say what others desire and have a premonition of. Thomas Aquinas, Bonaventure, Albert the Great, and Duns Scotus spoke admirably about Christian wisdom. All more or less felt that Christian wisdom secretly aspired to create a new people that would live upon the substance of wisdom, even in time, but Roger Bacon is the only one who saw it, the only one who received the personal mission of saying it and who did say it.[1] It is enough

1. St. Bonaventure is interested in the problem of assuring the sovereign authority of the Church and of its head, "universalis omnium pricipatus." *Quaestiones Disputatae de Perfectione Evangelica*, q. 4, a. 3, in *Opera Omnia* (Quarachi: Ex Typographia Colegii Sancti Bonaventurae, 1882–1902), 5:189–98 [There is an English translation by Thomas Reist and Robert J. Karris (St. Bonaventure, N.Y.: Franciscan Institute Publications, 2008)]. The pope is in charge of guaranteeing justice in all orders, even civil justice (5:194). He therefore possesses the two swords (5:196). Likewise, see Aquinas, *In II Sententiarum*, d. 44, reply to the fourth objection. We will see that Roger Bacon agrees completely with them on this point. Neither he nor they spoke of the pope's "indirect" power over the temporal realm, and Bacon even required the pope to use his authority to guarantee the Christian people's scientific development and its material well-being in all orders. The sense of his message is: because the pope possesses wisdom, he is responsible for everything and therefore has power over everything in the whole extension of the temporal realm. Thus Bacon's conception is no less unitary than St. Thomas's, who, although he subjects the temporal power to the supreme authority of the pope, leaves the princes in charge under the jurisdiction of the spiritual power (*Summa Theologiae* II-II, q. 10, a. 10, co.). However, precisely for this reason, St. Thomas conceives the pope as directing people by directing the princes who govern them in temporal matters (*De Regimine Principum* I, 15). After establishing the pope's supreme jurisdiction as vicar of Christ the King and heir to all his powers (*De Regimine Principum* I, 14), a pure theologian like St. Thomas does not try to offer a particular representation of the Christian people that must emerge from this hierarchy of powers. Thomas sees each prince governing his people in the temporal realm according to spiritual directives given by the pope. It does not seem that he then turned his gaze toward the temporal Christian society whose birth became inevitable. There is not even a society of Christian princes. In fact, we do not recall that Thomas ever mentioned the emperor. In Roger Bacon, by contrast, the Christian people are present everywhere, and their leader is the pope, who governs by wisdom. Bacon does not compare to St. Bonaventure or St. Thomas as a theologian. He is not in their class. But we see no one comparable to Bacon in the thirteenth century in his feeling for the particular relation of the Christian people. Like Dante, Bacon is irreplaceable for us, and is at the very heart of our subject.

to open Bacon's *Opus Majus* to discover his overall plan and ultimate intentions from the first chapter:

Two things are required for a complete study of wisdom: first, what is necessary in order to know it in the best way possible, then its relation to everything else in order to direct it by appropriate means. Indeed it is the light of wisdom that orders the Church of God, organizes the Republic of believers, works the conversion of unbelievers, and finally, by its power, represses those who are obstinate in evil and pushes them further back from the boundaries of the Church than by shedding Christian blood.[2]

Such words are clear, and if our reformer's zeal may sometimes have seemed indiscreet to his contemporaries, they could not fairly reproach him for not knowing exactly what he wanted. There is a principle and a means, Christian wisdom: there are three functions, and three ends direct the Church of God, organize the people of the faithful, and protect its frontier against the attacks of the enemy more efficiently and with less bloodshed than in the Crusades. Nobody ever conceived a moral ideal that was more completely Christian.[3]

2. Roger Bacon, *Opus Majus*, ed. John Henry Bridges (Oxford: Clarendon Press, 1897), 1:1. Although this facet of Bacon's thought is of fundamental importance, it has been little studied up to now. By contrast, Bacon as reformer of Christian wisdom has been the object of several studies. See particularly Raoul Carton, *L'Expérience mystique de l'illmination intérieure chez Roger Bacon* (Paris: J. Vrin, 1924). Bacon was probably born between 1210 and 1214 near Ilchester in Dorsetshire. The exact date of his death is unknown. It must have occurred at the end of the thirteenth century, after the composition of the *Compendium Studii Philosophiae*, which is dated from 1292.

3. The great theologians of the thirteenth century envisaged the problem from the Church's viewpoint. Nothing is more natural. At the time the Church dealt only with Christian princes, exercising an absolute power over peoples themselves Christian, and not only Christian but Catholic. Therefore, there was no reason for the Church to govern the people other than by governing the princes. The rest followed automatically. But there is no definitive solution for practical temporal problems, and that is quite apparent when, at the time of the Reformation and because of this very policy, the desertion of the princes brings with it that of the peoples. In politics today the Church deals mostly with States that are atheist, schismatic, infidel, or neutral, the neutrality being sometimes only another name for barely disguised hostility. The exceptions are few, and everywhere that they exist within a parliamentary regime, they are permanently unstable. If we wish, we can close our eyes to avoid seeing reality. It is possible to reason as if the Church still had

It is important to observe that for the first time a Christian thinker gives a precise name to a confused reality that his contemporaries often called *Christendom*, as we do ourselves. The term *Christianitas* was already widespread in the thirteenth century.[4]

---

to govern the same temporal realm as in the thirteenth century. Personally, we do not think that the medieval elements of the problem have disappeared irreversibly. They, or quite similar ones, may some day be reproduced. What do we know about the future? On the other hand, it is certain that the theological elements of the problem of the Church and its authority over the temporal realm are invariable and for all time. What changes is the temporal situation to which the truths of theology, itself immutable, are applied. In the present situation and for a future whose duration it is impossible to calculate, it is the peoples who sustain the Church without the princes, sometimes against the princes, and no longer the princes who perpetuate the fidelity of the peoples. Although every Catholic engages in the struggle in his own country, all the Catholics of the world are companions in the struggle. It is still the Church that leads it, but in new conditions where her action is more effectively exerted by the faithful upon a government than by governments upon the faithful. This is why the problem of the organization of Christian peoples with a view to guaranteeing the exercise of religious freedom, which was absent from the theological horizon of the thirteenth century, seems present on our horizon. Let us repeat: it is for the theologians to decide about it after examining the facts. To refuse to take democracy into account under the pretext that it is an evil would be like a physician who does not want to admit the existence of the plague because it is an illness. The Church can only exercise its authority over real temporal structures, not ones that exist only in books. Roger Bacon's Christian Republic is not completely a chimera. The Church might still want to organize what Bacon foresaw under a different form.

4. Jean Rupp, *L'idée de chrétienté dans la pensée pontificale des origenes à Innocent III* (Paris: Les Presses Modernes, 1939), on the different senses and the history of the term. As Rupp notes on 30–31, Augustine was already familiar with the expression *respublica Christiana*. The term *Christianitas* has a wealth of nuances but first designated primarily what we call *Christianity*. Only later does it seem to have taken on the sense of Christendom, that is, the temporal society formed by all Christians by the very fact they are Christians. According to Rupp's research, this meaning of the word goes back to the ninth century and it became clearly discernable in the writings of Pope John VIII (35–41). "From the time of John VIII there was awareness of the existence of a social reality labeled *Christianitas*, which is neither the Church nor the Empire, but which could be called the Christian universe: land, people, and things submitted to Christ's influence" (47). See Rupp's chap. 4, esp. 78n1, the text from William of Malmsesbury, on Pope Urban II and the effect of the idea of the Crusade. It is significant that the great Scholastics did not elaborate a theology of Christendom. They considered only the Church, which by the very fact of including the laity, that is, princes and their peoples, dispensed with any other notion. We still have no theology of Christendom. To our knowledge, Roger Bacon is the first who described the reality at issue under the name of *respublica fidelium*. His reflections upon the Crusade must have greatly helped him to distinguish it. In the first place, the Crusades made evident to Roger the distinction between Christian and non-Christian

Its sense remained vague. It sometimes designates the Christian religion itself, sometimes the Church and the totality of its faithful. Occasionally although in a slightly confusing way, it designates the diffuse temporal society that was constituted by the totality of persons connected by the same faith, whatever their nationality, language, or race. If Roger Bacon had used the term he would be known today as the Doctor of Christendom; at least he conceived the thing, this *respublica fidelium*. He spoke of it often and never stopped thinking about it. He wished neither to confuse it with the Church nor to separate it from the Church.

Roger Bacon certainly distinguished the Christian Republic from the Church because he explicitly attributed different ends to them. We see this beyond possible doubt in the way in which he defines the services that wisdom renders to them. When wisdom is involved in the service of the Church, it is in order to structure, stimulate, and direct her "in every order of spiritual good so that the faithful may win the reward of future beatitude." When that same wisdom serves the Christian Republic, it is in order to provide it with temporal goods that it needs (*ut disponatur respublica fidelium cum temporalibus*). Roger Bacon specifies on this subject: "to give to individuals as to peoples what they need to preserve their health, prolong life in a wonderful way, acquire the goods of fortune, virtue, discretion, peace, justice, and to triumph magnificently over what opposes them."[5] So, we are certainly dealing with a temporal people engaged in the pursuit of temporal goods with a view to temporal ends that are peculiar to it. Still, we are not dealing with such and such a people but with the Republic of

---

peoples. Next, it places a temporal community before his eyes, using temporal means with such a temporal thing as war for a proximate end, a community, nevertheless, whose existence is explained only by its members' having in common the fact of belonging to the Church. Of course, the Republic of believers is in the Church, which as wisdom includes everything but it constitutes a distinct order that is separately definable.

5. Roger Bacon, *Compendium Philosophiae*, in *Opera Quaedam Hactenus Ineditata*, ed. John Sherran Brewer (London: Longman, Green, Longman and Roberts, 1859), 3:395.

Christians spread over a large part of the globe, which wisdom will soon expand to the limits of the inhabited world. Shall we say, *World Republic*? Yes, no doubt, because it is not clear why any place on earth should remain outside its frontiers. Still, two reservations are necessary here. First, however worldwide the Christian Republic is, it is not universal. Heir to St. Augustine's City of God, the Christian Republic only includes the predestined, at least among Christians. No doubt it is very much open to pagans, but they only enter it under the condition of ceasing to be pagan. All that Christian wisdom can do here is to ensure that "all the infidel peoples predestined to eternal life should be converted most effectively and gloriously to the Christian faith."[6] As the people of the City of God belonged to it by the mysterious decrees of divine predestination, so also the frontiers of the Church draw those of the Christian Republic.

But a second difference distinguishes it even within its limits, from the world republic about which our contemporaries think so much. It is that while temporal, the Christian Republic expects its foundation, organization, and prosperity from a completely spiritual wisdom, dispensed by a master and power that are spiritual themselves. Let us remember that we are in the thirteenth century, at a time when *cleric* is a synonym of *scholar*, and *layman* is a synonym of *ignorant*. If there are scholars and sages, they are clerics and men of the Church. When Roger Bacon thinks of the Crusades and their leaders, he feels pity of the way in which these simpletons make wars. He calls them civil wars, which does not mean wars between fellow citizens for Bacon, but wars between laymen, and therefore directed by ignoramuses. Because they know nothing, these people fight randomly. If the Church possesses wisdom, she also possesses the art of war. The future extension of the Christian Republic, and above all the defense of its borders, will therefore primarily depend on wars that are carried out wisely

6. Ibid.

by armies furnished with the necessary machines that science and wisdom alone can provide:

> For, what is puffed up with lay ignorance only succeeds by chance, as we see in all the wars on both sides of the sea, while the wars of wisdom rest upon a definite law to achieve efficiently the end they pursue. Thus, formerly, sovereigns acted through the wisdom of philosophers. For we read that thanks to the prudence and knowledge of Aristotle, Alexander the Great destroyed rather than vanquished a million men in his first two expeditions against the Kings of the East. His armies only consisted of thirty-three thousand infantrymen and four thousand five hundred cavalry, so they fought one against twenty-six. Still, he lost only four hundred nine of his men, as can be absolutely verified in Trogus Pompeius, Titus Livy, Justin, and in the history Orosius wrote for Augustine.[7]

What a happy time, when it was easy to write history. Four hundred nine men lost, not one more or less, and we are sure of it, because Trogus Pompeius, Titus Livy, Justin, and Paulus Orosius said so.

Whatever his other discoveries may be, Roger Bacon did not invent historical criticism, but he had something else in mind. His personal mission was to convince the Church in the person of her head, Pope Clement IV, that she had the charge and responsibility of assuring, along with the world's religious unity, the well-being and prosperity of the peoples who inhabit it. Just one obstacle blocks the road to such a precious good—ignorance—and there is one sure guide: wisdom. Good cannot be accomplished without knowing it nor can evil about something of which one is ignorant be avoided. Even if he who knows the truth errs out of negligence, he has the way to correct himself, lament his errors, and keep away from them in the future. Nothing is more precious than the study of wisdom: wisdom disperses the shadows of ignorance, enlightens the mind, and permits it to choose good while avoiding evil. We will never

7. Ibid., 3:395–96. The Englishman Roger Bacon perhaps did not invent gunpowder, but he expected cannons and, generally speaking, scientific war, the only sure defense of the Republic of believers.

have too much of it, and Bacon already talks about wisdom as if the age of technicians and administrators had arrived in the thirteenth century. Except that, because clerics alone possess wisdom, all those technicians and administrators belong to the Church:

> They are preferred to govern the Church at every level, and when they are charged with directing princes [*principium rectores effecti*], they direct the whole herd of laity [*totum vulgus laicorum*], they convert heretics and other infidels, and they serve as counselors in repressing those hardened individuals who are destined to an eternal death. The good of the whole world depends on the study of wisdom and inversely, loss of wisdom is a source of universal confusion.[8]

Do we begin to see the nature and scope of the problem? If wisdom directs the universe, the world will be what wisdom makes it, and if wisdom itself is corrupted, how will the world not be corrupted with it? This is the evil that Roger Bacon unceasingly bemoans and tirelessly denounces.

As a person goes in the study of wisdom, so he goes in life. That is why so many come out of a corrupted education corrupted, so much and so thoroughly corrupted that when they are chosen to govern the Church or advise princes and whole peoples, infinite corruption falls upon the world. The life of the faithful is no longer conducted according to the requirements of faith. Infidels no longer feel invited to accept the Christian truth, quite the opposite. The guilty life of Christians is an indescribable scandal and pushes the infidels away from accepting the faith.[9] It is good to say those things, but they must not be repeated too much. At any time, those responsible for teaching wisdom do not like to hear that they perform badly. Later on, better informed than Bacon, Descartes will remember that reforming education is much more dangerous than reforming science. Less prudent or more zealous than Descartes, Roger Bacon provoked increasing distrust and suspicion. Con-

8. Bacon, *Opus Tertium*, chap. 1, 11.
9. Ibid.

demned by the order's General Chapter in 1279, which was held that year at Paris, he was imprisoned from 1278 to 1292, that is, almost until his death *propter suspectas novitates*. Novelties there certainly were, his works are full of them! That some of them are suspicious may be readily granted. They would have seemed much less dangerous if, instead of saying that only he was right, Bacon had less often repeated that other people were wrong.

Still, wisdom as Bacon conceived it is the heart and brain of the new society. But who conceived wisdom like Bacon in his time? When he considered his contemporaries, Roger Bacon saw himself alone in the midst of a crowd of bewildered individuals, deaf to the message he unceasingly repeated to save them. There were doctors everywhere. The mendicant orders had multiplied in every city for forty years, and the world had never been fuller of ignorance and error. The proliferation of sin could not be doubted, because sin is incompatible with wisdom, and when there is more sin than ever, there is less wisdom than ever.

Can the proliferation of evil be doubted? Bacon asks us to consider the papal curia that was formerly guided by God's wisdom as it ought to be. It is now directed by legal codes of lay sovereigns, made to govern peoples composed of laymen. This is what is called civil law. The Church suffers from this. The Church's rights are violated. Justice and peace have drowned in a sea of scandals, and, following them, disorder, pride, avarice, envy, and lust dishonor the whole curia. Everyone thinks only about eating. As if that were not enough, the Church is denied the vicar of Christ, and the world remains without a leader. For many years the Apostolic See remained vacant through envy, jealously, and hunger for honors that run rampant in that curia, full of people, each of whom only thinks about advancing himself and his own, as everyone who wants to know the truth knows. If the head is like this, what will the members be like? Look at how hungry prelates are for money and disinterested in souls! What interests them is the advancement of their nephews, their friends, and shady jurists who ruin everything by their bad advice. Do not count on them to encourage studies! Looking down on theologians and philosophers alike, they do everything to keep Dominicans and Franciscans from freely attending to the salvation of souls and from devoting themselves to the service of God.

It will be said, at least there are those two orders. Let us examine both of them impartially. Although new, they are terribly decayed from their first nobility. As for the clergy, it completely immerses itself in pride, lies, and avarice. At Oxford and Paris, at any place where clerics assemble, there are only fights and disorders that scandalize the laity. Princes, barons, and soldiers attack and despoil one another when they do not fall upon the poor populace to overwhelm them with innumerable violent acts. Dukes and kings are no better. No one cares about what will happen. As long as people get what they want, every means is good. Irritated by their princes, the people hate them and only keep their sworn faith when they cannot do otherwise. Corrupted by the bad examples of their leaders, simple citizens oppress each other, devoting themselves to gluttony and lust more than can be told. Besides, it is enough to open one's eyes to see. About merchants and workers, it is better not to talk. Everything they do or say is only fraud, trickery, and unmitigated lies.[10]

This would still be nothing if we did not know what this evil is, a decadence, and what is worse, the decadence of Christians in relation to pagans. The philosophers of the past lived without the sanctifying grace that makes humans worthy of eternal life and that we receive with baptism. Yet, they lived incomparably better than we do, in contempt of the world, of pleasures, wealth, and worldly honors. To be sure of this, it is enough to read the books

10. Bacon, *Compendium*, 3:398–400. One of the most beautiful pages on the sacrament of the Eucharist written in the Middle Ages is situated here, perhaps the most touching before the *Imitation of Christ*.

of Plato, Aristotle, Seneca, Cicero, Avicenna, Alfarabi, and others. But this high morality is precisely the secret of their wisdom and of the discoveries they made in every science. By contrast, we Christians are far from inventing anything worthwhile. We are not even capable of understanding the science of those philosophers. The reason for this is simple. We do not have their morals. If we did, we would have their wisdom instead of having the illusion of wisdom that the Devil's trickery gave us, while wisdom reaches the depth of decadence and corruption.[11] God can delay the punishment for some time yet, but that day will come, unless a providential event changes the course of things: the advent of a pope who will reform the study of wisdom and will clean up the corruption.

Here Roger Bacon reveals himself in his most intimate facet. The herald of a reform of the Church by the pope, Bacon's own doctrine puts the means to effectuate the reform in the hands of the head of the Church. Moreover, this is why his most personal writings, rather than expositions of wisdom and the sciences, are a discourse on the method to promote wisdom and set the world in order through wisdom. At the beginning of *Opus Tertium* nothing is more clearly his intention. This is the third attempt to convince Pope Clement IV, the third appeal to the papacy. Bacon had already written two other works, including *Opus Majus*, to Clement, whose high office is "to achieve the good of the whole world."[12] Bacon unceasingly comes back to this: to direct the "Republic of believers,"[13] and to that end combat the efforts of the Devil who seeks to ruin knowledge in order to prepare the coming of the Anti-Christ. He must be resisted, and this will be difficult, but at least a pope can do it, because such a high authority can overcome all difficulties: his power penetrates the heavens, opens purgatory, conquers hell, and dominates the whole world.[14]

11. Ibid., 3:401–2.
12. Bacon, *Opus Tertium*, chap. 1, 3.
13. Ibid., chap. 1, 3–4.
14. Ibid., chap. 1, 8.

Therefore, some hope remains, especially after the advent of Clement IV, whom Roger Bacon had met when they studied together in Paris as young men, and in whom all his hope is placed. Guy le Gros, a famous jurist, had served St. Louis as his private secretary. He married, became a widower and, although he had two daughters, was ordained in 1247. Fate elevated him to the Holy See in 1265. How could Roger Bacon fail to see some providential design in such a sequence of events? A man of such great knowledge could not have become head of the Church by chance. The world's happiness depended on the cultivation of wisdom. Clement IV knew, or at least Bacon did not let him be unaware or forget that:

> Blessed Pontiff and most wise Lord, may your glory deign to consider this, that you alone can provide a remedy to our ills, because no Pope has ever known the Law as well as you. I do not believe that there have ever been others, because there are those who know law well, but there is no hope of their becoming Pope. Now, for forty years prophets and numerous visionaries have announced that a Pope would come in our days who would purge Canon Law and the Church of God of the jurists' sophisms and frauds. Justice will be rendered everywhere without the din of quarrels. The Pope will be so good, so frank, and so just, that the Greeks will return to the obedience of the Roman Church, the majority of the Tartars will be converted to our faith, the Saracens will be eliminated, and there will be only one shepherd and only one sheepfold. This word has resounded in the ears of the prophet. There is one who has seen it by revelation, who has uttered it, and who, furthermore, has assured that in due time he himself will see the marvels. Certainly, if it pleases God and the Supreme Pontiff, this can be done in a year and even less. Therefore, it can be done in your time, and please God to preserve your life that it may be done by you![15]

Nothing is clearer than this appeal to the reforming pope, alone able to unite the world by wisdom. Roger Bacon reveals himself completely in the appeal, or at least he lets the deepest part of

15. Ibid., chap. 24, 86–87.

himself be seen: "The evil must be uprooted and the elect of God appear, or a most blessed Pope must take the lead, remove everything that corrupts studies, the Church, and the rest, so that the world may be renewed, so that the crowd of gentiles make come to her and the remnants of Israel be converted to the faith."[16] The pope has the Church of God in his hand. Directing the world corresponds to him: *habetis ecclesiam Dei in potestate vestra et mundum totum habetis dirigere*.[17]

Really, there is more exultation than precision in this, because it is not very clear how the Supreme Pontiff, even after having restored studies and wisdom to their purity, could proceed to the extermination of the Saracens and the conversion of the Tartars. Roger Bacon sometimes alludes to some alliance between pope and princes, but the project remains vague. "At present, when human malice is at its height, the Church must be purified by an excellent Pope and an excellent prince, thanks to the alliance of the material sword and the spiritual sword."[18] It would be difficult to extract any clear idea about the manner in which our reformer envisages this alliance. All he knows, and the only thing on which he expresses himself clearly, is that the times are unsettled, a decisive crisis has been opened, and it will only closed through a savior pope or the Anti-Christ or some universal conflict of the kings of the earth, perhaps by the Tartars or Saracens. The Church must be reformed, and she will be. Does it not correspond to the pope to take charge?

No doubt it does, but the pope can only reform the Church through wisdom, and because wisdom itself is corrupted, the reform must begin with wisdom. Here Roger Bacon is on his own ground, the only one for which he feels personally responsible,

16. Bacon, *Compendium*, 3:402. Pierre Duhem, *Un fragment inédit de l'Opus Tertium* (Quaracchi: Ex Typographia Collegii S. Bonvaventurae, 1909), 181.

17. Bacon, *Opus Tertium*, chap. 24, 87.

18. Bacon, *Compendium*, 3:403–4. Are we talking about the emperor or one of the reigning monarchs, and which one? We do not know.

and it is immediately evident that he has gone over it a hundred times in every direction. No avenue or path is unfamiliar to him. The first thing is to remove the natural obstacles that obstruct the road to justice. Human beings must become aware of the weakness, ignorance, and error in which they have been submerged since original sin. Because of this no one studies, and no one knows anything before the age of twenty. But there is also personal sin, especially mortal sin, which is contrary to wisdom by its very nature. Mortal sin abounds, lust above all, to which animals yield only during suitable periods, while human beings always yield. Look at students, but look at their professors. "This very year at Paris, many theologians and students of theology were banished from the city and from the kingdom of France for several years and publicly condemned for the crime of sodomy." After the age of thirty, when by the grace of God they renounce lust, spiritual sins possess them: ambition, avarice, and obsession with wealth. With all that, how could they still study?[19]

After the reform of morals comes the reform of Church administration. Lawyers have destroyed the study of wisdom because they have fraudulently thwarted prelates and princes, although they drain money from them and receive all benefices from them. Nothing remains for theologians and philosophers. These unfortunates have nothing to live on and not even a place to work. When we say lawyers, we do not mean canonists, who are billeted under the same flag as philosophers. If they manage to live, it is because they know civil law, not canon law. We should not be surprised to see those with the best talents in philosophy and theology escape those disciplines and go over to civil law when they see that lawyers receive all the honors and all the wealth from prelates and princes.

Roger Bacon does not stop talking about this point. Nothing is equal to his animosity against civil law, the heir to pagan Rome, made by laymen to govern laymen, though it is progressively be-

19. Bacon, *Opus Majus*, part I; *Compendium*, 3:404–13; *Opus Tertium*, chap. 22, 69–73.

coming Church law. The strangest thing is that those who teach it do indeed seek to pass themselves off as churchmen. They have themselves called clerics, but they are not. They are married, mere laymen who contribute in no small measure to corrupt the clergy, to which they do not belong, by mixing with it. Again, they are given the title of masters. They are not masters, because they teach error, while a master worthy of the name teaches the truth. Evidently, our cleric does not judge that civil law is made for him. Civil law does not contain the laws of his country, because on the one hand there is the populace of clerics, and on the other hand, everyone else. Each country has its own laws, and its particular civil law. As our clerics are natives of twenty different countries, if they are subject to civil law, they are subject to conflicting bodies of legislation. Therefore, what can the clerics of England, France, Germany, Spain, and Italy do, but to reject all these laws and claim another? As Bacon explicitly says, "Since a lay prince rejects the law of another lay prince, with much stronger reason, every cleric ought to reject the laws of laymen."[20] From the *Letter to Diognetus* to *The City of God* and on to Roger Bacon's *Compendium*, the general tendency is constant: like the fourth-century Christians, the thirteenth-century cleric does not belong first of all to his country, but to the Church.

A more philosophical reason is offered to justify this position. If it is unbecoming to see clerics apply themselves to the study of civil law, the fact is that it is not a science in any case. As it is taught in the schools and practiced by jurists, law is only the particular, contingent application of principles that stem from philosophy. Law is a practical art for laymen. It is not a science suitable to philosophers or clerics. Ordinary law is to philosophy as architecture is to geometry or making jewelry to chemistry, and the same goes for all arts for the use of laymen. The layman's law is like mechanics in regard to the civil law of philosophers and clerics, which

20. Bacon, *Compendium*, 3:420.

alone is part of philosophy. Indeed, these laymen apply their civil law mechanically without knowing why. Compared to philosophers, these laymen are draught animals who do not know the reasons or the causes of the laws they apply. When clerics lower themselves to such studies, they also become so many animals and beasts without souls. From the standpoint of wisdom, that is an unmentionable degradation.[21]

The degradation is not necessary, and the ancient philosophers were wiser in this than many clerics of our time, because they at least taught law as philosophers. There is more truth in Aristotle's *Ethics* and *Politics* than in all civil law, precisely because instead of saying what law is, Aristotle taught its principle and causes. Christian law harvests in philosophical civil law itself everything that deserves to be harvested and adds many things that infinitely transcend human science.[22] He who grasps Christian truth grasps the philosophy of law and law itself with one stroke.

That is why we said earlier that the most urgent task is to restore wisdom. The ancients valued nothing more highly than ethics. They hoped to save themselves by it, and, to tell the truth, it was their theology. By contrast, we to whom revelation was given know that faith alone can save us. Therefore our theology is the doctrine of faith. If it is our wisdom, it must necessarily contain all knowledge. Roger Bacon expands on this point with gripping expressions: "There is only one perfect wisdom given by the only God to the only humankind and for just one good, which is eternal life, completely contained in Holy Scripture, but which still must be developed by Canon Law and philosophy. For, everything contrary or even alien to God's wisdom is false and vain, and can be of no service to the human race."[23]

In the Middle Ages nothing is more common than this reduc-

21. Ibid., 3:420–21.

22. Ibid., 3:424.

23. Bacon, *Opus Tertium*, chap. 23, 73.

tion of the science and arts to theology, but here it is expressed in a very personal tone and a totally particular spirit, because these classical theses are now going to justify the ideal of a united world as far as is possible, in the unity of a single, unique wisdom. The modern expression "one world" is familiar to our reformer, of whom it can be said that he is a prophet. Only, for the world to become one, wisdom itself must be one and be given to everyone by a single authority. All wisdom has been given by a single God to a single world and for a single goal.[24] The other sciences necessary for revealed wisdom to develop its content are no less included, as the open hand is in the clenched fist. The pope has the deposit of them, and therefore he and he alone can confer order on the Church and unity upon the Christian Republic. There can be one world because there is one pope who possesses the truth.

Notwithstanding this, let us recall that this unified world will not yet be a truly universal society, because even when the Christian Republic is achieved, it will have boundaries that will be the same as those of the faith. Much can be done to propagate faith. It will always remain a faith, which is to say a truth that no method can effectively impose and that ultimately depends on free acceptance by the believer himself. Here Roger Bacon meets the difficulty that we have shown lies at the very heart of a problem: how to universalize a faith. The unity of the world is only possible in the measure in which faith is universalizable. The problem, then, is to know if and how the Church can cause faith to be universally accepted.

Roger Bacon did not completely despair. First, because God wants to save all humans, he cannot deny humankind the knowledge of the ways of salvation, all the more because, insofar as his goodness is infinite, he always grants humans some light that unveils the ways of truth to them. Besides, the problem is not so complex that its elements cannot be calculated. The number of principal nations and their respective religions is known. They are

24. Bacon, *Opus Majus*, part II, chap. 1, 1:33 and 66.

the Saracens, Tartars, pagans, idolaters, Jews, and Christians. Accordingly, there are six, and there can be no more before the end of the world, until the seventh appears, that of the Anti-Christ. However, let us add that there are sects composed of several others, different combinations of two, three, or even four but the fundamental religions remain those we have said. The possibility of an atheistic world is does not seem to have presented itself to Bacon's imagination.

The simplest method to distinguish religions is to consider the goals they present to humans. The Saracens get the best advantage of the present life and of the future life. Polygamists avid for all temporal goods, they do not think that the abuse of these goods must deprive them of eternal happiness. Bacon knew the Tartars through the letter of Güyük that Giovanni da Pian del Carpine brought to Innocent IV:

> If you want to keep peace with me, you, Pope, and you, Emperors and Kings who reign over cities and kingdoms, do not put off until later the conversations with me to arrange this peace. You will then hear our answer and what our will is. You, inhabitants of the West, you adore God, and you believe yourselves to be the only Christians. That is why you scorn others. But how do you know to whom God deigns to grant his grace? We also adore God, and with his help, we will destroy the whole world from East to West.[25]

Carpine's book on the Tartars contained ample clarification. This people is evidently possessed by the *libido dominandi*. Pure pagans, like the Prussians and other peripheral peoples, seek pleasures, wealth, and honors, persuaded that the more one has in this life, the more he will have in the next one. The idolaters only expect material goods in the next life and know nothing about spiritual goods. Nor do they think that it is necessary to deprive oneself here below in order to be rewarded in the future life. Still,

25. Ibid., 2:368n1.

their priests make a vow of chastity and abstain from pleasures of the flesh. Next come the Jews, who hope for temporal and eternal goods but in different ways. Those who give a spiritual sense to the Jewish law aspire to goods of the soul and to goods of the body. Those among them who interpret the law literally only expect corporal goods for the future life. Furthermore, they pursue them by all means in this life, but formerly they did so with God's permission. Consequently, they cannot be blamed. There remain the Christians, who pursue spiritual goods by spiritual means. No doubt by reason of human feebleness in this life they can possess the temporal goods required for the exercise of the spiritual life, but what they aspire to is an eternal life where, as their bodies themselves become spiritual, the whole human being will be glorified and will be with God and with the angels.

Those are the principal religious sects. How should they be classified? The lowest are the pagans, who know almost nothing about God, have no clergy, and render to God the cult that pleases each one. Then come the idolaters, who have priests, temples, and, like the Christians, great clocks to call them to services. They have regular prayers and fixed sacrifices, but admit several gods, none of whom is all-powerful. In the third level come the Tartars who adore an all-powerful God and render cult to him. It is true that this does not stop them from venerating fire and the earth of their place of residence. At the fourth level are the Jews, who according to their own law ought to know more about God and await the Messiah who is Christ. Finally come the Christians who follow the Jewish Law in the spiritual sense and complete it by the law of Christ. Let us not speak, says Bacon, of the sect of the Anti-Christ that will only ruin the others for a time, although the elect must hold fast in the faith of Christ despite furious persecutions. The sects can also be distinguished according to the planets on which they depend. All religions are placed under the sign of Jupiter: its conjunction with other six planets, without destroying human free will, exercises an influence on human hearts that favors the birth of new religious laws.[26] However they are counted, we always come back to the number six.

To establish, enlarge, and ensure the Christian Republic, evidently, the greatest possible must be won over. In this sense, the problem is reduced to propagation of the faith. As we have said, this is a difficult problem, because we cannot argue in the name of our faith or on the authority of scripture against people who deny the divinity of Christ and the authority of his word:

> Therefore, arguments must be sought through another way that we have in common with the infidels: philosophy. In great measure, here the authority of philosophy is in agreement with the wisdom of God. Better yet, philosophy is a vestige of divine wisdom left by God to humans in order to set them on the path of divine truths. There are not things reserved to philosophy, but common to theology and philosophy, to faithful and infidel, given by God to philosophers and revealed by them in order to prepare humankind for particular divine truths.[27]

Roger Bacon is faced with a rather complicated situation. On the one hand, the unbelievers possess philosophy and the sciences, products of reason. That is their peculiar good, *quae etiam propria est infidelibus*. Philosophy is even so much their property that we Christians must learn it from them, and not without cause because we have the certainty of faith on our side: *ab eis totam habemus philosophiam*.[28] Bacon does not hesitate on this point and, furthermore, his admiration for the Greek and Arab scientists and philosophers would not allow him to doubt it: all philosophy is pagan in origin, and as it is the work of reason, which is common to us and them, it is impossible for us to deny philosophy. Except that,

26. For the details of the religious astrology, see ibid., part IV, 1:254. The reservation regarding free choice is found in part VII, 2:371: "Anima excitatur, in quantum est actus corporis et inducitur ad actus publicos et privatos per coelestem constellationem, salva in omnibus arbitrii libertate."

27. Ibid., 2:373.

28. Ibid.

if it is true that this work is at the same time a divine invitation to search for Christian wisdom, we ought to be able to use it ourselves to lead the infidels to this wisdom. Even more, we ought to be able to do that without resorting to principles that are foreign or even external to faith, but, on the contrary, draw from its very roots.

How should we proceed? We could directly address the people, but the common people are so ignorant that the arguments appropriate for them would be unworthy of wise men. We can do better, because everywhere there are cultivated persons, apt for wisdom. Let us persuade the latter first. Then it will be easier to persuade the people with their help. Accordingly, we will begin by appealing to natural knowledge that belongs to all humans by virtue of their very nature. There is at least one that is in fact common to all sects. It is the knowledge of God. However much sin may obscure it, it is found among all peoples. By contrast, God's unity and his nature are not naturally known.[29] Like the geometer who draws figures before proceeding to demonstration, the "persuader" will have to begin by describing God's nature in general. He is the first cause, before which there is no other, uncreated, necessarily existing, infinite in power, wisdom, and goodness, creator of the universe and governor of every being that God creates according to its nature. The Tartars, Saracens, Jews, and Christians agree on the above. The idolaters and pagans remain, but when they are provided with the reasons for this, they will not be able to contradict it, nor consequently will the peoples of whom they are in charge and whose direction belongs to them. When the idolaters and pagans realize that they are in the minority and in the minority in relation to other peoples whom they know to be more educated than they are, they will rally to the majority. If that is not sufficient, we will recur to metaphysics, the impossibility of going to the infinite in the causal order, the necessity of a first cause that is itself eternal and the

29. Ibid., 2:375–76: "Sed cognitio de unitate Dei et quid sit Deus et qualis et cujusmodi non est nota naturaliter."

cause of everything else. Furthermore, it is unique, because there is only one world, and for one world, one God is enough, all the more as one God would still suffice if there were several worlds, because whatever their number, these finite worlds would never make an infinite.[30] When that is accepted, no one will dispute that the creature ought to obey his creator and serve him. More exactly, because only an infinite power can create from nothing, the gift of creation is infinite, like the distance from nothing to being. Consequently, the creature ought to feel infinite reverence for his creator. But that is not all, because the soul is immortal. Aristotle, Avicenna, and all the great philosophers teach it. Cicero and Seneca affirmed it many times in their writings, and all the religious sects expect a future life. As we have said even the pagans believe that they will live in body and soul after death, and the Saracens affirm the resurrection of the dead. If pagans and Christians, who are the two extremes, agree on that, it certainly must be that all in between have to be in agreement likewise. Therefore, once there is agreement on the future life, it cannot be denied that a just God would want to reward the good and punish the wicked. Therefore, every human being must do all possible to fulfill God's will and serve him in order to avoid unspeakable wretchedness and obtain infinite happiness. On all these points, the things that all humans accept ought to allow reason to lead them to complete agreement.

It is true that they are no longer in agreement on the remainder, but why? To discover those things, they would also have to know what God wants them to do in order to obtain this beatitude, but how would they know? Only humans are incapable of knowing what God wants them to do to obtain salvation. The proof is in the division of sects and even among Christians themselves on this point, because there are heretics, schismatics, and true Christians, and the diversity of heretics is infinite. Let us add that the other religions are no less divided among themselves, and nothing

30. Ibid., 2:380.

is less surprising, because we are dealing here with problems that the limited character of natural reason does not allow humans to resolve. No one knows perfectly the nature of the most modest material creature, what a blade of grass or a fly is. With much greater reason, humans are incapable of knowing exactly the nature of incorporeal beings like angels or what concerns the spiritual state of our future life and still less what relates to God or God's will. Avicenna acknowledges this in what he said about the sources of ethics. Revealed knowledge of God is necessary. The situation is clear for Jews and Christians. The Saracens similarly believe that Mohammed was given a revelation, and he himself claimed that in order to be believed. At any rate, if God did not reveal his doctrine to him, it was the Devil. Tartars, idolaters, and pagans all believed that God revealed the truth on these problems. The fact that they believe proves that God alone seems to them worthy of being believed in these matters.

From there, we come to the last problem: which of these revelations is genuine? Only three deserve to be taken into consideration, because they are the most rational: those of the Jews, the Saracens, and the Christians. It is self-evident that for Roger Bacon, the choice is inevitable, but reading his reasons, we feel some doubt about their suitability to persuade Muslims and Jews. No doubt, even Christian philosophers of our time would have difficulty in accepting them. Bacon's main argument, the one that is clearly decisive in his view, is that philosophy everywhere allows vestiges of Christian wisdom and of Christian wisdom alone to be seen. It is not possible here to review the long succession of texts where, through ingenious but risky exegeses that apply certain mathematical conclusions and the teaching of ancient moralists to the doctrine of the Church, Bacon tries to establish that noble testimonies can be found in this science and in those authors.[31] For

31. Ibid., 2:389. For mathematics, see part IV, 1:175; on ethics, part VII, 2:228–49.

Bacon we are dealing with very precise points—indeed, with almost everything. The list of articles of the faith that Bacon thinks he can rediscover in this way includes the Trinity, Christ, the Virgin Mary, the creation of the world, angels, the immortality of souls, the last judgment, eternal life, the resurrection of the body, the punishments of purgatory and hell, and still other things that Christian faith teaches. Inversely, Bacon prides himself on the certainty that philosophy does not bear this kind of witness on behalf of other religions, something rather strange, at least regarding the Jewish religion in the parts it shares with the Christian religion. However that may be, such is his firm conviction, and it is enough to give him victory. "We do not find this agreement between philosophy and the sect of the Jews or of the Saracens. The philosophers do not testify in their favor. Since philosophy is the vestibule of religion and disposes us to religion, it is therefore manifest that the Christian religion is the only one that ought to be accepted." Furthermore, as if this were not enough, Bacon invokes the testimony of Albumazar,[32] who teaches in Book I of his *Conjunctions* that Islam will not last longer than 693 years. Our prophet, who wrote in 1267, observes that 665 years have passed. Islam, thus, does not have much time left, and who knows whether it will wait out the twenty-eight years to disappear? For the rest, the Sibyls have proclaimed the divinity of Christ "and all the principal articles of the Christian faith."[33] The choice is necessary. It is done.

Accordingly, we will not follow Roger Bacon in the details of the proofs that he adds *ad abundantiam*. Still, when everything is said, the Christian Republic of his dreams is not a total success. Doubtless it will be magnificent, incomparably more learned, civilized, and happy than thirteenth-century kingdoms or principalities. Far in advance of his time, Bacon foresees, announces, and anticipates the age of experimental science, of instruments for ob-

32. [Translator's note: this is Abu Ma'shar, ninth-century astrologer.]

33. Bacon, *Opus Majus*, part VII, 2:390.

servations, machines, and medicine founded on genuine scientific biology. Bacon certainly has characteristics that link him as a precursor to Francis Bacon and Descartes. If they could come back to our world, modern machinery would give them great satisfaction, because they foresaw, announced, and wished for it. Even now we are far from some of what they anticipated. Roger Bacon foresaw an astrolabe set in motion by the same force that moves the celestial spheres. He was convinced that human life could be prolonged beyond any foreseeable limit by applying certain rules of hygiene, by delaying old age and by asking experimental science for the secret of better medicine than what was commonplace. He does not doubt that some day chemistry would allow the transmutation of metals, that perpetual lamps and terrifying explosives usable in artillery pieces could be manufactured, in a word, that innumerable inventions would be possible, thanks to which the Christian Republic would enjoy the benefits of peace and be assured of victory in wartime. Yet, even then, its triumph would not be complete.

Bacon knows there would still remain an irreducible remainder of infidels. It would be useless to ask him why, but we can easily guess where his ingenuity would seek the answer to this question: namely, in the secret of divine predestination. The Christian Republic must grow and expand to the limits of the world, but while waiting for Islam to disappear on its own, our reformer counts less on experimental science to convert infidels than to exterminate them. This is what he delicately calls "the conversion of infidels and the reprobation of those who cannot be converted." The expression is a bit vague, but its meaning becomes clear when he speaks of "converting the Tartars and destroying the Saracens." Certainly, that is a method to guarantee that there is only one flock and only one shepherd, but it is not at all the method that the Gospel had announced. However, perhaps it is the only method that those like Roger Bacon could envisage when they dreamed of making the City of God descend from heaven to earth and from eternity to time. As these two worlds have their elect, they must have their reprobates.

Bacon's doctrine signals the first blatant and hardly disputable metamorphosis of the concept of the City of God. It concludes a perceptible evolution since the twelfth century, whose origins were still older. In his *Chronicle*, the Cistercian Otto of Freising observed around 1150 that the Roman Empire still survived and announced its duration until the last judgment. In the prologue of Book V, Otto added that, after Constantine:

> Since not only all peoples, but also all emperors, except for a small number, have been Catholics and subject to orthodoxy, it seems to me that I have written this history not of two cities, but to all intents and purposes of a single city that I call the Church. Because, although the elect and the reprobate are found in the same house, I can no longer say that these cities are two, as I previously did. I must say that formally they are one, although the grain is mixed with the straw in it.

Otto reaffirms this thesis in the prologue of Book VII, then in the prologue of Book VIII. In his mind, the identification of the City of God with the people of the Church is an established fact.[34]

34. This view agrees with that of the canonist Stephen of Tournai in the preface to his *Summa Decretorum*: "In eadem civitate sub eodem rege duo populi sunt, et secundum duos populos duae vitae, secundum duas vitas duo principatus, secundum duos principatus duplex juridictionis ordo procedit. Civitas ecclesia; civitas rex Christus; duo populi duo in ecclesia ordines, clericorum et laicorum; duae vitae, spiritualis et carnalis; duo principatus, sacerdotium et regnum; duplex jurisdictio, divinum jus et humanum. Redde singula singulis et convenient universa." Quoted by Carlyle and Carlyle, *History of Medieval Political Theory*, 2:198n. The Carlyles' interpretation of this text does not seem obvious to us (2:225). The text can be understood as affirming a simple juxtaposition of powers, but that is not certain. In any case and to keep to our problem, Étienne de Tournay could not affirm more vigorously the reduction of two cities to one by the substitution of the historical, temporal city in place of St. Augustine's mystical and eternal *civitas terrena*. See 2:207n1 for the text of the canon lawyer Rufinus. The latent danger in this reduction is discovered by reading treatises, which, though attributed to Bishop Gerard of Rouen, it is better to attribute to an unknown author. If there were only one city, why would the supreme authority in the world not belong to the prince rather than to the pope? Because the world is now the Church: "Mundum hic appellat [Gelasius] sanctam ecclesiam quae in hoc mundo peregrinatur." As human nature is one, he who governs bodies well, governs souls well; from *De Consecratione Pontificum et Regum*, in *Libelli de Lite*, 3:663 [*Libelli de*

It is also identified in Roger Bacon's mind, to the point that he no longer talks about anything but the Church. Except that he finds himself in the presence of a much larger earth than that of the twelfth century and of a Holy Roman Empire that real, powerful pagan empires threaten from afar but effectively. At the death of Mangou Khan in 1259, his empire extended from China to the Danube. It was therefore necessary to be resigned to seeing the duality of the Cities reappear or else, by a supreme effort, to maintain their coincidence by absorbing into the Church the immensity of the earthly cities that Marco Polo and Giovanni da Pian del Carpine had just observed. Bacon does not hesitate. He chooses the second option, but this choice confronts him with a serious problem.

If the City of God becomes the Church, the States become the Earthly City. Consequently, the Church must absorb or assimilate the States in order to maintain the unity of a single City. To remove this difficulty, Roger Bacon seems to have felt the need to include effectively all human knowledge in Christian wisdom in order to assure the universal triumph of the faith. The suddenly revealed immensity of the field that was now offered to the Church's apostolic zeal, the power of the opposing forces that it was going to have to conquer, the temporal nature of the goals, like the peace of peoples that the Church now had to aim at, all prompted Bacon to multiply the paths leading to faith by natural reason, and at the same time, to include faith and reason in a revelation enlarged as much as necessary in order to contain it. Because the City of God

Lite Imperatorum et Pontificum Saeculis XI et XII Conscripti, *Monumenta Germaniae Historica*, 3 vols. (Hanover: Impensis Bibliopoli Hahniani, 1891–97; reprinted in Cologne: Böhlau in Kommission, 1969)]. In this unitary conception where the Church and kingdom are mixed, the king is no longer a layman but the anointed of the Lord (3:679). The system can slide completely into Caesaro-Papism or else into Papo-Caesarism. On these issues see Heinrich Boehmer, *Kirche und Staat in England und in der Normandie im XI und XII Jahrhundert* (Leipzig: Dietrich, 1899). See also Zachary Nugent Brooke, *The English Church and the Papacy from the Conquest to the Reign of John* (Cambridge: Cambridge University Press, 1931; reprinted 1989).

did not envisage any temporal good, it knew no difficulty of this kind. But because the Republic of believers wanted to seize the earth, it could not avoid them. Accordingly, it is not surprising to observe the first symptoms in Roger Bacon's work of a tendency to count on philosophy and science to win the world to this faith that St. Paul initially preached as folly for the Greeks. The least that can be said about this solution to the problem is that the equilibrium was unstable. The moment has come for the masterful simplification that Dante is going to propose: leave heaven, theology, and faith to the Church, reason to philosophers, and the earth to the emperor.

FOUR

The Universal Empire

AT A DATE that is not known precisely, but certainly in the early years of the fourteenth century, Dante tackled the problem of a universal society in a spirit quite different from that of Roger Bacon. Nothing would make us believe that he knew the work of our Franciscan reformer, but by its nature the problem occurred to many thinkers at a time when every kingdom had to adopt a position with respect to the empire, and the empire itself had to adopt a position with respect to the papacy. The son of a city tragically divided by endless dissention, banished from Florence following a decisive political reversal, Dante at least could not be unaware of the problem's urgency. A victim of division, Dante ardently yearned for unity. His *De Monarchia* is the proof, and although the treatise is considered inferior to the *Divine Comedy* with good reason, it can be said without exaggeration that it is not unworthy of him. *De Monarchia* honors Dante's genius, if not in literary beauty, at least in the breadth and astonishing originality of its views. It would be difficult to give it higher praise.

It has been said that this work naturally fits in with many others that date from roughly the same period. That is true, but *De Monarchia* is nonetheless unique in its thesis, and Dante knew it. Everyone naturally loves truth, he says at the start of the treatise. Just as work of the ancients enriched the truths that their works transmit to us, it is right for each of us in turn to strive to bequeath new riches to posterity. Anyone who thinks otherwise fails in his duty. This work is not like a tree nourished by sun and rain that bears fruit in the autumn, but an abyss that swallows and never gives back. He adds:

Often meditating with myself upon these things, lest I should some day be found guilty of the charge of the buried talent, I desire for the public weal, not only to burgeon, but to bear fruit, and to establish truths unattempted by others. For he who should demonstrate again a theorem of Euclid, who should attempt after Aristotle to set forth anew the nature of happiness, who should undertake after Cicero to defend old age a second time—what fruit would such a one yield? None, forsooth; his tedious superfluousness would merely occasion disgust.[1]

Among the truths still hidden but that it would be useful to uncover, the most hidden and most useful concerns temporal monarchy. If no one is interested in that truth, it is because its discovery can bring no benefit other than glory. The endeavor is difficult, but Dante proposes to attempt it. Confiding less in his own powers than in divine illumination, he is going to seek to reveal the nature, necessity, and role of the universal monarchy to the world.

What is temporal monarchy? To define it roughly, let us call *temporal monarchy*, or as they say, *empire*, a single leader's domination over all those who live in time and over all things measured by time. It thus involves goods such as persons, provided only that their condition is *temporal*, that it is *in time*. Three overriding questions are posed on this subject, which we will consider in turn: whether monarchy thus understood is necessary for the world, whether the Roman people claims this title rightfully, and whether the authority of the monarch, the leader of the monarchy understood in this way, depends immediately on God or on God's vicar on earth.

1. *De Monarchia*, book I, chap. 1. We will quote the treatise according to William Henry Vincent Reade's edition that reproduces Edward Moore's text of Dante, *De Monarchia* (Oxford: Clarendon Press, 1916) [Translator: I quote from page 4 of the translation by Aurelia Henry, *The De Monarchia of Dante Alighieri* (Boston / Cambridge: Houghton Mifflin / Riverside Press, 1904)]. It is superfluous to observe how much Dante's state of mind is completely medieval and like Bacon's directed to the discovery of new truths, in which he differs from a philologist like Petrarch, who sees nothing wrong with repeating twenty times what the ancients already said. Would it be paradoxical to say that humanism was a return to the past in regard to the present, and Scholasticism a return to the past with a view to the future? Perhaps there is a grain of truth there.

Regarding the first problem, let us begin by noting that we are dealing with politics here, with a question where the only object of speculation is to lead to action. We cannot change anything in the object of metaphysics. Thus it is a purely speculative science. But we can make some change in the object of politics, and if we desire to know it, it is precisely in order to be able to act upon it. Consequently, it is necessary first to speculate to clarify our question, because the correct solution to every other political problem depends on the response. But we are dealing with speculation ordered to action. Every action proposes a certain end in view of which it is accomplished. Therefore, the end is the cause of the action, and its end explains the action. When several actions are ordered, some in view of others—because all are necessary with a view to attaining a certain end—the latter is called a *final end*, and this final end explains all else. It cannot be doubted that there is a final end of all political activities. Each city, each political unity pursues its own end. What is that end? That is what we must learn, because it is evidently the final end of all human political activities, and will serve as the principle of all our demonstrations.

Accordingly, this time the issue is certainly a temporal and universal human society. *Humana civilitas, civilitas humani generis*, are different expressions to designate the people that all humans united under a single leader form or could form. Because we have said that the end of a society is also its cause, it can be admitted that, being different from other societies, this one pursues a different goal that is its reason for being. It consists of social groups that are like the parts of our body. Nature makes the thumb for a certain end, the hand for another, the arm for a third, and none of these ends is the same as that of a whole human. Likewise, an individual seeks a certain end, the family another and so on for a village, a city, the kingdom, and on up to the final end in view of which God created the whole of humankind by nature, which is merely God's art.

Here Dante recalls a remarkable Aristotelian doctrine, though one so often unknown to those who appeal to Aristotle that the poet's philosophical perceptiveness is to be admired, namely that every essence exists in function of its operation. Therefore, no created essence can be the ultimate intention of a creator. Because an essence is placed with a view to its operation, its end must be sought in the operation. Thus posed, the problem boils down to knowing whether an end exists that is peculiar to humankind, that is to say, an operation that neither the individual, nor the family, nor a village, nor a city, nor a particular kingdom can accomplish, but that the whole human race can. What is the operation that marks the ultimate limit of what humankind can do? Evidently, it is what humans alone are capable of achieving. It is not to live or feel, because other things besides humans can do those things, but to know intellectually. Let us be more precise: to know by the *possible* intellect, because below the possible intellect there are beings lacking understanding. Above the possible intellect, there are pure intelligences, whose act is uninterrupted understanding, because being is simply knowing for them. Accordingly, to acquire knowledge by the possible intellect is the operation that characterizes humans as humans, because the operation belongs to nothing that is above or below it.[2]

It is an operation of a particular kind. The possible intellect, this faculty of knowledge that we said is proper to humans, needs to be actualized by the agent intellect, and no individual intellect, however actualized it may be, knows everything that a possible intellect can know. Nor are any of the communities we have named capable of doing so. The only human community, once it is actualized, where all understandings taken together attain the totality of what the human intellect can understand is the whole human race. It is even for this reason that humankind exists: all this multitude of thinking beings is necessary, because it is required to actualized

2. Dante, *De Monarchia* I.3 [13].

the total possibility of the human intellect, first by speculation, then by action, which is only a kind of prolongation of speculation.

No one is more Greek, more Christian, or less of a pragmatist than Dante here. Acting is only an extension of knowing in his eyes, and the existence of such an immense multitude of humans is only justified because their number is necessary for the total possibility of the human intellect to be always completely actualized: *proprium opus humani generis totaliter accepti, est actuare semper potentiam intellectus possibilis*.[3] What one man does not know another man knows. What is unknown in one city is known in another, and all knowledge open to humans would be simultaneously known if all human intellects were free to attend to speculation simultaneously. But a condition would be required for that ideal to be achieved: peace. Humans acquire wisdom and prudence in calm and leisure, not in agitation and struggle. The same holds for humanity. Without a tranquil peace, humanity is incapable of carrying out its proper task, which can be called almost divine. Consequently, it is obvious that universal peace is the most important condition for our happiness, and the best means for that end, if it is permissible to say so. Besides what did the angels of the Lord promise the shepherds? Not wealth or pleasure or honors or long life or health or strength or even beauty, but peace. *Pax vobis!* Peace be with you! He who is the salvation of humans saluted them thus. The supreme Savior must necessarily direct the most perfect salutation to humans. It follows that universal peace is what is most immediately required to attain the end toward which all our acts tend. Therefore, we have the right to demand that the society of the human race should satisfy all the conditions required for peace finally to reign in the entire world.[4]

From this principle, we can establish by induction the neces-

3. Ibid., I.4 [17] ["The proper function of the human race, taken in the aggregate, is to actualize continually the entire capacity of the possible intellect" (15)].

4. Ibid.

sity of a single monarch reigning over all humans. In the individual, all faculties are ordered with a view to happiness under the direction of the intellect, the leader and guide of other faculties. In every family the father plays the same role. Each village, each city, each kingdom has its leader, without whom everything would be handed over to disorder and become the victim of unending quarrels. If we think that the human race itself also forms a society that pursues a determined end and is ordered to that end in its entirety, it must have its own leader who imposes laws on it and governs it, a monarch or emperor. A monarchy or empire is necessary for the common good of the world.[5]

Dante offers abundant proof on this point. He establishes that the order of each part stands to the whole order in the same relation as part to whole. So, if the order of each part requires a single leader, a single leader is similarly necessary for the human race as a whole. But humankind itself is not what is most universal, because it is included in the universe whose single monarch is God. Consequently, just as the more restricted groups included in the human race are small monarchies included in a larger one, likewise humankind must be a monarchy included in a still broader one, which is the universe. To deny this, it would be necessary to dispute that everything is in order when everything happens according to the will of the first cause of the world, who is God. That is evident, at least if we admit that divine goodness is perfect, because it enters into God's intention that each thing bears God's likeness in as great a measure as nature permits. Therefore, it is in making itself as like God as it can be that the human race will attain all the perfection of which it is capable. God is one. Consequently, humankind must be one, and it will be so only if it is entirely united under a single prince.[6] Conceived this way, the universal society would be like the world of which it is a part and about which

5. Ibid., I.5 [19].
6. Ibid., I.8 [26].

we know that God, its supreme leader, moves it in its entirety with a single movement.

These metaphysical principles have not only physical but political consequences, and it is right that peace is presented as tied to the unity of authority. Where there is contention, there must be judgment, at least if we want the evil to be remedied. There could be contention between two princes, either of whom is subject to the other. If we want to avoid war, the only way to solve this disagreement is to recur to a third prince with broader jurisdiction, who has the authority to arbitrate the difference. If this prince is the universal monarch, we have a conclusion. If he is not, he himself can fall into a conflict with another prince, whose authority equals his, which would make it necessary to appeal to another still higher authority, and as we cannot go on to infinity here, it is certainly ultimately necessary, directly or indirectly, to come to a first supreme judge whose judgment settles all differences at whatever level they are produced. This is the monarch or emperor. Therefore, the universal monarchy is necessary to the world, as it is required for the peace of the human race.[7]

In this way we are brought to one of Dante's most familiar and most beloved concepts, justice. Taken in itself, in its own nature, justice is an abstract essence for Dante, and thus an absolute that is not capable of more or less, a perfectly straight line that cannot veer right or left. That is what it is in itself, we should say, in the purity of its abstractness. However, in reality, these pure forms enter into composition with others, and being involved in different degrees in individual subjects, they become susceptible of more or less. Justice is justice entire. A human being can be more or less just. Justice is found in its most perfect form when it is less mixed with its contrary, either in its nature or in its operation. Its beauty is then such that no star is comparable to it. It might be called Phoebe looking at her brother across the heavens in the

7. Ibid., I.10 [30].

purple of a morning calm. For that, it is still necessary for nothing to tarnish its purity. There can be none of those inner contradictions, that, by setting the will at odds with itself, permits avarice to distort justice; nor can there be any of those weaknesses that so often make the just man incapable of rendering justice to others, because whatever desire he may have of doing it, he lacks the power. If things are thus, justice will reign, all the more perfectly over the world in the measure in which the world is subjected to a more powerful and more just leader. We are going to see that only a single leader of the human race meets these conditions, and that is why we call him necessary for human happiness.

Here Dante obviously is thinking of some supreme authority, who, by transcending the particular interests of all States, is capable of arbitrating their conflicts. This concept is familiar to us nowadays, although the means has not yet been found to make it come into reality. The principal difficulty does not come from each State's having to give up part of its own sovereignty in order to establish this supreme power. By the mere fact of not being alone in the world, no State is totally free, even inwardly, and although it may be pleased to maintain a fiction to the contrary, it can beyond doubt be gotten to recognize this fact openly. The principal difficulty is rather to find an arbiter whose justice and impartiality are sure enough for the particular States to agree to recur to his decision. We are not dealing with national pride, ambition, or cupidity here, but quite precisely justice, because it is not just that a State should sacrifice whatever sovereignty it may have, if the sacrifice to which it consents risks entailing some injustice to any of its members. This is why Dante is bound to specify that the single sovereign of the universe will certainly also be the most just. He will be so in virtue of his very uniqueness, because insofar as he has everything, he no longer has anything to desire. Passions are absent when their objects are lacking. What could a sovereign still want whose jurisdiction is not limited by another like that of the king of Castile by the king of Aragon, but only by the ocean? Not only will such a prince's justice be above all suspicion, but also we can be certain of the love he feels for his subjects.

What Dante writes sheds a very bright light on the way in which he conceives the universal monarch's relation to humankind, because we see clearly that Dante does not picture the elimination of other princes, but nonetheless judges that a supreme monarchy would be closer than the princes to their own subjects. This monarch does not govern humanity through the intermediary of the princes. The princes govern human beings by the monarch, because human beings are entrusted to their princes through the monarch. Because the monarchy is closer to individual humans than the princes are, that is why they love him most. As for his power, who could question it? To do that, it would be necessary not to understand even what his name means. He who possesses the supreme power by himself can have no enemies. In short, the sovereign of humankind lacks nothing to possess judgment, to want to apply it, and to be able to impose it.[8]

We see how Dante proceeds, and it would be a waste of time to ask him for unimportant details. What will be the relation of princes to the monarch legally and politically? Dante does not say, and we cannot even know if it is because he conceives them according to the still feudal forms that survived in his time, or because he devoted no thought to them. What must we understand by *humankind*? It certainly seems to be the totality of humans living on earth at a given time. Dante's whole argument implies this meaning. Yet Dante says nothing about the problem that haunted Roger Bacon's thinking: how, by what persuasion or what constraint, are the peoples of Africa and Asia to be united to those of Europe under the authority of the same leader? Dante's demonstration is that of a pure philosopher, as Bacon's was that of a pure theologian. When he arrives at some decisive point, we see him

8. Ibid., I.11 [40].

stop for an instant to check the logical solidity of his construction, and then continue as if the problem were definitively settled. Let us take our last conclusion as an example. Universal justice is best assured when the world is submitted to one supremely just man who is supremely eager to apply universal justice and supremely powerful enough to do so. Nothing is more certain, because this is a second-figure syllogism with the internal negation of the type: all B is A, C alone is A, and therefore C alone is B. This amounts to saying: all B is A, nothing but C is A, therefore nothing but C is B. That is why the whole world must obey a single leader.

Whatever the reason that this leader is desired, once he is in place, humans will finally enjoy a good that is precious among all goods, freedom. Philosophers speak about it a great deal. They even correctly define its principle, free will, as "a free judgment on the will," but do they always know what these words signify? A judgment is free when it moves the desire entirely without being moved by it at all. This is our freedom's root and the means of our happiness in this life as in the next. We attain human happiness here below by free choice, and in the other world, divine happiness, that is to say, first to be fully human, then gods. The best state of the human race that can be conceived is therefore that in which humans can use their free choice most completely, that is, where they possess themselves fully and exist for themselves and not in function of someone else. To use Kantian language, the notion that someone is free when he is treated as an end and not as a means is familiar to Dante, but, in his thought, it first of all evokes those little Italian republics, oligarchies, or tyrannies about which he says that they and their ilk "force mankind into slavery." The burning desire Dante feels to free humans from the State that subjugates them is evidently the primary reason that incites him to call for a super-State whose authority alone can forbid the several particular States to be served by their subjects instead of serving them. Precisely that would be the role of the supreme monarch whose necessity Dante proves. The living embodiment of the will for justice, full of love for his subjects, the supreme monarch will only want humans to be good in order for them to become happy. Just one political regime can attain is end, that whose goal is human perfection. That is the meaning of the expression: *to want humans to exist for themselves*. Not citizens for consuls, nor peoples for kings, but consuls for citizens and kings for their peoples. We have forgotten the authentic sense of the word *minister*, which means *servant*, and that is why, under a regime that is served by the people instead of serving it, the good person is a bad citizen. Under a monarch capable of remedying this disorder, the good person and good citizen are identified, because its good government has no other object than to make good persons. In that sense, its leader, the monarch, is the minister of all humans, and that is why monarchy is necessary for their happiness.[9]

If Dante does not believe he is bound to propose a universal constitution or a United Nations charter, he at least indicates the outlines of what ought to be the relations of the monarch to the other princes and consequently to their peoples. The universal society that Dante foresees will be pluralistic in the sense that it will be composed of different peoples subject to different authorities and following different constitutions or customs. The union our poet desires would thus be the opposite of unification. Each nation, each kingdom, and each city is distinguished from the others by its peculiar characteristics that require different regulations, because the law is the rule that directs life. These customs themselves are causes in the nature of things. Scythians do not live like Hindus, because they live in different climates. Still, whatever their habitat may be, all humans are human, and common needs exist for the whole human race. The monarch is responsible for these needs, and he must meet them by establishing a common law with a view to peace. Therefore, he establishes the law and trans-

9. Ibid., I.12 [44].

mits it to kings or princes to whom the task of applying it corresponds, just as theoretical reason gives practical reason the principles that the latter ought to put into practice in each particular case. Only one person can do this, and it is necessary that only one should do it if we want to avoid complete confusion. In this way unity will prevail in the world; unity, which is the attribute of being that immediately precedes the good. The further we are from the one, the further we are from being and consequently from the good. By contrast, where unity reigns, good reigns too. Harmony is a good because it is a unity. Because by its nature harmony is nothing but the universal development of several wills, the unity itself of these wills is what constitutes it. How could this unity be established without the authority of a single leader whose authority dominates and directs all the others? This is why the world needs a single prince, who alone is capable of making harmony and peace reign in it.[10]

If Dante awaits this future happiness, the fact is that he believes that the world enjoyed it at least once in the past when Rome obeyed Augustus, and the world obeyed Rome. The world knew peace in that unique century. The temporal order achieved its fullness then, because nothing that human happiness required remained unsatisfied. Such also was the time that the Son of God wished to await to become human in order to save humans. No doubt he did not merely await the time but wanted and prepared it.[11] Who believes that such a confluence is the result of chance? Nobody, but then we must go further, because we are no longer dealing with reasoning here, but with fact, and so to speak with an experience worthy of being remembered. Everything transpires as if God himself had predestined Rome for the empire of the world, and that is what Dante is going to demonstrate.

Let us first try to see the problem as Dante himself sees it. The

10. Ibid., I.15 [58].
11. Ibid., I.16 [59].

universal empire is not a chimera, because it already existed, but it was ruined by a kind of revolt of its peoples, and this is one of the facts upon which Dante has meditated longest. What could have been the cause? First, how did it happen that the Roman people had earlier achieved the world empire almost without resistance? Before having reflected on that carefully, Dante thought the empire was made by force of arms, but he now knows that the triumph was the work of providence. Here we are at the heart of the question, because if the Roman Empire had only existed due to violence, its past triumph would create no claim for the future, but if it was the work of providence, that fact confers a right on it.

This right is what Dante proposes to establish, because unless that is done, political disorder in the world will be irresistible. We speak of a rebellion of peoples against the empire, but we are really dealing with a rebellion of princes and kings whose wiles have mobilized the peoples against the empire with no other end than to begin to subjugate the peoples again.[12] Here the emperor is the only protector of the peoples against the princes, as the Tsars were thought of as protecting peoples against their own boyars. As Dante conceived it, the restoration of the empire could have the effect of liberating humankind from the yoke that kings and princes lay upon them. In modern language, we could say that the universal monarch is the only recourse of peoples against the totalitarianism of particular States. It still is necessary to be able to show that the monarch's authority is legitimate, or in other words, that it is lawful.

But where is the law? First of all, it is in the mind of God, and because everything that is in the mind of God is God, and God wills himself before all else, the law is willed by God. Even more, as will and what is willed are one and the same thing in God, it follows

12. Ibid., II.1: "Ad dirumpendum vincula ignorantiae Regum atque Principum talium ostendendum genus humanum liberum a jugo ipsorum" ["To break asunder, then, the bonds of ignorance for those kings and princes, to prove the human race free from their yoke" (69)].

again that the divine will is the law itself. From there it follows ultimately that, in things, the law is only a likeness of God's will. Nothing that fails to agree with the divine will in things could be law, so much so that to ask whether what happens is in conformity to law is to ask in different words whether what happens is in conformity to God's will. Let us posit in principle, therefore, that what God wants for humans is the very thing that is law. It is true that taken in itself God's will remains unknown to us, but it is manifested by signs, exactly as we manifest our own wills, and therefore we must determine it from signs. All these signs indicate the Roman people.

The first sign is the Roman people's nobility, because the right to the world empire belongs to the noblest people, at least if it is true that the honor ought to fall to merit. Is it necessary to linger over the proofs of Roman nobility that Dante supplies? Everything Virgil says on the subject in the *Aeneid* seems to establish that beyond dispute; it is as if a Frenchman, an Englishman, or a German, in order to prove that his country has the right to the universal empire, must compile a collection of national boasts extracted from their best national authors, something that would not be difficult and likewise not convincing. Not everything is vanity in the testimonies that a people gives about itself, but to make them the minor premise of a syllogism with Dante, a conviction is necessary in which logic has little place. We easily understand the illustrious poet when he writes, as if were self-evident, that Lavinia, born in Italy, came from the noblest country of Europe, but Greece also had its merits to put forward, and here Dante merely affirms what he should have demonstrated.[13]

There would be no reason to detain ourselves on the following proof either, if it did not pose an odd problem. Dante undertakes to establish that God himself confirmed Rome's imperial calling

13. Ibid., II.3: "Quod ultima uxor [*scilicet* Lavinia] de Italia fuit, Europae natione nobilissima" ["This last consort was of Italy, the most excellent region of Europe" (83)].

through miracles. St. Thomas says that a miracle is what God does outside the established common order of nature.[14] The major premise, indeed, is indisputable, but once more a much less certain minor follows. The minor amounts to this: we know through illustrious ancient writers that God worked miracles for Rome. Under Numa Pompilius a shield fell from the sky upon the city chosen by providence to dominate the world later. Titus Livy affirms this, and Lucan confirms it. When the Gauls attack Rome, a goose "unseen there previously" saves the city by giving the alarm—again Titus Livy testifies, confirmed this time by Virgil. Let us skip over the miraculous hailstorm that saves Rome from Hannibal and Cloelia's no less miraculous escape and so on. What is really interesting is Dante's general attitude toward what he considers to be facts. Instead of seeing a number of demoniacal interventions in the history of pagan Rome, Dante does not doubt for an instant that they are all divine miracles included in the general providential plan to assure the good of the world: "Truly it behooved him so to do, who through eternity foresees all things in the beauty of order. Invisible, he wrought wonders in behalf of things seen, in order that when he should be made visible, he might do likewise in behalf of things unseen."[15] Thus, according to Dante, there were genuine miracles wrought by God for pagan Rome, exactly as God had performed them for the people of Israel. In the Middle Ages few theologians would be found holding the same thesis, which nonetheless is laid out here unequivocally.[16]

14. Thomas Aquinas, *Summa contra Gentiles* III.101, cited in Dante, *De Monarchia* II.4 [84].

15. Dante, *De Monarchia* II.5: "Sic Illum prorsus operari decebat, qui cuncta sub ordinis pulchritudine ab aeterno providit; ut qui visibilis erat miracula pro invisibilibus ostensurus, Idem invisibilis pro visibilibus illa ostenderet" [87–88; the goose appears on 86].

16. The fact that no one can be saved without faith, even if the person could not have faith because he had never heard of Christ, is something that unaided reason cannot manage to see as just, although it can do so with the help of faith (ibid., II.8 [106]). Without St. Paul's phrase, "Impossibile est sine fide placere Deo" (Heb 2:6), Dante would certainly not hesitate to put a fairly large number of Romans in heaven. Moreover, let us note that Rome's military successes seemed to him to be an authentic "divine decree" (ibid., II.9

Moreover the empire has something to justify it, because when the Roman people subjugated the world, it had no other goal than to guarantee the common good and make law rule. Its acts are enough to make us see that was its intention: "We behold them as a nation holy, pious, and full of glory, putting aside all avarice, which is ever adverse to the general welfare, cherishing universal peace and liberty, and disregarding private profit to guard the public weal of humanity. Rightly was it written, then, that, 'The Roman Empire takes it rise in the fountain of piety.'"[17] Here we are very far from St. Augustine harvesting with the greatest care the cruelest denunciations of Roman decadence in ancient historians. Quite the opposite, Dante only remembers the praises given to the Republic, as if Cincinnatus, Publius Decius, and Cato were enough to justify Rome's claims to universal empire. This is the only conclusion that interests Dante, and he uses anything at his disposal to reach it: "The Roman people in subjecting the world to itself acted with Right, and consequently appropriated with Right the dignity of empire."[18] In short, because God willed it thus, he thus disposed nature, which is nothing but God's art. Things could not go otherwise, because if the universal empire is required for human good, nature has to work to establish it, and consequently to obtain the means for it. That is why we see that it produces peoples made to obey and others made to command. How would nature not have produced a people to exercise the universal empire required by that common good of humankind? Therefore, we know that there is one, and if the issue now is only to know where it is, everything that goes before guarantees that it is at Rome. Because

[115]). Dante views universal history as a vast tournament where the nations that are candidates to become the empire confront each other successively. Assyria, Egypt, Persia, and Macedonia failed, and finally Rome achieved the empire. Dante even tried to establish his thesis in the case where that history is understood as a "single combat" (ibid., II.10 [116]). The arguments presumptuously directed by certain jurists against the empire seemed to Dante to be refuted by this fact alone.

17. Dante, *De Monarchia* II.5 [90].

18. Ibid., II.6 [97].

the domination of the Roman people over the universe was willed by nature, once more it appears as in conformity to "Right."[19]

Such a thesis could satisfy neither the French jurists, who did not even admit that France was included in the empire, nor the theologians concerned about guaranteeing the pope's authority over the empire. For that is precisely what Dante questions here. If Rome owes having conquered the world empire to nature and God, it is not clear by what right the pope would have jurisdiction over the world empire. By natural law and by divine law, the empire existed before there were popes, so much so that even before Dante attempts his dialectical demonstration, he can already affirm that the empire directly comes under God alone.

He is all the more indignant to see Christians, clerics, and defenders of the Christian faith combat the emperor's rights. Does the misery of the poor people of Christ who are everywhere oppressed by princes leave those who combat the emperor indifferent? But the very Church patrimony is constantly pillaged and confiscated by the same tyrants, and that should interest those Christians. These people claim to want justice and they refuse the leader who alone can guarantee it.

This impoverishment of the Church does not take place without God's judgment, because the Church does not place the resources of its patrimony at the disposition of the poor people to whom it belongs, and although the patrimony comes to the Church from the empire, the Church shows the empire no gratitude for it. Accordingly, let this wealth return to where it came from. Well-given and badly possessed, the wealth arrived well; let it be returned badly. What does it matter to such shepherds? How does it matter to them that Church goods are lost, if it is to enrich their own goods? But enough on this point. Let us wait for God's help and conclude our remarks. Furthermore, nothing is simpler, at least if one addresses Christians, because it is certain that by obeying an edict, every-

19. Ibid., II.7 [100].

one testifies that he recognizes its justice. Christ wanted to be born in the empire of Augustus and to submit to the edict on the census proclaimed by the emperor. Therefore Christ recognized simultaneously the justice of the edict and the emperor's authority. Let us rather say that God issued the edict by means of Caesar. Nothing is more certain: here God's authority confirms the imperial authority.[20] This reason only holds for Christians, but one cannot be Christian and reject it.

There remains just one rival who can dispute the title of master of the temporal world with the emperor, namely the pope. Here we must choose between the two great luminaries. But which must be chosen? The problem is all the more difficult, because in both cases Rome is the only candidate. On the one hand there is the *Romanus Pontifex*, on the other, the *Romanus Princeps*. Is one subordinated to the other in temporal affairs?

Let us return to the principle that we have already used: because nature is God's art, God does not want what contradicts nature's intention. As for what does not contradict this intention, God can either love it or not love it without however hating it. But God can only hate what contradicts this intention, and he can only love what is in agreement with it. Therefore, it is obvious that God wills what is nature's end. If he wills the end, he also wills the means required for this end and the elimination of everything that can prevent nature from attaining it. Otherwise, he would not want what he wants, which is absurd.[21] The issue for us is to know what nature's intention is here and the problem would be simple if it were not obscured by political passions. There are cases where ignorance causes conflicts, but there are others where the

20. Ibid., II.12 [127]. Dante even sets out to prove (II.13 [128]) that if the emperor's authority under which Jesus Christ suffered death to save us had not been legitimate, if the author of punishment did not possess regular jurisdiction, the suffering of Christ would have been an injustice legally speaking, not a punishment. Adam's sin would not have been "punished' in Christ, and the task of redemption would not have been accomplished.

21. Ibid., III.2.

conflict causes ignorance, and this is one of them. Will precedes reason here instead of following it, and most people behave like blind individuals unaware of their blindness. This is why we see them go out of their territory without realizing it and enter that of others without noticing, and once there, no longer understand or are understood, which sometimes attracts the anger of others, sometimes their scorn, and occasionally their laughter.

The truth we are seeking has three kinds of adversaries. First, there is the Supreme Pontiff, vicar of our Lord Jesus Christ and successor to Peter, "to whom we should render not what is due to Christ but what is due to Peter."[22] We should carefully note this expression that Dante writes as if in passing, but that nevertheless cuts the knot of the theological problem. If the pope is the vicar of Christ on earth, it can be held with a number of theologians that we owe him all we owe to Christ, which would make it impossible to deny him a power of jurisdiction over temporal affairs. Yet Dante has just rejected that consequence. As Peter is the first of the vicars of Christ in time, Peter's successors have no right to any other power than that with which Christ invested the first of his vicars long ago. Ill-advised zeal for the Church and the power of the keys is doubtless what misleads the popes and their supporters rather than pride. They are no less mistaken, as will be seen.

Afterward come those whom avarice blinds and who deny the empire's temporal independence for no other reason than their love of money. They call themselves children of the Church, but the Devil is their father. The third group is the Decretalists, whom Dante detests. He has nothing against the Decretals themselves,[23] whose authority within the Church he regards as unquestionable. But these people do something completely different. Lacking any theology or any philosophy, they base themselves on the Decre-

22. Ibid., III.3: "cui non quidquid Christo, sed quidquid Petro debemus" [142].

23. A Decretal is the pope's answer to a question that has been posed. It is given in the form of a letter. The answer holds for all cases of the same kind.

tals alone to mount an attack on the rights of the empire. They attack much more, because Dante assures that he had heard one of them mention that the Church's traditions are the foundations of the faith, as if there had not been a Savior of humankind before there were traditions of the Church. Before the Church, there is holy scripture. With the Church, there are ecumenical councils, in which no one doubts that Christ took part, he who promised the disciples that he would be with them until the consummation of the world. After the Church, there are these traditions of the Church called Decretals. They certainly deserve the respect owed to the authority of the Holy See, but nonetheless come after scripture. To resolve the problem under consideration we ought to direct ourselves to scripture, not to the Decretals. As it would be pointless to take up with those whose blind avarice opposes reason, we will only have controversy with those whose ignorance misdirects their zeal toward the Church. That is to say, even while combating them, a child of the Church will observe the appropriate filial piety.

Moreover, their arguments are strange. The first says that according to the Genesis narrative, God created two great lights, one of which, the sun, is larger than the other, the moon, which gets its light from the sun. Interpreting this narrative in an allegorical sense, they understand by the two lights the two governments, spiritual and temporal. They say that just as the moon's only light is what it receives from the sun, likewise the temporal government has no other authority than what it receives from the spiritual government.

This abuses the allegorical meaning. Not all that scripture says involves such a meaning. Even where scripture has an allegorical meaning, it ought to be certain that the allegorical meaning drawn from it is in fact what it contains. Some make mistakes through simple ignorance, which is pardonable. But there are those who draw allegorically from scripture all that they would like to find and that they put there in order to justify their interests or their passions. They are tyrants who ought to be treated as such and criminals who falsify the intention of the Holy Spirit.

Whatever may be the case, the comparison that is established here is not meaningful. Spiritual and temporal authority can only belong to humans who had not yet been created when God created the sun and the moon. To maintain that God created those two authorities on the fourth day is to want accidents to have been created before their subject, which is absurd. Besides, without original sin, humans would need no government, whether spiritual or temporal. Are we going to maintain that if Adam had not sinned there would have been neither sun nor moon? On the fourth day, there were still no humans. The sun and moon were there nonetheless, even before sin was possible.

Still, let us try to give this comparison the most favorable meaning it can receive. At any rate, it is certain that even if the moon borrows its light, it does not get its existence from the sun. Besides, it does not borrow all its light. At least Dante is sure of that, because he points out that even during an eclipse the moon remains visible, which proves that it has some light of its own. What is true is that the light the moon receives from the sun lets it act better and more vigorously. The same holds for the two authorities. Temporal government does not owe its existence to spiritual government. It does not even owe its own power to it, because, just as the moon has its light, temporal government has its own power. But the emperor or universal monarch should act better and more effectively in the light of grace insofar as the Supreme Pontiff's blessing influences him in heaven and on earth. Our adversaries' syllogism is incorrect, because from the fact that the moon gets *light* from the sun, they conclude that the emperor gets *authority* from the Supreme Pontiff. No, the emperor only receives light that helps him spiritually in the exercise of his authority.[24] Let us ob-

24. Ibid., III.4 [149–50].

serve that Dante is at the heart of the problem here. Indeed, the whole problem seems to be finding out whether the source of light cannot be the source of authority at the same time.

The defenders of the pope's temporal primacy possess other arguments similarly extracted from scripture. Dante discusses them one after another guided by the same principle and always, like a good logician, specifying the type of sophism hidden in each syllogism. At bottom, the majority reason as follows: God is sovereign of the temporal and spiritual realms. The Supreme Pontiff is God's vicar. Therefore the Supreme Pontiff is lord of the temporal and of the spiritual realms, which would be very good if God's vicar were God. No vicar, divine or human, is the equal of him whose vicar he is. The proof is that the vicar can receive authority but not give it in turn. Let us add that the vicar can never do all that is leader can do, as we see evidently in the case of the pope, whose authority, which he holds from God, does not involve either the power of doing miracles or of creating. No leader can be substituted with a vicar who is his equal, and the very idea is absurd, because a vicar can do nothing except in virtue of his leader's power.[25]

Therefore, we must carefully distinguish according to each case. Christ says to Peter: "Whatever thou shalt bind on earth shall be bound also in heaven; and whatever thou shalt loose on earth shall be loosed in heaven." The fact is indisputable, but it remains to see what *whatever* means. We see that by what immediately precedes: "I will give thee the keys of the kingdom of heaven" (Mt 16:19). In short, Peter will have the power to do *everything* that stems from his office, but even there, not the power to do anything at all. To take an example, Peter cannot dissolve a properly consummated marriage nor allow a woman whose husband is still living to remarry. The power of the keys has not been given to Peter absolutely, but relative to his papal function. Therefore, it does not follow that the successor of Peter has the right to establish or

25. Ibid., III.7 [163].

rescind the laws of the empire, because as will be seen, the power to do so has no relation to the power of the keys.[26]

The same goes for the well-known argument of the two swords, where it is claimed that because Peter had both, and one represents the spiritual power, the other the temporal power, Peter's successor must possess both. But where do we find that Peter's two swords ever represented the two powers? First of all, where do we find that Peter had two swords? In Luke's Gospel we read: "And they said, 'Lord, behold here are two swords.' And he said to them, 'Enough.'"[27] But Jesus, nevertheless, had just told them a little earlier, "and let him who has no sword sell his tunic and buy one."[28] A sword for each one does not make two swords but twelve. Consequently, Jesus first advises the apostles to have one sword each, but when Peter answers him that they have two all together, Jesus simply tells them that, if each one cannot have a sword, two will be enough. Moreover, Peter was not a person to look for allegories. He took words in their literal sense, and all his answers to the Lord testify to that.[29] The swords of which Jesus spoke were literal swords, we may be sure of it, and not the pope's authority or the emperor's authority.

There remains the Emperor Constantine's donation of Rome to Pope Sylvester. Dante does not openly dispute its authenticity. He does not directly deny that Sylvester received the gift of Rome, seat of the Church, from Constantine, along with several other imperial honors, but he disputes the consequences alleged to follow from the fact. We are no longer dealing with scripture here, but with a simple event in Roman history, and with arguments based on these conclusions: no one can legitimately hold what belongs to the Church unless he holds it from the Church. Roman power belongs to the Church. Therefore no one can legitimately hold

26. Ibid., III.8 [167].
27. Lk 22:38.
28. Lk 22:36.
29. Dante, *De Monarchia* III.9 [171].

Roman power unless he holds it from the Church. What is defective in this syllogism is the minor. The *Romanum regimen* does not belong to the Church, because Constantine could not transfer the imperial dignity, nor could the Church receive it. No one can do what is contrary to his office in virtue of the office he holds. The peculiar office of the emperor is to guarantee the harmony and unity of humankind. Therefore, it is contrary to his office to divide the empire, even in order to entrust part of it to the pope. If, as they say (*ut dicant*) Constantine had transferred certain prerogatives of the empire, "the 'seamless garment' would have been rent, which even they had not dared to mutilate who with their spears pierced the side of Christ, the very God." The Church is founded on Christ, who is divine, but the empire is founded on law, which is human, and just as the Church would be ruined by shaking its foundation, the empire would destroy itself by shaking its own foundation. The empire is the very unity of the universal monarchy. The emperor could not be permitted to use his authority to divide the empire. Besides, how would this be possible? Jurisdiction always precedes the judge, because the judge is there for the jurisdiction, and not the jurisdiction for him. The empire is the universal jurisdiction that includes all temporal jurisdictions. The emperor is only there to exercise that jurisdiction, and because he is only emperor through it, he cannot modify it. If Constantine was emperor when he made this donation, he could not make it without destroying his peculiar function. If he was not, he could not make it either. He cannot have made it in either case.

Besides, had the emperor made the donation, the Church could not have received it, because the Gospel clearly says that the Church cannot possess either gold or silver. *Nolite possidere aurum, neque argentum, neque pecuniam in zonis vestris* (Mt 10:9). No doubt the emperor could delegate his possessions to the Church, but not transfer the property. The pope could be the usufructuary of the goods entrusted to him to help the Church or relieve the poor, but is in no case their owner.[30] All cases of this kind that could be cited ought to be settled in the same way: usurpation of a right never creates the right.[31]

The argument that claims to be based on reason alone is subtler. Basing themselves on Aristotle, the supporters of the pope's temporal powers argue as follows. Everything that falls into a single kind comes under just one term, the measure of what belongs to the kind. The Supreme Pontiff and the emperor are humans. Therefore they must come under just one and the same human, as being included in the kind *human*. But because the Supreme Pontiff cannot be ranked under another human, the emperor must be ranked under him like everyone else.

Here again Dante uncovers a sophism in the syllogism, because there is a shift in it from substance to accident in order to predicate of the accident what is only true of the substance. It is true that all humans as humans must be referred back to a single human, but it is a mistake to conclude that this individual is the pope, because being pope is accidental to the human being as, furthermore, it is accidental to be emperor, lord, or father. A human is human by virtue of his substantial form. He is pope, emperor, or father only in virtue of some accidental form, because he would remain human even if he were none of those things. Precisely, pope and emperor are those things only by virtue of certain relations. The pope is pope by virtue of his spiritual fatherhood, as the emperor is emperor by virtue of his temporal power. They therefore do not fall within a common genus. As emperor and as pope they are not reduced to any unity.

Really, we are faced with three distinct orders here, none of which collapses into another. As such all humans must be referred back to a single individual who is their measure and their idea, so to speak. This human, who is eminently human, is "the best."

30. Ibid., III.10 [177].
31. Ibid., III.11 [182].

As human, the pope and the emperor are, therefore, both measured by this standard of human excellence that we call *good man*. It is no longer the same if we consider one as pope and the other as emperor. From the point of view of these relations, one cannot be subalternated to the other, because being emperor is no more being pope than being anyone else, and being pope is no more being emperor. In fact, there is no common genus between the two, because we do not say that an emperor is a pope or vice versa. Therefore, the only way to unite them is to reduce them to a third term, and as they have nothing in common, other than that each designates a relation of superiority, we must find a term that is still superior, from which these two relations of superiority flow. In short, the pope and the emperor are measured by a certain term as humans and by another as pope and as emperor.[32] This last term, the pinnacle of all that exists, is God.

This way we reach the answer to the last of the three questions posed: in the order of relations within which the pope and the emperor preside, each depends directly on God alone. It is clear that the Church's authority cannot be the cause of the imperial authority. There was a universal empire and an emperor before there was a Church, and as the empire does not owe its existence to the Church, it does not hold its authority from her either. That is demonstrated formally: let A be Church, B empire, and C imperial authority. If, although A does not exist, C belongs to B, then A cannot be the case of C belonging to B. The priority of cause in relation to effect is patently necessary, above all in the order of efficient cause with which we are dealing here.[33]

The more Dante thinks about it, the less he sees a crack through which the power of confirming temporal authority on the emperor could slip into the Church. Might it come from God? That could not be except by virtue of the natural law or of the divine law.

32. Ibid., III.12 [185].
33. Ibid., III.13 [189].

It is not by virtue of the natural law, because insofar as the Church is not an effect of nature, but of God, the natural law cannot confer any power on it. Nor is it in virtue of the divine law, because this law is completely contained in the two Testaments, neither of which entrusts any temporal responsibility to the Church. Does the Church hold the power from itself? But if it does not have it, how can it give it to itself? On the other hand, as we have seen, it is certain that the Church cannot have received power from the emperor. The final possibility remaining is that the Church holds this power by universal consent of peoples. However, the Asians, Africans, and the majority of Europeans refuse to acknowledge it. If the Church does not hold the power from God or from itself or the emperor or the universal consent of peoples, it absolutely cannot be seen where it could get it.[34] Moreover, this would be against its nature, because every nature is principally defined by its form. The Church's form is none other than Christ's life taken in his words and in his acts, and we know by what words his life is summed up here. "My kingdom is not of this world." Of course, this does not mean that Christ, who is God, is not Lord of this kingdom. It simply means that as the Church's divine model, Christ does not take the responsibility for this world. Because Christ is the form of the Church, the Church cannot assume the responsibility without contradicting its nature.[35] Therefore, not only has the Church not received this responsibility, but also it would be impossible for it to receive it.

If the emperor does not hold his authority from the Church, he can only hold it from God. There are positive reasons to admit this conclusion. Of all beings, humans are the only ones midway between corruptible and incorruptible things, which is why philosophers compare humans to the horizon that marks the common limit of two hemispheres. Corruptible in body, humans are incor-

34. Ibid., III.14 [190].
35. Ibid., III.15 [194].

ruptible in soul. This is as much as to say that our nature is double, and because every nature has its peculiar end, it must necessarily be that humans have two final ends, one belonging to the body, the other to the soul. The final end of the body is happiness in this life, the figure of which is the earthly paradise. The final end of the soul is the happiness of life eternal that consists of seeing God face to face in the heavenly paradise, which humans cannot attain through their own powers.

As these two kinds of happiness belong to different ends, they can be attained only by different means. We attain the first end under the guide of philosophy, provided that we follow its teaching by practicing the intellectual and moral virtues. We attain the second end under the guidance of revelation, which transcends human reason, provided that we follow revelation's teachings by practicing the theological virtues of faith, hope, and charity. So we have two distinct conclusions, as it were, to which similarly distinct middle terms guide us. On the one hand, there is temporal happiness, which the philosophers have discovered completely (*quae per philosophos tota nobis innotuit*). On the other hand, there is eternal happiness, known to us through the Holy Spirit who has revealed the necessary supernatural truth to us whether by inspiring the prophets or sacred authors or through the mouth of Jesus Christ, Son of God, co-eternal with Father and Spirit, as well as by the teaching of his disciples. Therefore, we know everything we need to know to attain these two ends, but human greed is like lost horses who would stray far off the route if the bridle and bit did not subdue their animal nature and keep them on the straight path.

Accordingly, humans need a dual authority to lead them to their dual end: that of the Supreme Pontiff, who, thanks to the teaching of revelation would lead them to eternal life, and that of the emperor, who would lead humankind to temporal happiness through the light of philosophy. No human being or very few would attain that happiness, and even those few with great difficulty, if after torrents of cupidity had been calmed, humankind did not rest, free and in the tranquility of peace. It is God alone who imposes the responsibility on the emperor to do what the emperor has the power and means to do. It is God alone who elects him and God alone who confirms his authority, so much so that no one is above the emperor. Let us make no mistake. Even those who are called *Electors* do not deserve their title, because they do not choose. They only designate the elect of providence. Moreover, this is why these so-called Electors do not always agree in their designations, because greed makes them unable to discern God's plans.

Let us conclude. The temporal monarch's authority descends upon him directly without intermediary from the universal source of all authority. Authority is one in the simplicity of that source. It flows in different channels that its abundant goodness fills. On the one hand, the pope is the spiritual authority. On the other, the emperor is the temporal authority. It certainly cannot be maintained that the Roman Empire is not subject to the pope in anything, because this life's mortal happiness is in some manner ordered to the happiness of immortal life. Therefore, let Caesar demonstrate the respect for Peter that the eldest son has for his father, so that, illuminated by the light of paternal grace, he may project in turn more powerful rays on this earth, over whose government the emperor has been appointed by the one whom all things temporal or spiritual obey.[36]

However nuanced it is, Dante's political doctrine remains perfectly coherent and solid. At first sight this guiding principle greatly resembles the well-known Thomistic adage: *Jus autem divinum quod est ex gratia, non tollit jus humanum, quod est ex naturali ratione.*[37] At least, it is certain that Dante accepts this principle and yet that all the while, yielding to the overriding concern to maintain the autonomy of nature, he intends to assure nature the

36. Ibid., III.16 [206].
37. *Summa Theologiae* II-II, q. 10, a. 10, co.

full benefit of grace. The Supreme Pontiff can do a great deal for the emperor, and because the emperor expects a great deal from the Supreme Pontiff, he owes him filial respect. But precisely because the pope has the power to help the emperor better fulfill his function as emperor, the pope cannot confer the function upon the emperor. The supreme spiritual authority can help the temporal authority to achieve its temporal end. The supernatural authority can help nature realize itself as such, but it presupposes nature and so cannot be substituted for it. The moon only shines better thanks to the sun that gives it light. It still does not owe the sun either its being the moon or even shining.

This full autonomy of the temporal lets Dante formulate—it seems for the first time—the idea of a truly universal society of humankind, which owes its universality to its temporality, the reverse of what occurs in Roger Bacon's Christian Republic. Like Roger Bacon, Dante holds that the Church is a universal monarchy, but one whose universality comes precisely from its spirituality. As Dante conceives the Roman Empire, on the contrary, it is a strictly political society, coextensive with all humankind and thereby doubly alien to the City of God. In French Third Republic jargon, it could be said that Dante's universal empire is neutral and that its very secularity grounds its universality. All humans are called to be part of it without distinction of race or religion. Is not one of Dante's arguments against the temporal primacy of the popes that whole continents refuse to accept their spiritual authority? They nevertheless ought to acknowledge the emperor's temporal authority, all the same. In other words, although the emperor himself must personally acknowledge the pope's spiritual authority, it is not necessary that a people should belong to the Church for it to belong to the empire. We are no longer dealing with either Church or Christendom or City of God. All are called, all are chosen. Dante's Roman monarchy is the first modern expression of a single temporal society of all humankind.

As we are dealing with Dante it is no surprise that along with one possible solution of the problem, his genius discovered the only element that lets it be solved. For the empire to be freely constituted with a view to its peculiar temporal end, it must dispose of appropriate temporal means. That is why the distinction between empire and Church is coupled here with a corresponding distinction between philosophy and theology, reason and revelation. His "secularism," therefore, is coupled here with a "rationalism" that is its very condition. It is good to highlight these two constants of the problem, without forgetting that in Dante's own thought their distinction does not imply opposition or, absolutely speaking, separation. The temporal, the secular, and the rational are autonomous in their peculiar orders, as is nature in relation to grace, although it is in nature's interest to profit from the beneficial effects of grace, as it is for the temporal to profit from the spiritual. The complexity of these relations becomes possible in Dante thanks to the distinction he introduces between the orders. The perfect autonomy of each of them protects it from any intrusion on the part of other orders at the same time that it forbids it to invade the other orders. Therefore the autonomy allows the sovereign in each order to acknowledge the authority of other sovereigns without diminishing his own authority in any way. The sage is the measure of humans, the emperor the measure of citizens, the pope the measure of Christians, and so that each of them may possess alone the keys of his kingdom, he must acknowledge that each of the others is similarly alone in possessing the keys of his own kingdom. Accordingly, the pope may have no temporal authority that is not delegated to him by the emperor, nor the emperor any spiritual jurisdiction that is not granted to him by the pope. Theology cannot have authority over philosophy, or reason over revelation, although one can always freely appeal to the light of the other. In short, whatever mutual service empire and Church render to each other, the empire alone, nonetheless, guides humans to temporal happiness through reason, as the Church guides them to eternal happiness by revelation.[38]

If this is not a good theoretical solution to the problem, it is at least one of the possible answers. By making philosophical reason the peculiar light of the temporal, Dante removes the difficulty that religious particularism opposes to the establishment of a universal society of humankind. There is no reason to doubt that Dante holds that ultimately faith is universalizable, but he does not want to wait for the pope to have won all peoples for the Church in order to submit them all to the empire, and that is why the empire's universalism seems to Dante to be immediately linked to the universalism of reason. Consequently, a Christian ideal seeks to be achieved here by completely human means and, on a specifically human level, by denying to the Church's authority only what would delay the birth of the society of humankind. Therefore, Dante has brought out, it seems for the first time, the notion of the temporal as autonomous and sufficient in its order, endowed with its peculiar nature, with its peculiar final end and the means to attain the final end that are naturally appropriate to it.

As perfect as an architect's sketch, the solution proposed by Dante remains rather vague when it comes to means of application. Let us not reproach him for it, because he would certainly respond that as a philosopher resolving a philosophical problem, he was not responsible for the practical conditions required to achieve the solution. Organizing the empire corresponds to the emperor. All that Dante can do for him is to convert to his cause those adversaries, who ought to be his natural allies, and then to recall to the emperor, along with its nature, the nature of the

38. On this problem taken in itself, see Étienne Gilson, *Dante et la philosophie* (Paris: J. Vrin, 1939), 167–200 [English translation by David Moore, *Dante the Philosopher* (New York: Sheed and Ward, 1949), reissued as *Dante and Philosophy* (New York: Harper and Row, 1963, and Gloucester, Mass.: P. Smith, 1968); in addition to the works cited in the present book, see John Joseph Rolbiecki, *The Political Philosophy of Dante Alighieri* (Washington, D.C.: The Catholic University of America Press, 1921), 151–56].

means of which he disposes to achieve his end. We are in the twentieth century. There is no longer monarchy, and twentieth-century peoples are still asking themselves how to be united. Our very exalted poet cannot be reproached for not having found the answer to our questions in the fourteenth century.[39]

His political philosophy, nonetheless, marks a new stage in the history of our problem. Although it invokes the Rome of Augustus, Dante's universal monarchy is a temporal copy of the spiritual society that is the Church. Its emperor, whose authority is exercised according to philosophical truth, is an exact counterpart of the pope, whose authority is exercised according to theological truth. The emperor consults Augustus; the pope consults St. Thomas Aquinas. Accordingly, the society of humankind is a temporal Church in charge of the temporal happiness of humans, which guides them there by nature. By taking this decision, Dante im-

39. Unquestionably, by directly subordinating the emperor's political authority to God's authority, Dante envisaged an empire that was religious in its very roots and an ultimately Christian empire. Still, the fervor that certain advocates of the fusion of the orders dedicate to Dante's doctrine is hard to explain. In fact it rests upon a misinterpretation. Dante does not desire an emperor of the world in order to submit him to the head of the universal Church, but a universal empire, temporally independent of the universal Church, although in harmony with it in fact. Incidentally, let us observe that Dante's self-proclaimed disciples are generally fanatical nationalists. They do not want a universal empire at all unless, of course, their own country assumes the government of the empire. Dante's poetical universalism excludes all nationalist imperialism but it still does not rest on the universalism of faith. Its authentic foundation is an unlimited confidence in the power that natural reason and natural truth have of being universalized in and of themselves. This illusion is quite explicable at the end of the thirteenth century and still exists in many minds. The overall agreement on a new interpretation of Aristotle, achieved by theologians in the unifying light of faith, was offered as the effect of spontaneous agreement between purely natural reasons. In fact, in the thirteenth century, and still more in the fourteenth, there was conflict between the philosophers' philosophy and the theologians' philosophy. The weakness of Dante's position stems from his absolute confidence in the unity of philosophical wisdom working on its own under Aristotle's guidance to provide the emperor with universally valid ethics and politics. Dante grounded philosophy's sufficiency to guide the emperor in a union of reasons that were the work of theology and the Church. Nature constantly forgets that it owes the privilege of regaining its naturalness to the recreated work of grace, *opus recreationis*. To recreate nature is completely the opposite of suppressing it.

plicitly accepted two postulates of which he himself was not clearly aware, as often occurs in similar cases. The first was that natural reason, alone and left to itself, was capable of achieving agreement among humans about the truth of one and the same philosophy. Aristotle's triumph in the medieval schools favored this illusion. The least that can be said is that the illusion has become difficult for us. Even in the Middle Ages there were disagreements about Aristotle, sometimes profound ones. Which was this philosopher's truth? Was it that of St. Thomas Aquinas, of Siger of Brabant, of Duns Scotus, or of William of Ockham? Do we know whether the truth of Avicenna and Averroes, among others who could be mentioned, was that of Aristotle himself?

Let us prudently avoid the other disputed question: is it certain that Aristotle's triumph in the Middle Ages was purely philosophical and rational without faith and theology being involved at all? Whatever is the case on this point, the situation is different today. No known candidate to the universal monarchy appeals to Aristotle's ethics or politics to administer the world empire. Moreover, it is difficult to see which philosophy would play this role today, because theologians have never had an easier time using the classical argument in favor of the unity of faith based on "the contradictions of the philosophers." It is worth pondering, in fact, that the theologians are the ones who used to advise that the earth be governed according to the philosophical principles of the Stagirite. The point is not to find out whether the emperor of tomorrow should not follow this advice. It is to find out whether twentieth-century philosophers would agree to advise him to follow it. With the ingratitude toward faith that humans so often demonstrate, Dante's philosophy is based on what it owes to Christian revelation in order to justify its intention to do without Christian revelation in the future. We have the result before our eyes today. In the middle is the worst philosophical chaos that the world has ever known; to the right there is the union of reasons under the unity of the Church's faith; on the left there is the submission of reasons to the force of a new empire whose official doctrine hardly resembles Aristotle's. There is nothing in this situation that Dante foresaw in the slightest. Even the highest genius is not exempt from being mistaken in his predictions.

Still worse, the second error Dante committed stems from his way of understanding the subordination of the temporal to the spiritual. St. Thomas said and repeated that humans have a dual end (*finis duplex*). Dante said and repeated that humans have two ends (*fines duos*). That is a different thing. It is exactly what allows Dante, while he subordinates the Church directly to God through the pope, to subordinate the empire directly to God through his vicar in temporal matters, who is the emperor. By doing this, Dante misunderstood the fundamental principle that, very far from suppressing the autonomy of any lower order, its hierarchical subordination has the effect of grounding it and perfecting it, in short, of guaranteeing its integrity and maintaining it. Nature is only more perfectly nature by being informed by grace. Natural reason only becomes more integrally reasonable by being illuminated by faith. The temporal and political order is only more temporally happy and wise by accepting the Church's spiritual and religious jurisdiction. However direct it is, and although it extends into the political realm, the popes' authority over the temporal realm is not itself temporal or even political in the temporal sense of the term. It does not use the same means; it does not aim at the same end. Dante may be excused for having been mistaken here. The political struggles of his time set Italian cities in opposition to Rome and made it much more difficult than it is today for him to discern the true nature of the hierarchy of powers in dispute. But neither past confusions nor those that might actually be reproduced in the future can now hide the true elements of the problem from us. Can there be a universal empire, whatever its political form, unless it is subordinated to God by the Church's jurisdiction under which, far from losing its autonomy, it would find its being? There can be a Church without there being political unity on earth. But can there be political unity on earth without there being acknowledgment by the temporal order of the direct authority of the spiritual order, not only over ethics but also over politics? After Dante it is impossible to be unaware any longer that this indeed is the question.

FIVE

On the Peace of Faith

Dante proposed a solution to our problem that consisted of juxtaposing a universal temporal society and a universal religious society. But the immediate objective of *De Monarchia* was not to found the latter. Dante's work was satisfied to take it as given or rather to accept the idea just as it was offered in the Church of Rome. Dante had no illusions about the *de facto* universality of the Catholic, apostolic, and Roman Church. He knew well that it was rejected in certain regions of Europe itself and unknown in almost all of Asia and Africa, a vast expanse of the inhabited world. Still, if he wanted to specify the nature and rights of the universal empire, he never seemed to doubt that the Church of Rome, just as he knew it, one day was to become the universal Church. The only reform he desired in the Church was that it should cease to encroach upon the rights of the empire. Associated with a free empire in the temporal realm, a Church that is free itself in the spiritual realm doubtless seemed to Dante all the more surely destined to become the universal kingdom of the children of God.

Was this hope justified? A man of the Church asked himself this question in the fifteenth century, and his response is all the more surprising in that it did not come from an adventurer with no authority and still less from a heretic or schismatic outlawed by the Church for suspicious novelties. On the contrary, Nicholas of Cusa was one of its princes. Born in 1401 near Trier, Nicholas was ordained as a priest in 1428 and made a cardinal in 1448, with San Pietro in Vincoli as his titular church, an honor, as a historian of his time remarked, that was rarer for a German than a white crow.

There was no more respected figure in the Church at the time or afterward. His memory continues to be respected. When we learn how he conceived the universality of the Christian religion, we can only be surprised at such marvelous impunity.[1]

The message of Nicholas of Cusa is simple. Religion is a factor of unity.[2] But religions are factors of disunity. Consequently, there must be only one religion, and the cardinal does not doubt for an instant that it ought to be the Roman, Catholic, and apostolic religion, but neither does he doubt that certain adjustments are necessary for it to be able to win over the other religions of the

1. On Nicholas of Cusa, see Edmond Vansteenberge, *Le cardinal Nicolas de Cues (1401–1464): L'action, la pensée* (Paris: H. Champion, 1920) [reprinted in Geneva: Statkine Reprints, 1974, and Frankfurt: Minerva GmbH, 1963]. See also Maurice de Gandillac, *La philosophie de Nicolas de Cues* (Paris: Aubier-Montaigne, 1941), as well as Gandillac's translation of *Oeuvres choisies de Nicolas de Cues* (Paris: Aubier-Montaigne, 1942). On Cusa's political ideas, see Elisabeth Bohnenstadt, "Kirche und Reich in Schrifttum des Nikolaus von Cues," in *Cusanus-Studien*, Acts of the Sessions of the Academy of Science, Philosophy and History section, XXX–1, Heidelberg, 1939. Our analysis of *De Pace Fidei* is far from complete. Even the passages in quotation marks are sometimes only fairly free summaries with a public lecture in mind, rather than literal translations. Still, we hope we have never betrayed the author's meaning. For old editions of the original Latin, see Friederich Ueberweg, *Grundriss der Geschichte der Philosophie*, 12th ed. (Berlin: Verlag E. S. Mittler und Sohn, 1924), vol. 3 [Basel: B. Schwabe, 1983]. A German translation is found in Franz Anton Scharpff, *Des Cardinals und Bisschofs Nicholaus von Cusa wichtigste Schriften* (Freiburg im Brieigau: Herder, 1862).

2. What links the whole notion of the universal society to a philosophy that legitimates it is established in Nicholas of Cusa. His irenism spontaneously blends with his notion of God as the harmony of opposites and extremes. Because God is infinite, he is at the same time the maximum and minimum (*De Docta Ignorantia* I.4). He is being and nonbeing, light and shadow, and so on. From here comes a "circular theology" that, following Pseudo-Dionysius leads to a learned ignorance that is the mystical *intellectus*. From here too comes a notion of the Church as the union of souls in the faith of Jesus Christ (*De Docta Ignorantia* III.11 and 12). The *learned ignorance*, which is the intellection of faith, evidently makes the reconciliation of different religions easier, but this is only possible from the point of view of Christianity and through it. More precisely, it is possible through the Cusan theology of the Christian word and the philosophy that theology implies. This could not satisfy the dialecticians who accused Cusa of heresy for having dared to question the principle of noncontradiction. Yes, answers Nicholas in his *Apologia pro Docta Ignorantia*, it is a heresy for Aristotle's sect that regards the coincidence of opposites as a heresy, and yet it is certainly necessary to admit the coincidence, because recognizing it is the point of departure for the ascent toward the peaks of learned ignorance: *in cuius admissione est initium ascensu in mysticam theologiam*.

world.[3] This is precisely the thesis he maintains in his *De Pace Fidei* (1454).

From the outset of this curious fable, we see the principal element of the problem. Nicholas was painfully concerned by a fact whose tragic character stands out for a sincerely religious soul: the wars of religion. The news of cruelties recently committed by the sultan of Turkey near Constantinople deeply wounded the heart of a pious man who had once visited Turkey.[4] He ardently implored the creator to put an end to the ferocious persecutions that reigned in that country as a result of the diversity of beliefs and religious

3. Anyone who wants to understand Nicholas of Cusa's attitude must take into account the personal experience of schism he acquired at the Council of Basel, which inspired his *De Concordantia Catholica* (1433). The list of events that unfolded during the previous centuries did not invite friends of unity to easy optimism. Wycliffe (1324–84) and John Huss (1369–1415) foreshadow the Reformation. The Hundred Years' War between Christian peoples begins in 1339. The great schism occurs in 1378. The Serbs are defeated by the Turks at Kosovo in 1396. The Turks under Bajazet I defeat a French Crusade at Nicopolis in 1396. In 1415 there is a Hussite rebellion, against which Pope Martin V preaches a Crusade (a Crusade against Christians). Also in 1415 the Council of Constance proclaims that ecumenical councils are above the pope. Benedict XIII is deposed in 1417. The Turks under Amurat II capture Thessaloniki in 1430. The schism of the Greek Church becomes final in 1440. The Turks led by Mohammed II take Constantinople in 1453. This is the date historians choose to mark the end of the Middle Ages. Nicholas of Cusa was born in 1401 before the Hussite revolt and died in 1467 after the fall of Constantinople. He witnessed the disintegration of medieval Christendom. He needed great faith in unity to try to maintain it and even to try to extend it, being as it was in a state of dissolution at a time when everything threatened unity.

4. The importance of the problems raised by the Crusades against Islam must not be forgotten if we want to understand certain aspects of Nicholas of Cusa's position. On this point see Rudolf Haubst, "Johannes von Segovia im Gespräch mit Nikolaus von Kues und Jean Germain über die Göttliche Dreieinigkeit und ihre Verkündigung vor den Mohammedanern," *Münchener Theologisches Zeitschrift* 2 (1951): 115–29. See 119 on Nicholas of Cusa and his *De Pace Fidei*: "Therefore, through that, the treatise *De Pace Fidei* gets an authentic interpretation here. Nicholas not only wants to present the ideal relation of Christ's revelation to the partial truth of the content of other religions in a celestial congress of the nations in the presence of the Divine Word, he likewise wants to define religious peace as a requirement of divine and human law and draws this consequence directed against wars of religion: *Sola defensio sine periculo Christiano*." On the same page, Haubst describes the project for a real conference with the Muslims in Cairo, Alexandria, or Jaffa, dealing with the dogma of the Trinity. Dr. Joseph Koch informed us about the existence of this recent work, and we wish to express our gratitude for the indication.

confessions. Obsessed by this idea for several days, Nicholas ended by having a vision that revealed to him the means to put an end to this religious dissention. If there were a congress of some intelligent persons, well informed about the religions that are found throughout the world, would they not discover among themselves a minimum real agreement upon which lasting religious peace could finally be established? Nicholas of Cusa's treatise resembles the official minutes of this heavenly congress of religions.

At the height of his spiritual contemplation our man is suddenly transported to heaven where a council is held with the Almighty presiding. The king of heaven and earth takes the floor. The news from earth is bad. Sighs of grief rise toward heaven from all sides. Innumerable men take up arms and fight to force each other to abjure their traditional religion. Innumerable messages bring these complaints from all regions of the earth, which the king of heaven submits to the assembly of the saints. Moreover, everyone seems to know the messages, because the king of the universe himself posted them in the different provinces and regions from the start.

Speaking in their name an archangel addresses God as follows:

> Lord and King of the universe! What does your creature have that you did not give him? You formed his body out of the slime of the earth, and you animated it with a rational soul so that the image of your ineffable power might shine in it. Just one of them became the source of a great people that covers the surface of the earth. Immersed in the slime of the earth and surrounded by shadows, this rational spirit cannot see the light or guess its origin, but you have also created what was necessary so that, astonished by what it saw with the body, it would be invited to turn the eyes of its spirit toward you, creator of the world and to unite itself to you by the highest love so that enriched by this merit it might return to its origin. Yet, Lord, you know that such a multitude cannot be without differences. You know that almost all humans are condemned to lead a life of work, of cares, and of suffering in the servitude that kings impose on them. Very few of them have enough leisure to come to know themselves on their own and freely. Gripped by a thousand cares and toils of the earth, they

are incapable of searching for you, the hidden God. Therefore you gave your people kings and prophets who, mostly in your name and under your orders, instructed an ignorant multitude, ordered divine worship, and established laws. The multitude accepted these laws as if you yourself had spoken to them face to face, and as if it were your voice that they heard in your servants. You have sent different prophets at different times into the midst of the nations. It is human nature for custom to become second nature, and for humans to end by regarding it as truth. From there comes lack of unity, and that each religious society refers its faith to that of the others. Hasten to their aid, you who alone can help them. It is because of you, whom all venerate in their prayers, that this warfare goes on. In everything that each one seems to pursue, he seems nothing other than the good that you are. In all the wandering of his intellect, no one seeks anything other than the Truth that you are. What does a living being want but to live? What does an existing thing want but to be? Therefore, it is you from whom being and life came that different religions seek in different ways, you whom they call different names, although you remain completely unknown and ineffable in your true being. Creatures can form no idea of your infinity, because no relation is possible from the finite to the infinite. Still, almighty God, you can reveal yourself to all minds in a way that is understandable. Therefore, hide yourself no longer, oh Lord! Be merciful! Let your face be seen. Return salvation to all peoples so they may nevermore forget the source of a life whose sweetness they have hardly tasted, because only he who does not know you abandons you. Thus, hate, suffering, and war will end, and everyone will know that there is only one religion in the diversity of rites. If this multiplicity of rites cannot be abolished, or if it is preferable that it should remain in order that the rivalry of peoples should benefit the worship of God, may there at least be a single religion and a single divine worship, as you yourself are one. Lord, be forgiving! Your anger is love, and your justice is compassion. Take pity on your fragile creature! Those to whom you have confided the protection of your people make the request in all humility.

Some of the phrases in that passage have a novel tone that was literally unheard of at that time. First of all there is the expression of Nicholas of Cusa's ecumenical sentiment: different religions serve the one and same God in different ways and call him by different names. Then there is the very energetic affirmation of the fundamental thesis: despite the difference in religious confessions, there is only one religion. It is true that, in matters like this, intentions count less than the manner in which they are accomplished. Does Nicholas of Cusa speak sincerely, or are his words only the bait in an operation where all religious confessions would ultimately be invited to bear the cost in benefit of the Catholic religion? To find this out let us see how Nicholas conceives its realization.

After this prayer of the archangel, all the inhabitants of heaven bow before the throne of the Most High whose answer is that he created humans free and capable through their freedom of living in society with him. Unhappily, the prince of darkness plunged the earthly, animal humans into ignorance. They now wander in the sensible world and no longer live as spiritual humans in their native country. That is why, God says, I took care to send prophets to humans to call them back from their error. Because the prophets were insufficient, I sent my Word by whom the world was created. He donned human flesh to better enlighten humans, to teach them to live according to their inner humanity and savor the sweetness of eternal life. In taking on human nature, the Word manifestly testifies that humans can receive eternal life and that this is the only desire of the inner human. Of all God could do to save humans, what is there that he did not do?

At these words of the king of kings, the Word speaks in his turn. Assuredly, the Father's work was perfect. Accordingly, it did not have to be perfected. Still, humans had been created free, and because everything changes in this world of sensible things, points of view continually vary over time, and not only points of view, but also even languages and ways of expressing oneself. This is why frequent rectifications are necessary to dissipate the errors that crop up and to lead people back to the way of truth. Truth is one, and because minds are free, they must all be capable of seeing it. If everyone sees truth, the multiplicity of religions will be reduced to the unity of one and the same faith in one stroke.

The king of kings gave his approval to this discourse, and the angels who preside over the nations and the different languages of the world were immediately summoned with the order that each should present a particularly well-qualified representative of every people before the Word. By a kind of enchantment these eminent individuals immediately appeared before the Word, who addressed these words to them:

> The Master of heaven and earth has heard the sighs of persons put to death or thrown into irons just as of all those who suffer because of differences of religion. All those who carry out these persecutions, like all who suffer them, are convinced that the salvation of their souls demands this and that their creator wills it. Therefore, the Lord has taken pity on his people and decided to reduce all the different religions to one single religion through a peaceful understanding. You, Delegates, are the ones he charges with carrying out his design. To help you he will entrust your protection and your supervision to the angels of his court. He has designated Jerusalem as the most suitable place for this gathering.

At this point, the first human spokesperson intervenes, whom Nicholas of Cusa simply calls "the Greek." His contribution has the special interest of being more philosophical than religious in the confessional sense. Thus Nicholas of Cusa's horizon is even broader than simple ecumenism, which would already be broad enough. Greek wisdom, that is to say the wisdom of human beings *qua* human, does not seem to Nicholas to have been the simple search for abstract truth as might be that of a system. What rather catches the Greek's attention in the ancients is that they always sought truth from some master, as if wisdom had to be embodied to be accessible to us. Accordingly, thanks to the Greek, philosophy itself will be integrated into the universal religion, which is Christianity properly understood.

To be sure, the Greek himself initially doubts that the general assembly of religion could lead to harmonizing religions. How will a people accept another religion than the one for which it has already shed its blood? The Word assures that the issue is not for any people to adhere to a new faith, but to become aware of the common faith that unites us already. As all philosophers love wisdom, they necessarily hold it to be well established that there is only one wisdom. Even if there were several, all would come from a single source because multiplicity always supposes the unity in which it participates. The sensible world bears witness to the fact that this one wisdom is also infinite in power. Being invisible, it transcends all its visible works. The divine Word affirms it, as the Wisdom books already affirmed it, and the Greek does not contradict it here because he acknowledges that the philosophers in the past were also only led to accept wisdom by having perceived and admired the sweetness of the sensible world whose artisan is wisdom. Who would not give his life to attain the source of all sweetness and of all beauty? With this, carried away by his passion, the Greek throws himself into a eulogy of wisdom, whose power bursts out in the human body, in the harmony of its organs, in the form and movement of its members, in the life that animates them, and finally in the mind, capable of the most surprising arts and with a wisdom in which the image of its divine cause shines, by which it is nourished and which it unceasingly approaches, although it can never attain it in any other thing as it is in itself. "You are on the right path that leads to the end toward which we are moving," answers the Word. "Even if you profess different religions, you all place something that you call wisdom ahead of your differences. Answer then: does this one wisdom include all that can be expressed?"

The Word himself responds to the Italian, who takes the floor after the Greek and observes that there is no "word" outside of wisdom. The Word answers that it is a matter of indifference to say that everything is created in wisdom or that everything is created in the Word. Indeed, the Italian admits, the Word of the creator, in which he created everything, can only be his wisdom, and not a creature, but uncreated wisdom by which every creature is what it is. Eternal principle of everything, absolutely simple as is everything that has no cause, it is consequently eternal. There cannot be several eternities, because eternity is at the origin of everything, and unity always precedes multiplicity. Therefore, wisdom is God, the One, the simple and eternal God who is the principle of all things. With this the Word concludes that coming from so many different schools, all philosophers still agree in confessing the existence of only one God.

On this point the Arab is in agreement. He recognizes that all humans naturally desire wisdom, which is the life of the mind, and that an absolute wisdom exists that is the one God, but, as the Word asks him to conclude from this that there is only one religion and only one worship prior to all distinctions of religious practice, the Arab hesitates. This representative of monotheism is made uneasy by polytheism. "You are Wisdom," he says to his divine interlocutor, "since you are God's Word. So I ask you how those who adore several gods can be in agreement with the philosophers about one single God." The Word responds that those who adore several gods have always presupposed the existence of one unique divinity. They prayed to that divinity in all their gods as if the latter participated in its divinity. Just as there can be nothing wise if there is not Wisdom, there cannot be gods without a divinity. To speak of several gods is to suppose a divine principle that is prior to them, just as admitting that there are several holy people presupposes that there is a Holy of Holies in which the other participate and thanks to whom they are holy. Besides, there has never been a people so limited as to believe in several gods, each of whom was the first cause and creator of the universe.

The Arab concurs without difficulty, because he judges that

it would be contradictory for there to be several first principles. The first principle could have no cause, even himself, because he would need to be before being able to cause himself. That would be absurd. Therefore, he is eternal, unique, and the cause of the universe, he whom no people could doubt. The Word does not ask for more, because if polytheists simply directed their worship to this divinity whom they really adore in all the false gods, and if, as reason demands, they explicitly took as the object of their religion this divinity whom they implicitly worship, the disagreement would be smoothed out. Still, the Arab doubts that those who adore several gods would allow themselves to be persuaded easily to renounce worshipping them. How is a people to be persuaded to direct itself no longer to familiar divinities to which it has the custom of asking for help? That is not impossible, answers the Word, because if the people are taught that all their divinities presuppose only one single divinity, without doubt they will be persuaded that it is in their interest to ask for help from the author of being, who is the supreme Savior, rather than from those who have nothing of themselves that they have not received from him. Besides, there is no objection to people in their illnesses or distress invoking humans to intercede with God, humans who are commendable because of their holiness, or that people should venerate them as friends of God or as examples worthy of being imitated. Provided that divine worship goes exclusively to the only God, there will be no contradiction with the single religion about which we speak. In short, the Word proposes worship of *dulia* given to saints as a substitute for the worship of *latria* given by polytheists to the divinities they adore. Thus, he assures, the people will be satisfied.

So be it, the Hindu says then, but what will we do with the statues and images? The Word sees no problem in their being used, provided that what they represent is compatible with the worship of a single God. It would be different if the statues and images turned people away from that worship, by letting it be believed that stones contain something divine. This will be difficult, answers the Hindu, because the worship of statues is rooted in the people's heart, especially by reason of the oracles they emit. But the Word knows the remedy for that evil. In theory, these oracles come from priests who make them pass for words of the divinity. This is very clear in the ambiguity of their predictions, which often makes it difficult to make them admit to lying or to prove that, if they are not completely mistaken, they have only told the truth by chance. The Hindu objects to this as a matter of experience that a spirit who dwells in the statue sometimes responds for it. But the Word replies that there we are dealing with the evil spirit himself, not the spirit of a person, of Aesculapius, or of Apollo. The enemy of humankind recurred to this trick in the beginning, but he has renounced it. After the trick was discovered, the statues stopped speaking. Consequently, it will surely not be difficult to get the East to renounce the worship of idols and for its people to join other humans in the worship of one single God.

The Hindu concedes this point. As the Greeks, the Romans, and the Arabs have given up the worship of idols, why will the Orientals not do it in their turn? The difficulty will not be to convert them to the worship of one God, but of the Trinity. To say Trinity in the divine essence is to say multiplicity at the same time. How can it be simultaneously true to say that there only exists a single divinity and that nonetheless it includes a certain multiplicity? But the Word, who seems to have read Nicholas of Cusa, has his answer ready. As creator, God is one and three, but as infinite, he is neither three nor one, nor any attribute that can be conceived. All the names that we attribute to God are taken from creatures. He himself is ineffable and above any perfections that can be attributed to him. The world is his handiwork, and it is true that the parts are multiple, but the source of this multiplicity of parts can only be the unity of their cause. Likewise, if there is dissimilarity between the parts of the universe, where none resembles any other, it springs forth from the equality of unity. Therefore, prior to any diversity, we posit eternal equality. Moreover, we observe in the universe a distinction or separation of parts. Yet before any distinction there is the connection between unity and equality. This connection is eternal, and as there cannot be several eternal beings, in eternity we necessarily find unity, equality of unity, and the connections of equality and resemblance. Thus the unique, simple principle of the universe is one and three. Let us leave to the experts the task of evaluating this theology where God is only Trinity as creator, a theology that hardly seems to be worried about the distinction of divine persons. It is still legitimate to wonder whether in his zeal for the establishment of universal peace among religions, Nicholas of Cusa proceeds to a reconciliation where Catholic dogma pays the whole price and ultimately risks vanishing.

However that may be, the Hindu does not respond further. The Chaldean takes the floor in his turn. As the Word has said that the stamp of the Trinity is found in all the effects of God, the sage asks him to explain this point more clearly. If there are not three gods, but only one that is three, does not the Word simply mean to say that this one God is three in his action? The Word responds that God, being all-powerful, is supreme in every order of causal efficacy, but because his efficacy and his presence are one, to speak of a Trinity of his efficacy is to speak of the Trinity of his essence. The same goes for his power. Therefore, there would be nothing absurd in saying that the divine omnipotence, which is God, contains in itself unity, which is essence, plus equality and relationship. Consequently, on everything that possesses being, the power of unity confers at once being and unity. A thing only is insofar as it is one. Likewise, the power of equality confers equality and form on everything that is, because what equality consists in for a thing is being no more nor less than what it is. Without this equality it would be nothing. Lastly, it is the power of relationship that unites and reconnects unity to equality. Thus the omnipotence of unity draws being from nothing; the efficacy of equality informs it; and the efficacy of relationship unites it. Unity, equality, and their connection consequently would have appeared in that order when God created being, which amounts to saying that nothing can be unless it is *one*; what is must first be one.

Here the Word engages in a long metaphysical development, made exactly to confirm us in the certainty that he is Nicholas of Cusa's spokesman. The creature's equality, he specifies, is its very essence, because equality is the development of the form in unity, in consequence of which it is human unity that is produced, not that of a lion or any other essence. Equality can only stem from the unity of an essence with itself and from the mutual love or relationship that unites them. Going back from beings to their source, the Word finally establishes through a scholarly metaphysics of number that the divine Trinity is not a numerical plurality but the simplest unity. To believe in one God, therefore, is not to reject the Trinity, which is God himself, all-powerful principle of the creation of the universe. Let us note with what care Nicholas of Cusa's Word maintains the divine Trinity's relation to the creative work. If it were not Trinity, the first principle would not be, as it is, the simplest, most efficacious, and most powerful principle.

The Chaldean admits that he is convinced, but he still has a scruple. At least, he recalls that the Catholic Church's language is a little less vague than what the Word uses here. That God has a Son and shares his divinity with that Son is, he objects, what the Arabs and many others with them challenge. The Word responds that some people give the name *Father* to unity, the name *Son* to equality, and the name *Holy Spirit* to their relation. These terms are not to be taken literally, but they express the Trinity appropriately, because equality is born from unity, as the Son is born from the Father. From the Father's unity and the Son's equality proceeds love, or the Holy Spirit. Yet, the Word adds, if simpler expressions were found, they would be still more suitable. It is impossible to be more accommodating about the letter of dogma. The unity of faith that the Word imagines no longer even requires that we speak of Father, Son, and Holy Spirit. An exegetical commentary by Nicholas of Cusa on the letters of St. Paul would be extremely interesting.

After this we at least understand that the Jew himself comes around to the dogma of the Trinity without discussion. The Word continues: how will the Arabs and all philosophers say "no" here? To deny the Trinity thus understood is to deny God creative fruitfulness and power, while by accepting it, we avoid recurring to the hypothesis of several gods to explain the creation of the world. The overriding concern of Nicholas of Cusa is clearly perceptible here. If Nicholas insists so strongly, through the Word's authority, on the unity of the Christian God, it is in order that the dogma of the Trinity should cease to appear to Arabs and Jews as an insurmountable obstacle. Nicholas quotes the words of their prophets to Arabs and Jews in order to convince them that their prophets themselves speak of the divine Trinity, although without realizing it. In the sense in which Arabs and Jews reject the divine Trinity, it certainly ought to be rejected by everyone, but in the sense in which the Word himself has just said it ought to be understood, the Trinity cannot fail to be accepted by all. The Scythian, who follows the Jew, also agrees. That only requires a small effort of him, because without it being clear why, he becomes the spokesman for a doctrine of three divine substances analogous to Plotinus's doctrine: one God from whom a creator Intellect is born, which is his Word, to whom God is united by a World-Soul, who is none other than love. This refined Scythian easily confirms that all philosophers have known something about the Trinity of God in unity.

The intervention of the Frenchman, who supports what went before by invoking Nicholas's own doctrine, at first only perfects the general agreement, but thereafter he soon threatens to break it by posing the thorny question of the Word's incarnation. There, he remarks, we are far from being in agreement, because some maintain that the Word was made flesh to save humans, while others deny it, and it is a point on which harmony will be difficult. At this point the Word announces that the apostle Peter is in charge of clarifying the issue. Peter indeed appears and speaks in his turn, but initially he limits himself to establishing something that is not the most difficult point, namely, that if it is agreed that God's Word becomes human, this human who incarnated the Word of God is also God. But here the Persian protests because the difficulty that holds him back is completely different. For him the issue is knowing how God, who is immutable, could become human, that is to say, in short, non-God. There, he says, is what we all agree in denying. Indeed, even some among us who bear the name of Christians acknowledge like us that it is impossible that the infinite should be finite and the eternal should be temporal.

Peter does not dispute this. On the contrary, he explicitly acknowledges that such propositions must be denied. But because those Persians who profess Islam acknowledge that Christ is God's Word, in which furthermore they are right, they also ought to admit that Christ is God and not just a man inspired by God's Word, as nobody had been before him, but rather God himself. The Persian at least cannot dispute that Christ had a human nature, which Christians similarly admit, because he was truly human like other humans and mortal like them. But it is not according to this nature that he was God's Word. If the Persians themselves acknowledge that Christ was God's Word, in what sense could he have been it? Not by nature, they say, but by grace, that is to say, like a prophet, and even, if we wish, the greatest prophet.

Yet Peter judges that this is not enough. Christ was not simply a messenger of God but his Son, the Word born of the Father and heir to his dignity, just as to his power. So, although the Son is not the Father, he is no less the king than the Father is. As for saying that God cannot have sons, nothing is more certain, at least if we want to take such a comparison literally, because then we would come to say that the Son is a different God from the Father as the king's son is a different man from the king. But let us set aside the persons and only consider that power that is based on the royal dignity of the Father and of his heir the Son. Then, how will we not see that this royal dignity is one and the same in the Father, who is ungenerated, and in the Son, whom the Father generates as his Word? If that is agreed, why not admit that this engendered royalty should take on an alien nature to associate it individually to its own royal authority, so that the inheritance that one possesses by nature, the other possesses by adoption? Here adoption is not separable from the filiation that alone makes it possible. Therefore, it is necessary that the adoptive heir should be the same as the natural heir. Indeed, if the adopted one is not the same person as the authentic son, how could he share in this indivisible inheritance? Consequently, let us conclude: the human nature is linked to the Word's divine nature by an indivisible union that, while respecting their distinction, unites them in the divinity of a single person.

Despite the Persian's good will, because he begins to find this rather clear, he asks that the point be explained with the help of an example, and Peter immediately devotes himself to satisfying him, not without warning that no really appropriate example is conceivable here. Let us imagine a man endowed with the greatest wisdom possible. Human nature would be united in him in the most directly possible way with the Word of eternal Wisdom. For that union to be the closest possible, it would be necessary that the human nature should be then personally united to the divine nature by a grace such that a greater one could not be conceived. Surely, even if it is admitted, as it should be, that the grace is included in this man's nature, he would still remain human and would not be God. What distinguishes Christ from all other humans, even the greatest prophets, is the unique greatness of his person that alone has permitted his union with the divine nature. In Christ alone human nature is united to divine nature in the unity of a single supposit.

Perhaps the Arabs, who acknowledge that Christ is the Word of God and the Most High, will be encouraged by this image to acknowledge that Christ is God without God's unity being broken. The Persian, however, is not yet completely assured because, though now reassured about the integrity of the divine person in the incarnation, he is concerned about the integrity of the human person. To completely convince him, Peter invites him to imagine a piece of iron, attracted by a magnet. The iron loses its weight but conserves its nature. Thus, in the inseparable union with the divine nature, Christ's human nature still remains what it is. The comparison is a stretch, as Peter himself affirms, but the Persian declares he understands and this time seems to consider himself satisfied. Besides, those Arabs who admit that Christ rose from the dead and performed other miracles certainly must understand that he can only have done that by the power of his divine nature. With the Jews this will be more difficult, because they do not want to yield any ground on this point. They certainly have their scriptures, where they are told everything about Christ, but holding to the letter they refuse to see the sense. However, their resistance will not prevent religious harmony, because they are only a minority and will never be able to perturb the peace of the world by force of arms. Therefore, there is no ground to be concerned.

The Syrian, who follows the Persian, poses a completely practical question: how, in fact, is agreement between religions to be achieved on this precise point? To this Peter responds: here is the way. Are not all religions, whether of Jews, Christians, Arabs, or many other peoples, in agreement that after death the mortal nature of a human being will resurrected to eternal life? If it is really thus, they must likewise admit the union of human nature and divine nature in the person of Christ, who is the pledge of our resurrection and our immortality. Once again, the Jews raise an obstacle, because they will object that the Messiah has not yet come. But Arabs, Christians, and all those who have signed their testimony with their blood would unite to assure that he has come. Because they affirm it on the strength of his miracles and of the prophets, who can resist them?

With equal success, Peter defeats several other objections. The Spaniard is afraid lest many should be held back by the virginal conception, but if Christ is the pinnacle of perfection, whose son could he be but God's? He can only have been born of a virgin. The Turk observes that according to Christians, Christ was crucified by the Jews, something Arabs refuse to admit. But the Arabs would no longer refuse, if they understood that Christ wanted to die to seal with his blood the promise of the kingdom of heaven and of the happiness that he brings to humans. The German objects that it is precisely on the nature of this happiness that religions disagree. The Jews count on sensible and purely temporal goods. The Arabs expect carnal but eternal pleasures. Christians hope for spiritual joys like those of angels. How are they be made to agree? Simply by making them understand that all the Koran's descriptions are only manners of speaking. The issue is to use unsophisticated images in order to make a unsophisticated people understand that God has promised us the highest good that is achievable by human nature. Their wise men have seen this very well. For example, does not Avicenna say that the happiness of seeing God is infinitely better than the pleasures that the Koran announces to the people? Besides, which pleasures? The dark maidens with large eyes that it promises would say nothing to Germans, even if they were offered to them in this life. Accordingly it will not be difficult to put all religions in agreement on this point. It will simply be said that this happiness surpasses anything that can be said, because it consists in the satisfaction of all desires in the enjoyment of the very source of good during eternal life. It is true that once more the Jews will be recalcitrant. They will claim to await happiness only in this life.

But would they accept dying for their faith if they did not expect some future happiness? In fact, they do not say that there is no eternal life. They do not even count on their works, but on their faith, and we have said enough that faith presupposes Christ.

The issue of the sacraments appears with the Tartar. His compatriots profess the existence of one single God, and what surprises them in other religions is the multiplicity and diversity of their rites. They are all the more amused that to honor a single God, some have themselves baptized, whereas others have themselves circumcised. Consider marriage! Certain peoples only admit monogamy. Others allow one legitimate wife and several concubines. Still others permit several legitimate wives. Similar diversity is observed in sacrifices, something that produces conflicts, enmities, hatred, and wars.

This time Peter, the guardian of divine truth, yields to Paul, the apostle to the gentiles, who will really go very far on the road of reconciliation. Nothing is easier for him, because we know that, according to him, it is not works but faith that saves. He whom faith justifies will live in eternal life. If this is agreed upon, rites will no longer be an obstacle, because they are only sensible signs of the truth itself of faith. The signs can vary but not the faith that they signify. After having explained to the Tartar, who had raised the question, about what justification by faith consists in, and that it suffices to gain eternal life, Paul proceeds to a short exposition of God's commandments, whose fulfillment is love to which all of them lead. That said, the problem of the sacraments no longer offers insurmountable difficulties. Baptism is certainly necessary, but it is a sacrament of faith. It rests upon the trust that if Jesus Christ can justify humans, he must be able to cleanse their sins. That is why faith is necessary in adults, who cannot be saved without receiving this sacrament, unless it is impossible for them to receive it. As for children, having them baptized will be accepted all the more easily, as even the Jews have infants circumcised when they are eight days old. No doubt it will be agreeable to them to replace circumcision by baptism. Moreover, if baptism does not please them, they will be left with the choice.

The Bohemian then raises the question of the sacrament of the Eucharist. We know what controversies it had provoked in his country. How, he asks, will all people be made to accept transubstantiation? Paul makes an effort to explain it to him, but he finds it difficult to understand. No, Paul answers, it is easy through faith, because this sacrament is a sensible sign that signifies the food of eternal life. That is even why, if there is faith, the sacrament is not so necessary that beatitude cannot be attained without it, because to attain beatitude it is enough to believe and to be thus nourished with the bread of life. We also see why no restrictive law determines whether, to whom, or how often this sacrament should be given to the people. When one has faith but judges himself unworthy of the table of the supreme king, it is praiseworthy humility to abstain.

As the ecclesiastical authorities have complete power to regulate these matters in terms of places, times, and circumstances, a peace agreement among peoples can be established in a common respect for faith in which the law remains necessary. Doubtless heartened by this extraordinary amplitude of viewpoint, the Englishman asks finally what will be done about the other sacraments: marriage, priestly ordination, confirmation, and extreme unction. His patience is not disappointed, because the apostle Paul answers that human wisdom has to be taken into account in all things, as long as it does not raise an obstacle to faith. To want perfect conformity in these matters would be rather harmful to peace. Nevertheless, it can be hoped that an agreement might be reached about marriage and ordination because peoples seem to tend spontaneously toward monogamy, and the priesthood is an institution common to all religions. Furthermore, these two sacraments have such purity in Christianity that understanding on this subject will be easy. Nobody says a single word about the sacrament of penance, which certainly simplifies the problem, and as for fasts, abstinences, formulas for prayers, ecclesiastical functions, or other similar institutions, St. Paul liberally grants all nations the right to continue in their practices of piety and their customary ceremonies, provided only that peace and faith are protected. Moreover, perhaps religious piety has more to gain than to lose in there being some diversity in these things, as each nation would want to outdo the others in piety and zeal to assure itself of more glory in the eyes of the world and more merit in the eyes of God.

It would be impossible to be more optimistic. With the discussion over, a certain number of works will be prepared on the practices of the ancients. Its composition is entrusted to eminent writers in each language, chosen among those who, like Varro among the Latins or Eusebius among the Greeks, had compared the different religions with each other. Their examination will reveal that all the differences occur rather in religious customs than in the worship of a single God, because all religions suppose him and worship him, although, seduced by the spirit of darkness, the simple people have often done so without knowing it. Thus, the agreement of all the religions of the world ends up being clinched in heaven. Angels were put in charge of communicating it to humans in the expectation of a council to gather in Jerusalem so that one single faith might be accepted in the name of everyone for eternal peace to be established upon its common faith, and, through this peace, for the creator of all to receive the praise and honor that are due him for eternity. Amen.

Thus ends the book *On the Peace of Faith* by Cardinal Nicholas of Cusa, whom no one will accuse of having a timid mind or narrowness in his views. This little book is doubly surprising in that it was written and that the Church never condemned it, but we must reserve all our attention for the undertaking that it recommends.

In the first place, an exposition of what Nicholas himself held to be the Catholic religion cannot be found in the book. Personally, he had no other faith than that of the Church. Here the center of his interest is not the Christian faith, which is not at issue, but the religious peace of the world, which he hopes to obtain by a kind of concordat among the most varied beliefs. In the second place, his irenics does not consist of sacrificing Christianity to the other religions to obtain their agreement, but, on the contrary, of making them become aware of the *de facto* agreements that already united them to Christianity, and of the spiritual progress they would achieve if they came closer to Christianity by making an effort to purify the meaning of their own truth. It cannot be doubted for an instant that Cardinal Cusa ardently desired the complete Christianization of the world. It is even probable that the peace of the faith came to mind as a necessary means to reach total Christianization, except that, unlike Roger Bacon, Cusa no longer anticipates it after some foreseeable waiting period. That is why, instead of eliminating opposing sects and religions, he accommodates them. The Republic of believers is no longer exclusively composed of Christians linked by the unity of one and the same wisdom. Rather, in order to legitimate the coexistence of different religions within the common peace, Cusa recurs to his personal concept of wisdom in sheltering the coincidence of opposites and the union of contraries. The central fact remains that after Cardinal Cusa, the cognition of faith unites what faith divides. Perhaps he himself would not have accepted this expression. Seen from the height of his mystical contemplation and his metaphysical theology of the Word, our distinctions tend to be erased and our orders tend to be blended. Without at all losing its unity, Christian faith progressively absorbs all the superficial differences in the measure in which we better penetrate into its depth. But, to be precise, the Christian faith is no longer universalized as it is directly, according to the letter of its dogmas, the conceptual determinateness of its theology and of its rites. Comprehension of the faith rather than the faith itself tends to become the principle of peace and of religious organization of the earth. The moment approaches in which the universalism of reason will offer its services to the architects of future humanity. Theology is going to become metaphysics in Campanella's dream.

SIX

The City of the Sun

THE MEANING of *The City of the Sun* has been debated at great length. That is legitimate, because it is not immediately clear whether Campanella is satisfied with imagining the utopian model of a society of limited size or whether the reform he imagines ought to be gradually extended to the whole world.[1] In fact, the Solarians are only a small people established on an island where four

1. Born at Stilo in Calabria in 1568, Campanella enters the Dominican convent at Placanica in 1582. He continues his studies at the convents of Nicastro, 1586–88, and Cosenza. He is swept off his feet by Telesio's universal animism on which he publishes a book. A first heresy trial is followed by abjuration in 1591–92. From that moment on, Campanella is almost always involved in such trials, several of which are connected to his plans for reforming the Church. In this realm, let us note the following works: *Commentaries on the Monarchy of the Christians* (1593–94), *Discourse to the Princes of Italy* (1595), and *Ecclesiastical Government* (1595), which defends the pope's claim to be universal monarch. In 1599 he is implicated in the anti-Spanish uprising in Calabria and jailed from November 8, 1599, to May 23, 1626. After being freed, he is arrested again and condemned to life imprisonment by the Holy Office. Pardoned on April 6, 1629, by reason of insanity, he goes to Rome and makes contact with French circles there that arrange for him to go to France in October 1634. In 1635 in his *Monarchy of the Nations* he offers the scepter of universal monarchy to the king of France. At the birth of the future Louis XIV he draws up his horoscope. Below we will read the supposed account of this event. Campanella dies in Paris on May 21, 1639, at the age of seventy-one. [Translator: With the exception of *The City of the Sun*, the titles mentioned above are my translation from Gilson's French. There do not seem to be published versions of these works in English.] For the life and works of Campanella, see the excellent study by Luigi Amabile, *Fra Tommaso Campanella, la sua congiura, i suoi processi e la su pazzia*, 3 vols. (Naples: Morano, 1892). It remains the standard biography of Campanella. On Campanella's doctrine, see Léon Blanchet, *Campanella* (Paris: Alcan, 1920) [reprinted in New York: Burt Franklin, 1971]. For the *City of the Sun*, we have followed the Italian text, which seems to be the original version: *Città del Sole, Testo critico, introduzione e note*, ed. Giuseppe Paladino (Naples: Genanaro Giannini, 1920). On occasion, we have completed Paladino's critical text with the often more explicit Latin translation: F. Thomae Campanellae, *Civitas Solis, Poetica idea reipublicae philosophicae* (Utrecht: Waesberge, 1643).

other peoples live, with whom they have come to be at war. On the other hand, the complete title of the Italian text is "A Dialogue on the Republic," where "the idea of a reform of the Christian Republic" is proposed, which supposes a much larger plan. Campanella himself suggests very different interpretations of his work, according to what the circumstances invite him to do, and, no doubt, the wisest course is to let the idea present itself in its true light.[2]

At the opening of the dialogue a knight of the Order of Hospitallers asks a Genoese sailor to recount his whole voyage. The sailor recalls how, going around the world, he reached the island of Ceylon, had to disembark and, fearing the ferocious natives, took shelter in a forest from which he ended by coming onto a vast plain situated, he observes, just under the equinox. This geographical marvel is only the prelude to several others, because our Genoese seaman suddenly finds himself surrounded by an armed band of men and women, many of whom understand his language and lead him to the City of the Sun.

The greater part of the city is built on a hill in the heart of an enormous plain onto which the city's outer neighborhoods spill. The city itself is over two miles in diameter and more than seven miles in circumference, but because it is built on a hill, it has more houses than if it were flat. Divided into seven enormous circles, each one of which bears the name of one of the seven planets, access is gained through four doors and four streets, each of which points in one of the four cardinal directions. The seven circles are, first of all, fortifications, because the walls are more and more difficult to conquer, so much so that it would be necessary to enter the

2. Campanella, *Città del Sole*, 30. Written in 1602 and retouched in 1613, *Civitas Solis* was published as an appendix to *Realis Philosophiae Epilogisticae Partes Quatuor* (Frankfurt: Impensis G. Tampasii, 1623). Its title then was *Civitas Solis, Appendix Politiae, Idea Reipublicae Philosophicae*. The project aimed at submitting Flanders to Spain also dates from 1602. It would be published in the *Monarchia di Spagna* of 1620. The *Monarchia Messiae* was written in 1605 and published in 1633. For Campanella's ideas regarding the Universal Monarchy, see Blanchet, *Campanella*, 515–21.

city by assault seven times to overcome it. The first wall alone is so well defended that it seems impregnable. Let us skip the picturesque details in which Campanella delights. Let us cross through all these walls and climb up to the plateau that crowns the mount and the city.

An enormous circular temple without walls rises here. Beautiful and strong columns support its cupola. Under the center of the cupola is a single altar. Around the temple, outside the area enclosed by the columns, there is a series of walks or cloisters. On the altar itself, two globes are visible. One is a map of the heavens, the other of the earth. Moreover, the cupola vault has the principal heavenly bodies with their names and an indication of their different influences on earthly matters summed up in three verses per star. The poles and circles are indicated on the vault first and then underneath, on the altar globes. Seven perpetually lit lamps bear the names of the seven planets.

Like the cupola of St. Peter's in Rome, the main cupola of the temple contains a smaller one that contains some cells, but many other large cells are located above the cloisters, in which forty monks dwell.[3] A banner floats over the cupola showing wind direction. It can indicate thirty-six directions and in every season, the inhabitants always know which wind is blowing. Lastly, there is an extremely important book there, written in gold letters, to which we will have to return.

The city government is as follows. Its leader is a priest called *Hoh* in their language, that is *Sun*, whom we call *Metaphysician* in our language. As the spiritual and temporal leader he has final say in everything. Three principal colleagues, *Pon*, *Sin*, and *Mor*, that is, Power, Wisdom, and Love assist him. It is surely unnecessary to point out that Campanella entrusts the City of the Sun to the earthly image of one God in three Persons, who are the all-powerful Father, the Word or divine Wisdom, and the Holy Spirit or divine

3. The Latin translation has forty-nine, i.e., seven times seven.

love. Campanella's whole theology of divine "Primacies" is put to work for the greater good of the City of the Sun. The *Podestà* (Power) is concerned with peace, war, and the armed forces. In case of war, he is the commander-in-chief, though still under the Sun or Metaphysician.

Wisdom presides over all the sciences, professors, and teachers of the liberal and mechanical arts. Under him works an official for each science: Astronomer, Cosmographer, Geometer, Rhetorician, Grammarian, Physician, Politician, and Moralist. A single book contains all the sciences, and everyone has to read it, as the Pythagoreans used to do. Furthermore, Wisdom has arranged for all the sciences to be depicted on every available wall. The curtains, which are lowered between the temple columns to keep the voices of the priests from being lost when they preach, represent the stars with their names, their sizes, and their movements. Inside the first circle are all the geometrical figures, including a large number that Euclid and Archimedes did not draw. Outside is a map of the whole earth, then the individual maps of the different countries, with their rites, laws, customs, and the alphabets they use, compared to that of the City of the Sun. The interior of the second circle teaches mineralogy and petrography. Everything is painted in images with two explanatory verses for each picture. The exterior face of the circle teaches everything about liquids, lakes, seas, rivers, wines, oils, and all kinds of liquors with their effects, origins, and qualities. There, they keep flasks full of different liquors from a hundred to three hundred years old, with which they can cure all illnesses. There also, meteorological phenomena are depicted: winds, rains, hail, thunderstorms, and rainbows. They are not only depicted but also reproduced as well in the respective laboratories. Let us go by the third wall more quickly. Its inner face is devoted to biology and its outer face is devoted to ichthyology. One side of the fourth wall depicts birds and the other side insects. Land animals occupy both faces of the fifth wall, but let us stop for a moment before the sixth where the visit raises a rather odd problem.

The inner side of the wall depicts all mechanical arts, the various kinds of machinery known, and materials used in different countries of the world but on the outer face one sees "all the inventors of Laws, Sciences and weapons." There, our seaman reports, "I found Moses, Osiris, Jupiter, Mercury, Mohammed, and many others. Then, in a place of honor are Jesus Christ and his twelve apostles (to whom they give great importance), Caesar, Alexander, Pyrrhus, and all the Romans."[4] The enumeration is somewhat disordered and confused. The author or his translator believed they should redo the order in the Latin version of the little book where Mohammed, though always mentioned, is presented as the lawgiver of a base, deceitful religion, whereas Jesus Christ and his apostles acquire superhuman dignity.[5] We should no longer be surprised to see Jesus Christ, whether raised above human rank or not, take a place with Mohammed among the Great Initiates. After Roger Bacon and Nicholas of Cusa, religious diversity appears to some as a fact with which it is quite necessary to reckon. What is curious here and new, at least for us, is that the Great Initiates, whoever they are, are now mixed with the group of heads of state and founders of empires. Jesus Christ and his twelve apostles are in less strange company, with Osiris and even Mercury, than with Caesar and Pyrrhus, because evidently we are dealing with the Hermetic god. However that may be, the sixth wall marks the end of the pictorial encyclopedia thanks to which skilled teachers impart the totality of knowledge to children, who assimilate it before the age of ten, because they learn without effort while amusing themselves.

4. Campanella, *Città del Sole*, 7–8.

5. See the table of variants for the 1623 edition in *Città del Sole*, xi. See, for the 1643 edition: "At in loco dignisssimo Jesu Christi vidi effigiem, ac duodecim apostolorum quos dignissimos reputant, magnique faciunt; ut supra homines vidi Caesarem" (11), and so on.

There remains the third minister of this governmental trinity, Love, who is in charge of education strictly speaking, medicine, agriculture supply, and reproduction. To be exact, he is in charge of eugenics, because he makes sure that the union of men and women benefits the race.[6] Moreover there are male and female instructors in charge of eugenic education. The Metaphysician deals with any of the ministers that come under his jurisdiction. The Metaphysician meets with the minister, or rather with them all, because the four share their difficulties, but nothing is done without the Metaphysician, and all agree upon the solution he favors.

In this City of the Sun, which strictly speaking is neither republic nor monarchy, nor oligarchy, the rule is that property and women are held in common, not at all pure and simple promiscuity, but a kind of organized and regulated holding in common. One would be rightly surprised that Tommaso Campanella went so far, if it were not necessary to say that this was his point of departure. All evils that affect society seem to Campanella to come from the kind of avarice that is the desire to possess, as one's own, the largest possible amount of goods. Against the tenacious desire to appropriate, our reformer opposes, with equal tenacity, a determined effort toward "disappropriation." According to him this appetite for private property under all its forms springs from the same root, which is the wish to have a house for oneself, children for oneself, and a wife for oneself. A man desires wealth for that, and he seizes it for that, if he is powerful enough to do so; or he accumulates it by avarice and trickery, if he is weak. If men lose this personal love, common love alone will remain, and with it all the virtues will flourish. Here again, the analyst hesitates before such a complex position, where monastic hostility against the *proprium*, that which is one's own, invades a realm that even the impetuous

6. For the Solarians' eugenic methods see *Città del Sole*, 18–25. The right of male over female will be noted. The female there is only a natural good, whose "common" character is affirmed without limitations.

Tertullian believed ought to be left aside. Everything is common among Christians, said Tertullian, except women. Campanella corrects him: women are included.[7] Furthermore, he observes that if the clergy of his time exhibited a less acute sense of private property, it would be great progress. "I think that if our priests and monks had no relatives or friends and no ambition for honors, they would be more detached, more holy, and more charitable toward all. To this remark in the Italian original, the 1637 Latin edition adds prudently, "as they were in the time of the apostles, and still are for the most part."[8]

This State, where all virtues flourish, does not owe its perfection either to the authority of a king or to the government of the people or to an oligarchy, but to the knowledge and wisdom of its leader. Everything depends on the choice of leader, and this is why Campanella surrounds it with many precautions.

No one can be the Sun, if he does not know the history of all peoples, the rites, sacrifices, republics, and inventors of laws and or arts. He must also know all mechanical arts, one of which he learns every two days thanks to practice and to the images. He should also know all the mathematical, physical, and astronomical sciences. As for languages, it is useless to worry about them, because this people possess interpreters, who are its grammarians. But before everything, the Sun must be a metaphysician and theologian. He must thoroughly know the principles and demonstrations of all the arts, the likenesses and differences of things, and the necessity, destiny, and harmony of the world, and the power, wisdom, and love of God that are encountered again in everything. He must know the hierarchy of beings, the relations of the celestial bodies to those of earth and sea. Lastly, he must study astronomy and the prophets at length. That is what the Sun must be. No one can become the Sun before the age of

7. On this restriction offered by Tertullian that irritates Campanella a little, see *Città del Sole*, 26–27.

8. Ibid., 10. See, for Campanella's protest against useless officials who are the ruination of the State and for his completely modern praise of the artisan and the worker: "Whence they laugh at us, those whom we artisans call base" (12); see also 25–26 for the praise of manual labor and sports.

thirty-five, but the post is permanent as long as a wiser person or one more suited to governing is not found.[9]

Entirely won over to government run by philosophers, Campanella resolutely follows Plato on this point. Even if he were not a good statesman, the Sun would at least never be cruel, criminal, or tyrannical. He knows too much for that. Above all, what he knows he knows too well. For the Sun does not have his head full of grammar or Aristotelian logic. He has not slavishly burdened his memory with what this or that author teaches. He studies things not books. He is not one of those who only knowing one single science, do not know well either it or the others. With an open, free mind, the Sun is always ready to learn about everything he needs to know, especially in a city like his where sciences are learned with such facility that one is taught more in a year than in ten or fifteen years in our cities. The descriptive method that is used in teaching allows the supreme leader to learn everything, and allows his three ministers to learn what they must know to discharge their functions well. At least they are all philosophers and, furthermore, historians, naturalists, and humanists. Wisdom never sees itself granted more absolute confidence nor is more unreservedly entrusted with the supreme direction of the State.

The most evident defect of the City of Wisdom is to be at the same time the City of Professors. There are professors for everything and they are in charge, each one in the place that corresponds to him by law in a governmental hierarchy that is confused with the hierarchy of technologies and sciences. The Sun, who is a Metaphysician, possesses wisdom. Consequently, he commands all Solarians, just as metaphysics, the architectonic science, commands all other sciences. Under the Sun's authority are placed the Grammarian, the Logician, the Natural Scientist, the Physician, the Politician, the Economist, the Moralist, the Astronomer, the

9. Ibid., 13.

Astrologist, the Geometer, the Cosmographer, the Musician, the Perspectivist, the Arithmetician, the Poet, the Orator, the Painter, and the Sculptor. Under Love are, among others, the Geneticist, the Educator, the Tailor, the Agronomist, the Breeder, the Shepherd, and the Chef. Under Power we see the Head Military Engineer, the Ironmaster, the Armorer, the Finance Minister, the Head of the Mint, the Engineer, the Cavalry Master, the Artilleryman, and still others. Each of them has artisans at his orders, who are under him by a strict law of talion: death for death, eye for eye, tooth for tooth, except in the case of a quarrel that was not premeditated, where the three great Ministers, and they alone, can pronounce sentence, with the right to pardon reserved exclusively to the Metaphysician. The laws are few. They are all engraved on a bronze tablet at the door of the temple of the columns on which the essences of quiddities of all things may be read: what God is, what an angel is, and so too for the world, a human being, and so on. There, the judges from every order hold court, and when they emit their sentences, they limit themselves to saying: "Very well, since you have sinned against this particular definition, read it." So they condemn for ingratitude, laziness, or ignorance, and rather than punishments, this kind of condemnations are mild remedies.

After the judges and the tribunals, there are the priests and the worship. This government of wise men and professors is simultaneously a government of priests, because the Sun is the Chief Priest, all the high officials are priests, and have as their duty to cleanse consciences. Everyone confesses his own sins, and even sins of others, if they are great and harmful for the common good. Thus, they learn what kinds of sins are committed most often. In turn, these high dignitaries confess their sins to the three First Ministers, telling their own sins, and in a general way, the sins of others, without naming the sinners. Nothing remains then but for the three First Ministers to confess to the Sun. Informed by them about the kinds of faults most often committed, the Sun takes appropriate measures, offers prayers and sacrifices to God, confessing his own sins to God, and even, each time it is necessary, publicly confessing the sins of the people at the altar in order to correct them, but without naming anyone. At the pinnacle of the temple, twenty-four priests take turns night and day to sing psalms whose models are found in Campanella's own Italian poems, and in order to observe the stars and thanks to this observation to infer the changes that are produced in the people. They indicate the favorable times for the procreation of children, the days for sowing and harvesting; in short, they serve as intermediaries between God and humans.

The Sun is generally chosen from among these priests. Scholars and writers only frequent women exceptionally and for hygenic reasons, with occasional exceptions. Every day, the Sun climbs up to speak with them about the research they have carried out in benefit of the City and of all other peoples of the world. In the temple below them there is always a priest who prays and who is changed every hour, as Catholics do during the forty-hour devotion. After meals, the priests thank God in music, "since the exploits are sung of Christians, Hebrews, and pagans of every nation" along with hymns of love, wisdom, and virtue. Each one sings the hymn he prefers, and all participate under the cloisters at magnificent balls. Without turning into Rabelais's Thelma Abbey, because the life of the City of the Sun remains fairly strictly regulated, the City excludes all ascetic excess from its cloisters, and the strangely liberal religious syncretism that is cultivated within them is not hostile to love affairs or pleasures.

It is nevertheless a religion, because the Solarians adore only God, and it is he alone that they still adore in nature, where they see his temple above all. Enemies of Aristotle, whom they consider pedantic, they still recognize his physical principles: the Sun, who is the father, and the Earth, who is the mother. For them the world is an immense animal, within which we are, as worms are in our body. Subject to God's providence, not to the world's, humans have rational souls that after death join the good or bad spirits according to what they have merited. As for the places of rewards and punishments, it seems reasonable that they are heaven and hell, but the Solarians are not absolutely sure. Very curious about whether those punishments are eternal or not, they are at least certain that there are good but sad angels, as occurs among humans. The Solarians know nothing exactly about whether there are other worlds or not, but they hold it absurd to say there is nothingness, because nothingness is not in the world or outside the world or in God, who is infinite being. Nothing is only the lack of being.

It can nevertheless be said, with their metaphysicians, that there are two principles of things, being and nothing, in the sense that if there were no lack of being, then nothing could be born or be corrupted, and we would see neither evil nor sin occurring, which themselves are only lack of being. Having no revelation, the Solarians are ignorant of the relations of the divine Persons and do not know the names that we give them. It is only all the more surprising to see them adore God and the Trinity and say that there is the supreme power from which the supreme Wisdom proceeds, as the supreme love proceeds from them both. Furthermore, that is why in their view all things, insofar as they are, are composed of power, wisdom, and love, but also, of impotence, lack of wisdom, and lack of love, insofar as things are subject to nonbeing. It is thus that things incur merit or demerit, which they do to such an extent that it cannot be explained without admitting that a great disorder has been introduced into the world. How? It is difficult to say, but they judge happy the Christian who is satisfied to believe that it arrived through Adam's sin. To be accurate, they believe that here the children inherit the punishment rather than the fault, and that the fault itself rather goes back from the children to the parents. Let us think of the negligence parents demonstrate when, after having conceived children outside the times and places that are appropriate, in the state of sin, and without choosing the father or the mother according to the rules of eugenics, they bring up children badly and teach them worse yet. On the contrary, the Solarians take great care about the procreation of children and their upbringing, and if they behave badly in either regard, they say that the punishment as well as the fault falls, beyond children and parents, on the city itself. Here true religion must play its role, because it consists in knowing the world in order to honor God in his handiwork, and to use all the laws that control it to produce other works that likewise honor him.

The Solarians are not Christians, because they have not yet received Christ's revelation. They do nothing but follow the law of nature, but this is also why we see them so close to Christianity, "which adds nothing to the natural law except the sacraments."[10] This remark defines as exactly as possible the meaning of the *City of the Sun* as well as Campanella's own position. Doubtless it would be an exaggeration to say either that he imagines a natural religion replacing Christianity or that he wants to reduce Christianity to the limits of natural religion. It will be granted all the more readily that the problem has not been perfectly delineated in Campanella's thought, inasmuch as his thinking hardly shines by its precision. At least one point seems sure. Here, Campanella envisages the reform, if not of Christianity, at least of theology and of Christian life through the elimination of everything that has been introduced contrary or alien to the natural law except for the sacraments. The Solarians, their ideas, and their morals constitute a decisive experiment for us here, precisely because, while not Christians, they are nonetheless very close to Christianity. From this it follows that, as the Christian religion in no way alters the law of nature, their doctrines and their morals can certainly call for Christian supplements, but not corrections. Consequently, in Campanella's utopia, he proposes the project of a reform of ideas and morals by

10. Ibid., 59.

returning to the natural law, certainly with the understanding that Christianity will remain there to sanctify them.

It is difficult to see things from Campanella's standpoint and still more difficult to hold to it. According to whether we pay attention to one or the other of the two moments of his thesis, we sometimes see him as a sincere Christian in search of reform, and sometimes as a deist who works to undermine the very basis of Christianity. What is peculiar to his position is to suppress the alternative. However we judge Campanella, he certainly sees himself as a reformer who, making Christianity a simple complement of the natural law, proves just because of that fact that Christianity alone is indisputability the true religion. Everything rides on just this sentence: "Christianity adds nothing to natural religion except the sacraments; for me this relation is the proof that Christianity is the true law and that once abuses are removed, Christianity will be the mistress of the world."[11] When we weigh these terms, we see that this declaration says everything.

Still, Campanella does not imagine that, even purified, Christianity is to conquer the world by the pure light of truth. Conquerors will have to fight for it and win the world empire. But as at the

11. Ibid., 69. There would be nothing new in maintaining the agreement or harmony between Christianity and the law or nature, or in maintaining that Christianity has the effect of restoring the law of nature so as to perfect it. Every expression of this kind would be normal. What is not normal is to maintain that repairing the abuses introduced into the law of nature suffices to give us Christianity. It would be a mistake to refuse to believe in the sincerity of Campanella's Christian sentiments, or in his fervent attachment to the Church, despite what he suffered. He is not a deist. What characterizes our reformer's position is its very ambiguity. He regards his philosophy as the rediscovery of authentic Christian truth, and precisely this allows him to hope that once the Church recognizes his philosophy, it can become the law of a universal republic. From there stems his *Atheismus Trimphatus, seu Reductio ad Religionem per Scientiarum Veritates* (Rome: Apud Haeredem Bartholomaei Zannetti, 1631). The acknowledgment of this truth would not exclude the teaching of Christian dogmas. On the contrary, it would permit theology's improvement by putting true philosophy at its service. It would already be a great gain to expel Aristotle's corrupting doctrine from theology. It is unfortunate that only the beginning of Campanella's "Summa Theologica" has been published so far. However, we see clearly enough in it the sense in which dogmatic theology still seemed possible to Campanella, as the confluence of theology and metaphysics, of religion and reason.

time when Augustus's empire had united all the peoples of the earth in peace and law, it happens precisely that the context is favorable to Christianity. It is even much more favorable than it was then. The Roman Empire had only united a narrow swath of the globe. Now we are dealing with the whole globe. After the Genoese Christopher Columbus discovered America, the Spanish took it over and, whatever particular ends they sought, these uniters of the earth are only in fact God's instruments. They know what they think they are doing, but they do not know what they are doing, because the real end of their efforts is to unite the whole world under a single religion. Moved by avarice, they go seeking new countries to find gold there, but God proposes a very different goal. See the sun. It tries to burn the earth, not to make plants and humans spring up, something, however, God makes it do. Likewise, God uses these discoveries and founders of empires in order to establish the kingdom of one, single truth. The philosophers chosen by God will bear witness to this, because God uses the former as well as the latter, and may he be praised for it.

Campanella takes leave of his dear Solarians in apocalyptic passages where the list of modern inventors supports astrological conclusions to establish that the time of great transformations is near. A clairvoyant witness, Campanella observes that the earth has just lived through more history in a hundred years than it had lived in four thousand. The inventions of the compass, the printing press, and of firearms are the preludes to the unification of the earth. The Solarians have already discovered the art of flying like birds, the only art that humans still lacked. Thanks to the telescope, unheard of planetary conjunctions and new stars are discovered that foretell the appearance of a great monarchy, the reformation of laws and arts, the advent of prophets, and the restoration of the earth. Certainly, it is necessary to weed before planting and to demolish before reconstruction. That will happen, but the very fact that the heavenly bodies announce a time when women will dominate is a sign of fruitfulness. The Amazons rule between Nubia and Monomotapa. Roxelana, Suleiman the Magnificent's favorite and later wife, rules in Turkey. There is Elizabeth in England, Mary in Hungary, Catherine de Medici in France, Margarite in Austria, and Mary Stuart in Scotland. Isabel the Catholic rules in Spain, which has just discovered a new world. There are so many other women who could be mentioned. They all announce a new era in the world, which can now be traveled. Thanks to the voyages of sailors and explorers, religions are spread through Africa and Asia. They conquer the earth in the measure that empires grow whether the religion is pure like Christianity in Spain and Italy or soiled by heresy as in Germany and England.[12] Moreover, all of this can be read in the stars, because although they do not determine the will and although they leave free choice intact, they can act upon humans enslaved to their senses rather than subject to reason. Consequently, there was a constellation that made harmful vapors rise from Luther's corpse, and one that made the perfume of virtues rise from the corpses of Jesuits of the period, and lastly,

12. Campanella's apostolic fervor sees the light of day in the long treatise *Quod Reminiscentur et Convertentur ad Dominum Universi Fines Terrae* (Psalm 21), ed. Romanus Amerio, vol. 1 (Padua: Cedam, 1939). We do not know whether vol. 2 has been published. On this work, which Campanella wrote in prison (1615–18), see Enrico Carusi, "Nuovi documenti sui processi di Tommasso Campanella," in *Giornale critico della filosofia italiana* VIII (1927), fasc. 5, doc. 72, of May 22, 1621. Carrying forward Nicholas of Cusa's project, Campanella decides to summon all peoples to meet in order to reestablish religious unity (12). See the moving passage (23–28) regarding Campanella's life in prison. He is the chime (i.e., the *campanella*) that summons men to put down their arms, "quibus bestiarum more defendimus dogmata" (29). He wants only one flock and one shepherd (33). The spectacle of the ruin of Christianity saddens him: "Ubi est Ecclesia Anglicana? Ubi Pannonica? Ubi Suetia et Gothica? Ubi Dalmata?" (47) He calls all the religious orders to the common struggle: "Vexillum crucis capiamus et exeamus de claustris et litibus ineptissimis," and so forth (51–54). Campanella's zeal is unquestionable, and some of the recommendations he gives to reform abuses are excellent (58–60). Like Roger Bacon, Campanella favors the abolition of civil law in favor of canon law (59, a. 10). He wants to replace pagan philosophy with Christ's philosophy (59, a. 11). Finally, he claims the universal monarchy for the pope (68–71). The important point is the idea Campanella forms about the philosophy of Christ. Naturally, it is his own philosophy that he offers to both the pope and to Richelieu as the bond of a universal monarchy to be led by them.

that of Hernán Cortés, who promulgated Christianity in Mexico in this same era. For, as St. Paul says, heresy is the work of the senses, and this is why the stars incline sensual humans to heresy, as they incline those who use reason to the holy and true laws of the First Reason, may it be praised forever, amen.

Like his predecessor Roger Bacon, this unifier of the earth spent a number of years in prison. Neither individuals nor institutions like being reformed, and it is not surprising that the reformers feel that painfully. Moreover, Campanella was not a simple reformer. He was an agitator whose political adventures have nothing in common with the purely speculative risks run by the worthy Roger Bacon. The Franciscan was only involved with the pope. Our Dominican, who was not afraid to get involved in conspiracies on occasion, attached the success of his own reform to that of several temporal sovereigns in turn. The nationality of the protector was unimportant,[13] provided that he was useful for the

13. Campanella successively offered the universal monarchy to the king of Spain (*Discorsi ai principi de Italia*, 1595), then to the pope (*Il governo ecclesiastico*, 1595), and later to the king of France (*Monarchie delle nazioni*, 1635). The 1637 edition of his *De Sensu Rerum et Magia* is dedicated to Richelieu. Campanella proposed the founding of the City of the Sun to Richelieu: "Et civitas solis a me delineata, perpetuo fulgore nunquam eclipsata, ab tua Eminentia, splendescat semper." In 1638 he drew up the horoscope of the Dauphin, the future king of France Louis XIV, who had just been born. As a curiosity, here is the anonymous undated text reporting the episode. It is found in the Engravings Room of the National Library in Paris, documents, "Dauphin," Q b 1, 1638–39. It is written on the back of an engraving according to C. LeBrun, representing the *System of the World at the Moment of the Birth of Louis the Great*. The title by itself discloses a later date. "Campanella, a Spanish [sic] Jacobin, who was also a good philosopher and knew how to predict the future, while detained in the prisons of the Milan Inquisition, obtained access through his friends to Cardinal Richelieu, who had him released and brought him to Paris. During this time Queen Anne of Austria gave birth to Louis XIV, surnamed the God-given, and she was curious to know what the destiny would be of a prince so dear to France and so long desired. She spoke about this to Cardinal Richelieu, who sent to have Campanella queried. The Cardinal knew Campanella's talent for predictions and ordered him to draw up the Dauphin's horoscope without concealing the truth in anything. The philosopher could not deny the Cardinal anything because of the great obligation he was under to him. He had the Dauphin stripped completely naked, and having considered him thoroughly from all sides, had him clothed again, after which he withdrew to his home to formulate his observations there. Some time went by without any word from him. Impatient to learn

endeavor, but the spirit of the enterprise itself is what concerns us, and first and foremost, the kind of form Campanella wanted to impose on the Christian religion to make it into the bond of a new type of political society.

Campanella scholars are not in agreement on this point. Basing themselves on Campanella's still partly unpublished theology, some scholars see him only as a more or less orthodox theologian, scarcely freer than his predecessors. Others conceive his work as an attempt to naturalize dogma completely and thus give humans something upon which to build a universal society. This disagreement is explained by the nature of the doctrine. It is certain that for Campanella himself the truth is found in his own interpretation of Christian dogma, and this was a rationalist interpretation. But his natural philosophy, like that of other reformers of his time,[14]

the Dauphin's destiny, the Queen demanded an answer. Campanella returned to court, again had the young prince stripped completely naked to examine him once more and verify whether the observations he had made were correct. As the Cardinal finally pressed him to say what he had observed he answered: 'Erit puer ille luxuriosus sicut Henricus quartus, et valde superbus. Regnabit diu, sed dure, tamen feliciter. Desinet misere, et in fine erit confusio magna in religione et in imperio.'" If the date and the text of the horoscope were trustworthy, one would be tempted to believe in astrology.

14. Consider, for example, Guillaume Postel (1510–81). See Pierre Mesnard, *L'essor de la philosophie politique au XVIième siècle* (Paris: Boivin, 1936), book V, chap. 1. A novice in the Society of Jesus, which he regarded as having been given the responsibility of conquering and unifying the world under the reign of Christ, this former teacher of Greek, Hebrew, and Arabic language and literature at the College des Lecteurs (Collège de France), he went to Venice, where he fell under the influence of a visionary nun. Out of that came the book *Les très merveilleuses victoires des femmes du Nouveau Monde et comme elles doivent à tout le monde par raison commander et même à ceux qui auront la monarchie du monde civile* (1553). Indeed, Jesus Christ has already redeemed the intellect (*vir*). The Holy Spirit will redeem reason (*femina*). The Inquisition arrests him but releases him on the grounds of insanity. He goes to Basel and makes contact with the Reformers, but having observed that their reform is not the one he envisages, he goes to Dijon, where he teaches mathematics, then to Paris, where he spends several years under a kind of house arrest until 1581, the year of his death. Among his works let us mention: *Alcorani seu Legis Mahometi et Evangelistarum Concordiae Liber* (1543); *Quatuor Librorum de Orbis Terrae Concordia Primus* (Basel, 1544). He states that world religious unity will be achieved by converting the nations of the earth to Catholicism in *Cosmographiae Disciplinae Compendium* (Basel, 1561); see the dedication, where he undertakes to account for everything that until then was unbelievable. Ultimately, Postel dreams of a French Republic whose sovereignty the

contained as many mysteries as revealed theology. He lived in a marvelous world full of analogies, secret connections, and magic, where everything, even stones, had life, perception, and feeling. Let us add that Campanella expresses himself differently according to the different audiences he addresses. His *Theologia*, finished in 1624, is aimed at theologians. Campanella stays as close as possible to dogma there. But in the *City of the Sun*, where he is certainly the speaker, he expresses his inner thoughts freely. He himself will later write, in his *Questioni sull'ottima politica*, that his utopia was not a revelation from God, but "a philosophical discovery of human reason to show that the truth of the Gospels is in agreement with nature."[15] In fact, natural reason was never less reasonable than as presented by Campanella, but his dreams all drifted in the same direction: that of the personal revelations he had in 1598–99 at Stilo in Calabria, which assigned him to complete Christ's revelation. Thereafter he foresees the disappearance of religious sects, the birth of rational faith, the restoration of nature, and the development of a communal way of life that, all things considered, was only a secularization of monastic life paralleling the rationalization of dogma. Lastly, Campanella foresees the advent of a universal republic, just as St. Bridget and St. Catherine had promised him.

All that was taking place; all that was certain; all that was near.

---

other peoples of the world would gradually accept thanks to the pope's support. Recalcitrant peoples would be subdued with the help of secret weapons (portable fortifications, unsinkable ships). Having failed to convince Francis I and then Ferdinand I, emperor of Austria, Postel becomes angry and directs his message to the Shiites. See Mesnard, *L'essor*, 451, for passages that are strangely reminiscent of Roger Bacon: "In order that there should be just one world in fact and desire, under one single God and under one single King and sovereign bishop, one faith and one law and one common happiness," and so on. Except that to attain this goal, Postel rationalizes faith instead of drowning reason in Christian wisdom. It is easy to understand that St. Ignatius did not admit this novice whose methods differed too much from those of the Society of Jesus. It should be noted that, like Campanella and, later on, Auguste Comte, this universalist fights the Protestants and tries to enlist the Jesuits. The Jesuits once more did not listen and the Protestants saw clearly that Postel's natural religion betrayed Christianity. See Blanchet, *Campanella*, 439–40. This is one of the constant elements of the problem.

15. Blanchet, *Campanella*, 73.

For the year 1600 would be a decisive juncture in the ages, as it is composed of 9 + 7, number under whose influence, according to Plato, republics and empires perish.[16] His most important biographer has spoken about madness in connection with Campanella. That may be the case, but the epithet proves no more against his project than it will prove later against that of Auguste Comte. Let us not forget G. K. Chesterton's remark: a madman is not someone who has lost his reason; he is someone who has kept only his reason. Campanella's reason believed it made at least two discoveries. First, that the spiritual society of the Church ought to be transformed into a temporal society of all the peoples of the earth and that, if a sovereign capable of taking that initiative were found, Europe was ripe to begin this transformation. Next, that this transposition of the City of God onto the level of the city of men implied another transposition affecting the future society's common bond. This bond could no longer be faith, unless faith itself accepted to become reason. Two developments were now possible: replacing charity by law on the temporal, political level, and replacing faith and theology by natural reason and metaphysics on the spiritual level. The next two chapters will show the forms in which these two developments took place in fact.

16. Ibid., 36.

SEVEN

The Birth of Europe

United Europe was born about three hundred years ago as a result of a vehicular accident. During the winter of 1706 a priest was traveling over the roads of Normandy when his carriage overturned, broke, and dumped him into the mud. The accident was unimportant. The traveler was much more important. While the vehicle was repaired, our Abbé reflected on the causes of the episode, and as soon as he returned home, he composed a "Memorandum on Highway Repair," which would be published in Paris on January 10, 1708: "I was giving the final touches to this memorandum," he tells us,

> when a plan for an organization came to my mind that left me astonished by its great beauty. It monopolized my attention for two weeks. I feel all the more inclined to go into depth the more I consider it, and for different features, the more I find it advantageous to sovereigns. It would establish permanent arbitration between sovereigns to end future differences without war. I may be wrong, but there are grounds to hope that a treaty will be signed someday, when it can be proposed at any time, to one or to the other interested party alike, and when it is easy for all of them to see that, everything considered, it would be much more advantageous for them to sign it than not sign it. In this hope I commit myself with passion and joy to the highest endeavor that could occur to the human mind. I do not know where I will go, but I know what Socrates said, that we go far when we have the courage to travel for a long time and in the same direction.[1]

1. For this passage and for all the biographical data and anecdotes contained in the first portion of this lecture, we are entirely indebted to the work of Joseph Drouet, *L'abbé de Saint-Pierre* (Paris: Champion, 1912). The passage we have just quoted is found on 108–9.

This strange clergyman was not that in his first incarnation. He was Charles François Castel of the family of the barons of Castel. But because he was born February 13, 1658, at Saint-Pierre-Église, not far from Cherbourg, he styled himself the Abbé of St. Pierre. It is easier to understand that the bad state of the road inspired his arbitration project if we recall that it was a road in Normandy. Normandy was the land of lawsuits. In 1673, at the age of fifteen, Castel interrupted his studies with the Jesuits, without regrets, in order to study law. He hoped to become qualified in this way to establish peace among the residents of the family domains by arbitrating their differences. He already had a calling to arbitration, and material was not lacking. His biographer tells us that at the age of eighteen, he was handling the mediation of a dozen lawsuits.

I have said that he was a priest, and I believe he was. But the title of Abbé suits him better, and even, if Rousseau is to be trusted on this, the title of *gentleman abbé*. But this is not our business. Castel was a man of his time. For him religion was practically reduced to philanthropy. He becomes part of Fontenelle's circle in Paris in 1680. He takes interest in scientific popularization, reads Descartes, and against Descartes's explicit intention, proposes to introduce the Cartesian method into political problems. In 1694 he is elected to the French Academy, thanks to the support of Madame de Lambert, who, he tells us, had created half of the academicians of her time. He had not yet published anything, and he would have done better to persevere in his silence, because his first book, *Polysynodie*, which appeared in 1717, brought him great troubles.[2] As his criticism seemed to strike at the regent's ad-

The older study by Édouard Goumy, *Étude sur la vie et les écrits de l'Abbé de Saint-Pierre* (Paris: Hachette, 1859), is still very useful.

2. See *Oeuvres complètes de J. J. Rousseau* (Paris: Baudouin, 1826), 6:456–99, for an analysis followed by a "Jugement sur la *Polysynodie*." Rousseau considers the piece to be the best of Saint-Pierre's writing. Although he praises its moderation and cleverness, Rousseau clearly sees that it is a criticism of the regime: "Thus, it was the hope of remedying these various defects that involved him in proposing another *polysynody* entirely different from the one he pretended to wish only to perfect" (6:485). Here as elsewhere,

ministration, the court was outraged, the book was confiscated, the publisher was imprisoned, and his colleagues expelled its author from the French Academy on May 5, 1718. If an academician is absolutely committed to writing, he can dabble in it, but never in politics. Our academician was consoled in the salons, but he became very reserved in his language. "The soup," he said, "is a little to salty *for me*," or "French music is more pleasant *to me, for the present,* than Italian music." The masterpiece of the genre is: "I do not yet see that as you do." But above all, Saint-Pierre invents. He never stops inventing plans.

Saint-Pierre proposes the creation of a Political Academy; it exists. He proposes the establishment of awards for virtue; they exist. He proposes the manufacture of "wigglers," that is mechanical armchairs, delightfully imitating the jolts of a stagecoach, and like stagecoaches, evacuating bile, liver, spleen, and intestines. The size and intensity of the shocks can be regulated at will and offer the stagecoach cure without leaving home. "Wigglers" were manufactured. Voltaire bought one. They are still manufactured today, except that they are electric. Lastly, so as not to enumerate every invention, let us come directly to the invention that interests us directly, the idea of a European alliance with the object of establishing and maintaining peace.

Like all inventors, the Abbé had predecessors. The idea had floated in the air since the sixteenth century. Emeric Cruce, who died in 1648, had published *The New Cyneas*, a curious book inspired by the deepest repugnance toward war. He found only four conceivable causes for war: honor, a worthless sentiment unless it is in the service of law; profit, which is absurd, because in any case war brings ruin; violation of territory, which for once is se-

---

Rousseau reproaches the "good Abbé of Saint-Pierre for always seeking a small remedy for each particular evil instead of going to their common source" (*Émile*, book V, 5:265). What is more remarkable, he reproaches *Polysynodie* for proposing nothing less than a revolution whose dangers he denounces, like most conservative politians, in terms that recall Descartes ("Jugement," 6:488).

rious, but which can be remedied differently; and lastly fondness for conflict, which, it must be acknowledged, seems innate in certain persons. But why not send the latter to satisfy their propensity among savages? They will be at home. As a remedy, Cruce proposes a general agreement among all Catholic peoples under the protection of the sovereigns cooperating in the maintenance of perpetual peace, through the initiative of a leader like the king of France, who is powerful enough to impose this on Muslims.[3]

A much more important project was conceived by Henri IV immediately after the peace of Vervins between Spain and France in 1598. The valuable *Memoirs* of Henri's minister the duke of Sully inform us about the fundamental ideas that guided the king. The primary evil of the period was wars of religion, which Henri had just ended with the Edict of Nantes. The example of what Sully calls "the Germanic Body" would suggest that peace can be maintained among sovereigns of different religions provided that they form a society. That was not the difficulty. The difficulty stemmed rather from "the great inequality that existed between the powers of Europe." The king saw that "the ability of the strong to oppress the weak and to enrich themselves with their plunder would always be a great obstacle to the maintenance of peace." How could this danger be remedied except precisely by organizing what the king called a *European Society*? Here again, the example of the Germanic Society makes it clear that such a thing must be possible. Ultimately, it is certain that in this body, "there are members who are twenty or thirty times more powerful than others who are their neighbors and that the weaker continue in the peaceful possession of their ancestors'

3. The Congress of United Europe, which met at The Hague in 1948, was the first visible effort to achieve this dream. We were there, and it was a pleasant surprise to hear Winston Churchill recall *The Great Cyneas*. As for the priest of Saint-Pierre, nobody that we know of mentioned him a single time. He was completely forgotten. A portion of Emeric Cruce's project is reproduced in the beginning of the following collection: *Les Français à la Recherche d'une Société des Nations* (Paris: Bibliothèque de la Civilization française, 1920). The essence of Saint-Pierre's project, whose original text is hard to find in libraries, may be seen there.

sovereignty after six centuries." How could a similar but more extended society be organized? By establishing perpetual arbitration between European nations? But how was this arbitration to work?[4]

If Sully is to be believed, the king had completely developed plans for "the European Union," which he would have communicated to "all Christian sovereigns" and even obtained their approval. Unfortunately, observes Saint-Pierre, these memorandums are lost, and little is known about what would have been the operational method or more exactly, about what was called "the great scheme." One of its bases, already defined by Cruce in *The Great Cyneas*, was that it would start from the status quo, with each State limiting its ambitions to what it already possessed. The second was the necessity of a contribution from each State to the common expenses. The duke of Sully called it "proportional contribution." Lastly, to assure the union of all European States in a single "Christian Republic," it would be necessary to create a General Council of sixty members that would have some centrally located European city as its seat, like Nancy, Metz, Cologne, or some other. Sully almost named Strasburg![5]

That is what our reformer calls the plan for European Union as Henri IV had conceived it, by Sully's account. Sully's modesty does not allow us to discern the part he himself had in the notion of "the great scheme." At least one thing is sure, because Saint-Pierre himself says so: the great scheme was the material for Saint-Pierre's own reflection. As the memorandums prepared by Henri IV on the means for carrying out the plan were lost, it was necessary to replace them. "It is," says Saint-Pierre, "in order to compensate in some measure for this great loss, that I have tried to place myself on the path to rediscover them."[6]

Of course, once the idea came into his head, the Abbé began to

4. Saint-Pierre himself reproduces the passages from Sully's *Mémoires* that inspire him. So, there is no need to look for his sources on this point.

5. Saint-Pierre, *Projet*, 1:567.

6. Saint-Pierre remits to *Mémoires de Sully*, 2:22.

talk about it to those around him. He attracted much ridicule, but that did not discourage him. In 1712 he published at Cologne *A Memorandum to Achieve Perpetual Peace in Europe*. It was a trial balloon. The work drew objections to which Saint-Pierre made responses. From that came a second version of the work, *Plan to Achieve Perpetual Peace in Europe*, in two volumes published by Schouten at Utrecht in 1713. A third volume printed by Deville at Lyon, though with the indication Utrecht, is also dated 1713.

Let us open the two volumes published by Antoine Schouten. On the back of the endpaper of the first volume, an engraving represents Henri IV unveiling a statue of peace before an assembly of princes and high Church officials. With it, there is an inscription in two verses that passed for poetry in those days.

> May his name be blessed! May it shine forever!
> He alone has made us see where peace resides.

We already know why Henri IV receives this homage. Opposite on the title page the map of a new country, "Europa," adorned with bunting, bears this epitaph: "*Gloria in excelsis Deo et in terra pax.*" The first volume consists of six discourses; the first three justify the plan, which is set out in the last three. The Abbé's general idea is simple: "My purpose is to propose the means of achieving perpetual peace between all Christian States." Perhaps it would be better to say: his expression is simple, because after reflection, the idea is not so simple as it might seem at first sight. Let us try to analyze it.

In the foreground we find the idea of peace. Peace is the goal, that which gives meaning to the endeavor; everything must be organized with a view to peace. The means to this end is Europe or, again, a "European Union," a "European Society." The latter expression seems to be what our Abbé uses most readily. To get this society, it must be organized, because it will never be established by dint of wars and treatise. The vanquished always sign with the idea of making their move again at the first favorable moment, and even if no one violates the treaties, there is no organism to guarantee their fulfillment. Balance between the great powers is not enough to ensure peace, because supposing that the balance is not altered, it gives no security to the small powers. The issue is really to obtain a society that unites the weak and the strong without harming the sovereignty of the weak. The examples presented by Saint-Pierre are striking: Holland constituted as the Republic of the United Provinces, and Switzerland, behind which he already saw what we call the Helvetic Confederation today. Lastly, there is, of course, Germany, more split up than ever, whose confused unity Saint-Pierre could perceive. The European Society will also unite weak and strong. Saint-Pierre pictures that already. He enumerates eighteen members in advance, and each time that one reads the book, one begins to dream: France, Spain, England, Holland, Portugal, Switzerland with its partners, Florence and partners, Genoa and partners, the Papal States, Venice, Savoy, Lorraine, Denmark, Courland with Danzig, the Germanic Empire, Poland, Sweden, and what Saint-Pierre modestly styles as Muscovy. How simple and yet how strange, almost unreasonable this Europe seems to us! What will our Europe seem like in 250 years? Allow me a short parenthesis here. When we speak of federation, we think of union, and rightly so, but one of the surest effects of federation is to perpetuate the division by uniting the divided parts. Once federated, these parts become irreducible. We even see thereafter some who entrench themselves more ferociously in their individual differences. For, ultimately, if the European Society had been achieved in 1713, we would still have a Republic of Genoa dealing with Courland, and a Republic of Venice exchanging ambassadors with Savoy, but we would not have Belgium. In short, the date the treaty of union is signed marks the end of national histories or at least establishes a portrait of the nationalities that must not be changed. The same thing would happen today, and this is not an objection to the plan but it is a remark about one of its implications about which people seem to think least.[7]

7. In Rousseau's *Extract* from Saint-Pierre's plan, the list of associated European

Let us come back to our inventor. As promises are not enough to establish this European Society, "permanent arbitration" is necessary, a "treaty of union," and a "permanent Congress," which is a third idea. From there comes his plan of the Great Alliance in five principal articles: (1) commitment to maintain the territorial status quo and fulfillment of the most recent treaties; (2) the proportional contribution already mentioned for common security and expenses of the Great Alliance; (3) absolute renunciation of the use of arms to settle differences and commitment henceforth to follow always the path of reconciliation through the mediation of the other Great Allies in place of the General Assembly and, in case of failure, through the judgment of the plenipotentiaries of the other permanently assembled allies; (4) in case of violation of the regulations of the Great Alliance, the Alliance will use military or economic sanctions against the offender; (5) once the fundamental articles are settled by the plenipotentiaries sitting in their permanent assembly, they cannot be changed except by unanimous consent of the Great Allies. In a word, nothing is missing, not even the veto.

This is not everything. In the course of his explanation, the Abbé of Saint-Pierre constantly uses an expression that the reader must have noted in passing. In his *New Cyneas* Emeric Cruce spoke of a general agreement among all *Catholic* peoples. The Great Scheme of Henri IV (or of de Sully) enlarged this plan to the totality of *Christian* States. The Abbé of Saint-Pierre even assures that the Holy See would have approved the plan in this form. "It would want to gather thus perfectly all Christendom so that it might be just one body that would be and would be called the *Christian Republic*." This is why Saint-Pierre himself, in the Third Discourse of his plan, speaks of his European Society as destined to obtain peace for Christian princes, not only Catholics and Protestants,

States is already modified, and not only the list but the order and names (Rousseau, *Oeuvres complètes*, 6:420–21).

but also Orthodox, as his Europe included Muscovy. Let us note that he did not mean to exclude the rest of the world from his society. At one point he had even composed his text with an eye to including Africa and Asia, but after his friends convinced him that his plan was too long-range, he had accepted reducing it to the dimensions of Christian Europe, which, being almost ripe for this reform, would lend itself to the plan's realization of its own accord.

It is also true that supplementary ideas are introduced into the great scheme at this point and with them serious complications that still hinder it today. Here are at least two of them. First, the desire is to produce Europe, which is excellent, but why only Europe? It is not surprising that Saint-Pierre immediately thought of Africa and America, because, if his reason for wanting to found a European society was to ensure peace, the key concept of the undertaking transcends the framework everywhere. Peace is not a European good, but a human good. Was not the first idea of our dreamer correct? From the outset of his undertaking, what was really in his mind was a society founded on an international legal order that was universal in its scope. Here we touch on one of the intrinsic difficulties in the concept of Europe, which is certainly not meant to turn us away from it, but about which it is good to reflect. Namely, when Europe attempts to reflect on itself and formulate its own essence, it tends to be dissolved in a broader society than itself, for which in fact it recognizes no other limits than those of the globe. Accustomed as Europe is to appeal to universal values, here peace through law, the justification that it gives of their outline abolishes Europe's boundaries at the same time. Europe is so constructed that it is buried along with its triumph each time it tries to define itself.

This is still clearer if we consider the second notion that our precursor has just introduced, that of the Christian Republic. It is the old notion of Christendom, but subjected to the narrowest constraints that have ever been placed on its boundaries, because ultimately, even if it were true to say, as we have heard in our time, that "Europe is the faith," it certainly is not true to say that the faith is Europe. Europe may well be marked off by the faith, but not the faith by Europe. We hope nobody will be scandalized by the bold proposition: Jesus Christ was not a European. Bethlehem is not in Europe. Neither is Tarsus. As for the faith itself, what Christian could conceive of the salvation of one of the five parts of the world to the exclusion of the other four without being horrified? Nobody thinks so upon reflection, but a number of our contemporaries speak as if they thought so. By identifying the two notions of Europe and Christian Republic, the Abbé of Saint-Pierre gave the example of the error common nowadays of justifying the layout of boundaries by a universal principle. If the essence of Europe is to be a Christian society, it ceases to be Europe. It is dissolved into Christendom.

The oddest thing is that this same idea should have haunted the brain of an illustrious reader of our Abbé, none other than Jean-Jacques Rousseau. We are indebted to Rousseau for an *Extract from the Plan for Perpetual Peace of the Abbé of Saint-Pierre*, written in 1756 and published in 1761 with reflections that may be read at the end of this work, where Rousseau's personal thinking surfaces.[8] Among the many friends of United Europe, one of the most interesting spiritual families is that which encourages us to achieve United Europe for the strange reason that it is inevitable anyway, or rather that it has already been achieved. This is exactly Rousseau's thesis, and he defends it with remarkable perceptiveness. Let us hear him: "All the powers of Europe form a kind of system among themselves that unites them by the same religion, by the

8. The passage in *Émile* that concerns Saint-Pierre's plan seems to have been written after the *Extract* and before the *Judgment* (*Émile*, book V, 5:261n). *L'Extrait du Projet de Paix perpétuelle de M. l'abbé de Saint-Pierre* is found in *Oeuvres*, 6:397–439. It is immediately followed by *Judgment on the Perpetual Peace*, 440–55. The *Extract* is less of a summary than a personal appeal in favor of the plan. There, Rousseau is found as much as Saint-Pierre. The *Judgment* offers the arguments against the plan.

same law of nations, by customs, by culture, by commerce, and by a kind of equilibrium that is the necessary result of all that, and which, without anyone thinking in fact about preserving it, would still not be as easy to break as many people think."[9] This is a truly admirable optimism. Rousseau's confidence in the excellence of nature is such that the problem here is not the establishment of Europe; it would rather be to keep it from existing.

Still, Europe has not happened all by itself. In any case, it has not always existed. There has not always been a Society of the Peoples of Europe, and it is as important to discover its origin, because the forces that formed it still serve to maintain it. They are what make us distinguish Europeans today from Kaffirs and Americans, as Greeks, in another time, distinguished Hellenes from barbarians.[10] What are these forces? First of all, they are the community of peoples created by the Roman Empire. One and the same political yoke subjected these peoples to one and the same authority, so it conferred a kind of civil and political unity on them. "This union," Rousseau notes, "was thoroughly bound together by the maxim, either very wise or very rash, of granting to the vanquished all the rights of the victors, particularly by the famous decree of Claudius that incorporated all these subjects of Rome into the number of its citizens." Here again we have an idea that is surely true in its order, but that in the very measure in which it is true imposes limits on Europe that are simultaneously too broad or too narrow. They are too broad, because if Europe continues the Roman Empire, what will we do with Roman Africa and Asia? They are too narrow, because it will be necessary for us to cut Germany in two following Domitian's famous boundary, and renounce Muscovy, the eighteenth of the Abbé of Saint-Pierre's European states. Still, let us hold onto this idea that the current

9. Rousseau, *Extract*, in *Oeuvres*, 6:400. In agreement with one of the constant traits of his thinking, Rousseau believes that the problem consists of making Europe, which is given *de facto*, pass from the state of nature to the political state.

10. Ibid., 6:401.

rubble of the Roman Empire is united *de facto* in a community of civilization that predestines it to become the nucleus of a society of peoples broader than theirs.

Roman law was the second unifying force of Europe. It increases, reinforces, and sometimes replaces the political bond, which was a *de facto* force, by a juridical bond, which was a bond of principle. With time, this purely moral force proved to be capable of compensating for the failure of the old political force. "The code of Theodosius and later Justinian's books are a new chain of justice and reason deliberately substituted for the Sovereign's chain that was very markedly relaxed. This supplement greatly delayed the dissolution of the empire, and for a very long time preserved a kind of imperial jurisdiction over the very barbarians who laid waste to it." Here again Rousseau is right, and we know that today, in a time when we wonder whether there is not a certain naïveté in speaking the language of law to peoples for whom the very idea of law, nearly alien to their history, is not yet meaningful. However, we return this way to a universal Europe that could not be established without abolishing its own bonds. Europe is perhaps law, but law is not Europe. What is typically European is to conceive law not as the foundation of European civilization, but of civilization pure and simple.

"A third bond, stronger than the previous ones, was that of religion," Rousseau tells us. "It cannot be denied that even today Europe owes the sort of society that has become perpetuated among its members to Christianity, so much so that a member of Europe who has not adopted the sentiment of the rest on this point has always remained an alien among the members of this society."[11] The latter is Turkey, of course, and nothing is more logical. From the instant Europe defines itself in terms of religious belief, it is inevitable that Islam should mark its eastern boundaries, just as in the thirteenth century it marked Christendom's boundary. We are

11. Ibid., 6:402.

in a circle here. Let us admit that a people must be Christian to become part of Europe. Will it be enough that the people be Christian to become European? If Asiatic Turkey becomes Christian, will it become European Turkey? Albania is Muslim. Must it be called Asiatic Albania? Unless we are satisfied with oratorical flourishes or gushes of sentimentality, the question has to be examined more closely.[12]

Neither the eighteenth nor the nineteenth century did so, nor, as far as we know, has the twentieth. What do we want? Who are we? It would be time to ask ourselves if we want to calculate our action with an eye to a foreseeable future.[13] For ultimately, when

12. Here we see the dual concept of Europe appear, into which all the current discussion about the spiritual essence or soul of United Europe slip. There is a particular geographically situated, politically organized Europe and an abstract Europe defined by a common "spirit" or by the acceptance of certain shared ideas. When someone believes he has fixed an opponent in one of these two Europes the opponent immediately takes refuge in the other. Therefore, we have Europeans in the first sense (Marx, Hitler, Mussolini, etc.) who are not Europeans in the second sense. Inversely, certain ideas originating in Asia (Christianity) or that have come back to us after having been developed there (Arab mathematics and optics), although they are not European in the first sense of the word, become European in the second. The confusion reaches its peak when we talk about America. Whatever Canada, the United States, Mexico, or the South American republics are, how can we place them in Europe? But also how can we attribute a spirit to them other than the European spirit, given that their local nuances are often less marked than those observed in Europe?

13. Rousseau's *Judgment* begins by approving, and surely quite rightly, the plan of a political union of the peoples of Europe. "If ever a moral truth has been demonstrated it seems to me that it is the general and particular utility of this plan" (*Oeuvres*, 6:440). But he judges it chimerical to count on the princes to achieve it (6:442–43). What interests them is despotism, which puts up with war quite well, although the situation of the winners is not better than that of the losers. "I have beaten the Romans," wrote Hannibal to the Carthaginians. "Send me troops. I have taxed Italy. Send me money" (6:444). In short, acknowledging the possibility and greatness of the goal, Rousseau reproaches Saint-Pierre for the childishness of the means he proposes. Rousseau does not doubt: "The project of the Christian Republic is not a chimera" (6:448). Henri IV prepared it secretly and through skillful negotiations (6:450–54). Those were efficacious means unlike the ones Saint-Pierre offers in his book. "No doubt permanent peace is an absurd project at present, but if we get a Henri IV and a Sully, permanent peace becomes a reasonable plan. Or rather, we admire such a fine plan, but we console ourselves for not seeing it carried out, because that can only happen through violent means, dreadful for humanity" (6:454–55). Here again, Rousseau's practical conservativism finally gets the upper hand:

our contemporaries talk about establishing Europe, they are certainly thinking of the future. Rousseau himself, who believes that Europe exists, holds it only to be the stuff of a possible society. More exactly, following his own division of the human order into two states, he understands that Europe would be brought from the state of nature to the political state by organizing it by a pact very much like that of the Abbé of Saint-Pierre. The past would make a legal system, in a word, a real society, out of that nationalist aggregate. There the thing that is called by such a fine name, *the European Republic*, will be born. But what is this European Republic of Rousseau but the daughter of the Abbé of Saint-Pierre's Christian Republic, which is itself the daughter of Roger Bacon's Republic of believers, which is an avatar of St. Augustine's City of God? Here we are exactly in the middle of what has been called "the heavenly city of the eighteenth-century philosophers."[14] But when we look

"We do not witness federal leagues establishing themselves other than through revolutions. On this principle, which of us would dare to say whether this European league is to be desired or feared? Perhaps it will cause more harm at one stroke than it will prevent for centuries" (6:455). In short, Rousseau is not entirely certain that we can obtain peace through law without paying rather dearly for this result.

14. Carl L. Becker, *The Heavenly City of the Eighteenth-Century Philosophers* (New Haven, Conn.: Yale University Press, 1932), 29–31: "We are accustomed to think of the eighteenth century as essentially modern in its temper. Certainly the *Philosophes* themselves made a great point of having renounced the superstition and hocus-pocus of medieval Christian thought, and we have usually been willing to take them at their word. Surely, we say, the eighteenth century was preeminently the age of reason; surely the *Philosophes* were a skeptical lot, atheists in effect if not by profession, addicted to science and the scientific method, always out to crush the infamous, valiant defenders of liberty, equality, fraternity, freedom of speech, and what you will. All very true. And yet I think the *Philosophes* were nearer the Middle Ages, less emancipated from the preconceptions of medieval Christian thought than they quite realized or we have commonly supposed. If we have done them more (or is it less?) than justice in giving them a good modern character, the reason is that they speak a familiar language. . . . Their negations rather than their affirmations enable us to treat them as kindred spirits. But, if we examine the foundations of their faith, we find that, at every turn, the *Philosophes* betray their debt to medieval thought without being aware of it. They denounced Christian philosophy, but rather too much, after the manner of those who are but half emancipated from the 'superstitions' they scorn. They had put off the fear of God, but maintained a respectful attitude toward the Deity. They ridiculed the idea that the universe had been created in six days, but still believed it to be a beautifully articulated machine designed by the Supreme Being

around us, what do we see? We see some houses still standing in the enclosure of a city in ruins that still attempt to bear the city's name. We see a body that claims a soul too big for it, a soul made to dwell in another body, not only greater, but of a different kind. This false perspective has consequences today. In those emotional gatherings where so many great minds hopefully scrutinize the future of United Europe, how many times have we not heard it said: Gentlemen, others are in the process of giving a body to Europe, but if we do not give it a soul, how will this body live?

There is no doubt about that, but which soul do we mean? Everyone proposes his own, but it is always the soul of something other than Europe, something that Europe is not and never will be. Does anyone dare to point this out? He will immediately be accused of not believing in Europe, of not having faith in Europe, in short of delaying the birth for which he should be working. His thoughts may be completely different. Perhaps he simply judges that even if it were in our power to create souls, it would be a wise precaution to make sure about the body before getting to work. Rousseau and the Abbé of Saint-Pierre were too close to their discovery to discern its nature clearly, but we have no excuse for perpetuating their illusions.[15] At the moment when their divinations

according to a rational plan as an abiding place for mankind. The Garden of Eden was for them a myth, no doubt, but they looked enviously back to the golden age of Roman virtue, or across the waters to the unspoiled innocence of an Arcadian civilization that flourished in Pennsylvania. They renounced the authority of Church and Bible, but exhibited a naive faith in the authority of nature and reason. . . . In the following lectures I shall endeavor to elaborate this theme. I shall attempt to show that the underlying preconceptions of eighteenth-century thought were still, allowance made for certain important alterations in the bias, essentially the same as those of the thirteenth century. I shall attempt to show that the *Philosophes* demolished the heavenly City of St. Augustine only to rebuild it with more up-do-date materials."

15. Those illusions about the particular point we are examining do not affect the positive contribution by Saint-Pierre and Rousseau to the problem of United Europe. International law is one of the most important of the necessary elements of this solution. After Saint-Pierre and Rousseau, Kant establishes this with remarkable depth in his *Project for a Perpetual Peace* (1795), *Projet de paix perpetuelle*, trans. Jean Gibelin (Paris: J. Vrin, 1948). Kant remains faithful to the Christian notion of "people." Only the practical will

finally solidify and take flesh in reality, the time has come for us to measure exactly both their greatness and limitation. Modesty is a beautiful virtue, because it does not aim at smallness but at the measure that follows the exact dimensions of reality. When the body of Europe is small, it will receive its soul, and those who come after us will know what it is, after living it. It will be scholarly, but it will not be science. It will give birth in beauty but it will not be art. It will be just, but it will not be the law. We hope it will be Christian, but it will not be Christendom.

---

can create a republic of peoples by creating a law. Nature cannot do so. Yet, nature already does for peoples what they normally ought to want, through a harmony that recalls Leibniz's harmony of nature and grace. On this curious teleology see Kant, *Projet*, 38–39. Kant quotes Seneca: "Fata volentem ducunt, nolentem trahunt." Or again, "Nature wills in an irresistible way that power should ultimately devolve upon law" (46). On the influence of Rousseau and Saint-Pierre here, see Victor Delbos, *La philosophie practique de Kant* (Paris: F. Alcan, 1905), 280. The "cosmopolitan society" whose history Kant retraces or foretells retains profound connections with the City of God: "The history of nature starts with good, as a work of God. The history of freedom starts with evil, as the work of humans" (Delbos, *La philosophie practique*, 293). Only, here the naturalization of the City of God is complete. Consequently, Augustine's city is metamorphosized into the kingdom of ends, the concept of which is already completely developed in the *Critique of Practical Reason*. This *mundus intelligibilis*, intelligible world, inhabited by persons, each of whom acts as legislator, is at least "possible" although no one can be compelled to enter it. The universal society of peoples, governed by a common law, owes its universality to the rationality of its moral and legal foundation. Yet, by way of preparation for the timeless kingdom of ends, it still exercises a function analogous to that of the Church conceived as the presence of eternity in the time, preparing the City of God. Kant's influence on the Reformed Churches would have been less deep if so many previously naturalized Christian notions were not found in his ethics.

EIGHT

The City of the Philosophers

When we approach the priest of Saint-Pierre after so many theoretical reformers, the political, concrete, and almost directly practical character of his plan strikes us. The Europe of his desires, as he calls it, can exist tomorrow, provided only that the sovereigns want it, and this is why, even before proposing his plan, we see him strive mightily to prove that it is necessary. Leibniz's reaction was the reverse of ours, or at least very different. After Saint-Pierre addressed his work to Leibniz, he read it, was pleased by it, and on February 7, 1715, wrote the author to congratulate him. The compliments are sincere, but they belong to the very peculiar species of compliments that a reader directs to the author of a book when he has his own ideas on the matter. "Humans need only willpower," remarks Leibniz, "to free themselves from an infinity of evils. If five or six persons willed it, they could end the great schism, of the West and put the Church in good order."[1] What an adjustment! How high this lifts us above the worthy Saint-Pierre! With Leibniz we have a man to whom people talk about organizing European society politically but who responds about the schism and reorganization of the Church. When Saint-Pierre sent his book to Leibniz, he could not doubt that he was addressing a genius of the ages, obsessed by the same problems, but who distinguished the real elements with much more profoundly. Leibniz's real answer is the perfect exemplar of letters that we

1. Louis-Alexandre Foucher de Careil, *Oeuvres de Leibniz, publiées par la première fois d'après les manuscrits originaux*, 7 vols. (Paris: 1859–75). The letter is found in 4:324.

write but do not send. We still have it under the title *Observation on the Plan for Perpetual Peace of the Abbé of Saint-Pierre*.[2]

This outline of an answer is most interesting, if only in what it teaches us about the problem's history or rather about what we ought to know before undertaking to narrate it. After praising Saint-Pierre for his courage in the face of "outburst of mockers," Leibniz pays tribute to his predecessors. There is Emeric Cruce, of course, whose *Le nouveau Cynée* Leibniz had read earlier without knowing its author and which he had almost completely forgotten except for its general thesis.[3] There is Henri IV, who, being a great king, could permit himself to propose a plan for which lesser princes would not dare to take responsibility. In this regard, let us note a remark by Leibniz that I am afraid is accurate: we can suspect Henri IV of conceiving his project rather "with a view to overturning the House of Austria than establishing the society of sovereigns." This shadow over the past slightly darkens our present. Behind our love of justice there is often fear and the desire to overwhelm some House of Austria in our federations. In the absence of a bond of common love, one is satisfied with a bond of common fear. Perhaps that is the original sin of Europe and like all original sins, we will have to pay for this one some day.

But let us return to our narrative. Besides these two predecessors whom we already know, Leibniz cites a third who is much less familiar. It seems that Landgrave Rheinfels of Hesse had written a work in German entitled *The Discrete Catholic*, which contained a plan similar to Saint-Pierre's. This prince envisaged a tribunal

2. *Observation sur le Projet d'une Paix Perpétuelle de M. l'Abbé de Sainte-Pierre*, in Leibniz, *Oeuvres*, 4:328–36.

3. "When I was very young, I knew of a book entitled *Nouveau Cyneas*, whose unknown author advised sovereigns to govern their States in peace and to make their States be judged by an established tribunal. But I can no longer find this book, and I no longer remember any details. We know that Cyneas was a confidant of King Pyrrhus, whom he advised to rest at once, since, as the king himself confessed, his goal was to do that once he had conquered Sicily, Calabria, Rome, and Carthage." *Observations*, 4:328–29.

of sovereigns whose seat would be at Lucerne.[4] We meet this same Landgrave again corresponding with Arnauld precisely on the subject of Leibniz and his attempts to reestablish peace between Protestants and Catholics. Indeed, Leibniz is certainly thinking about these religious problems when he reads Saint-Pierre's plan. He tells us that there were times when popes half-formed a plan that was "close" to Saint-Pierre's, by proposing the organization of a universal Church that would teach a universal religion under the direction of a spiritual leader, the pope, and a temporal leader, the emperor. Leibniz has many reservations about the temporal structure of Europe as Saint-Pierre anticipates it. It seems to him that by separating Savoy from the Empire and Courland from Poland, one provokes difficulties from those two powers. After all, the German emperor could still go to Rome to have himself crowned emperor of the Romans and king of Lombardy. Thus, there are practical difficulties, but what troubles Leibniz very much more is the undertaking's spiritual dimension. Saint-Pierre speaks indiscriminately of Europe and of Christian society. On that score, Leibniz has doubts, because, after all, the popes tried to create this society. The project was acknowledged to be impossible after the Council of Constance, and the obstacle upon which the plan foundered has continually become more insurmountable, namely, the Reformation. No Protestant was ever more in love with religious unity than Leibniz, and when someone preaches such facile unity to him as does the priest of Saint-Pierre, Leibniz immediately perceives the shoal toward which this plan travels under full sail. To have a Christian society, a genuinely united Church and Christendom are necessary. Where are they? For Leibniz this is the crux of the matter.

So we have returned to a familiar clime here. Leibniz, a philosophical and mathematical genius, invites us to reengage a prob-

4. *Observations*, 4:329; see 330 on the ulterior motives of King Henri IV.

lem whose meanings and elements he understands marvelously, yet we see him search for the solution other than where it is found. Leibniz sees lucidly what is at stake in the debate. Before grounding the unity of peoples upon Christianity, it is necessary to reestablish religious unity. Here the weapons of piety are needed more than those of warfare. If the gentleman of Saint-Pierre "could make us all Romans," Leibniz says, if he could "make us believe in the pope's infallibility, there would be no need of any other empire than that of the Vicar of Jesus Christ." Consequently, at the moment when the priest has just lowered the problem from the philosophical and religious level to the political level, a philosopher accustomed to diplomatic subtleties elevates the problem to the religious level. The two levels are necessary, but the one to which Leibniz holds is not only as real as the other, it is deeper.

Leibniz and the Religious Organization of the Earth: the title of this splendid book by Jean Baruzi is a program by itself.[5] The book came too early for its time. It revealed an almost unknown Leibniz to its readers. That Leibniz seemed outdated and consequently of no interest, but he has become more relevant than ever today. In 1676 our philosopher was installed at the court of Hanover, a Protestant country whose sovereign had been converted to Catholicism. We know him at least by what Bossuet says in the funeral oration of Anne de Gonzaga: "Johann Friedrich, Duke of Brunswick and Hanover, a mighty ruler who joined knowledge with valor, the Catholic religion with the virtues of his house, and . . . the service of the Empire with the interests of France." It will be easily understood that in this environment the reconciliation of Protes-

5. Jean Baruzi, *Leibniz et l'organisation religieuse de la terre* (Paris: F. Alcan, 1907). At that date Baruzi saw and recounted the historical setting in which Leibniz's work naturally takes place: "Viewed in depth, Leibniz's religious endeavor renews a medieval dream. To believe in a 'Christendom,' to desire universal monarchy, to annihilate the 'infidels,' and, on the other hand, to construct a Church among the sects, to describe a supreme arbitration, to spread Christianity and civilization beyond the old world . . . is this not the persistent centuries old aspiration for a Christianity to be achieved on earth? Indeed, Leibniz discovers a living expression of Christianity in Europe" (267).

tants and Catholics was a vital problem. It was desired not just for Hanover but also for all Germany, where religious unity had to be reestablished for a Christian Republic to be possible. In 1678 Duke Johann Friedrich was assigned to take charge of the realization of a plan that envisaged doctrinal reconciliation beyond mere reestablishment of good political relations. The Landgrave had a letter of approval from Pope Benedict XI and hence the support of Rome. Leibniz is in the Landgrave's service and will become the undertaking's mainspring. From there, among many other endeavors, comes his correspondence with Bossuet.

It would be impossible to choose the interlocutors better for this fascinating debate. Leibniz is ready to suggest all possible solutions but one. Bossuet is deaf to all possible proposals except the only one Leibniz refuses to accept. Still, let us note that in this exchange with no possible outcome, the philosopher is certainly on the high road that descends from St. Augustine toward us across the centuries. Leibniz hears talk about a society among States. He is not certain that the plan has sense in that form, because there is no society without friendship and no friendship without souls. Consequently, there can be only friendship or society between persons, who alone have souls. States do not have them. "There is only a soul for natural persons, not for juridical persons" writes Leibniz in his answer to Saint-Pierre. Among juridical persons there can be neither friendship nor hatred; in a word, there cannot be society. Leibniz knows well that this intimate union of souls that was once on the verge of existing thanks to the Church will be the work of Christianity or it will not be. But as a Protestant, he holds the experience of the Reformation to be decisive. As the papacy did not create the doctrinal unity without which no society worthy of the name is possible, experience proves that it will never do what it missed the opportunity to achieve. Accordingly, it is necessary to start over without the papacy or at least by persuading the papacy to abdicate its doctrinal privileges whose retention makes the birth of a universal Christendom impossible. Leibniz's attempt can be summed up in a simple expression: can Christianity be catholic, which is to say universal, without being Roman? Nothing is more instructive than to see this great mind grappling with this question.

To find the answer, Leibniz must necessarily soften the concept of Church. If he does not do so, how can he have two Churches or ten or a hundred in the same Christian society? In fact, the new approach to the problem implies a radical separation of the concept of Roman Church and the concept of Christendom. Let us assume it, *dato non concesso*. The immediate consequence of this approach is the loosening of spiritual unity and, by that very thing, of the social unity that the spiritual unity must ground. The relation is relaxed instead of being extended. This lack of substance is perceptible in a significant passage of Arnauld's letter of March 2, 1684, to Landgrave Rheinfels of Hesse. I do not know what to tell you about your friend, wrote Arnauld to the Landgrave, because "since he declares to you that if he had been born into the Catholic religion, he would remain there, I do not see how he can have his conscience at ease if he does not set himself on the path to reenter it." Indeed, but precisely what Leibniz means is that because he was born into the Protestant religion, he will remain there, and for no other reason than that he was born there. What Arnauld, as a Catholic, cannot understand is that someone should not see that choosing a Church is choosing the truth. Leibniz already no longer sees it, which would be important only for him, if this weakening of the concept of Church did not jeopardize beforehand his chances of resolving his own problem. It is a bit amazing that he did not see this, he who delighted to repeat that it is the same thing to say "one *being*" and "*one* being." If there is no being without unity, ought we not say similarly, it is the same thing to say "one *Church*" as to say "*one* Church," and it is the same thing to say "one *Christendom*" as to say "*one* Christendom"? In the instant when Leibniz undertakes to found a Christian society, he breaks the relationship by which he himself announced that he intends to unite it.[6]

Failing that, will he find another? Our philosopher naturally wonders about this, and he finds one, even several, but not without summoning us to new sacrifice, and it is no longer the concept of Church but of Christianity that will have to consent to the sacrifices. To resolve his problem, Leibniz needs a Christianity that is acceptable to all those who would agree to call themselves Christians in any sense. This is what led him, in fact, although perhaps not in his deep intentions to naturalize Christianity in order to universalize it, and to empty it of its properly religious consent in order to make it the religion of all humans.

Leibniz was not the only one to attempt the feat. Campanella's example found innumerable imitators. Deism's extreme thinness makes it almost impossible for us today, and, when we try to read those insubstantial books, we have difficulty understanding that the seventeenth and eighteenth centuries could have found any nourishment in them. In a word, the issue is to show that almost all that the Christian religion teaches is true, although the Christian religion itself is false, as are furthermore all religions. Toland had explained it very well in his *Christianity not Mysterious*.[7] Specifically, a text written in Leibniz's hand has just been published, whose ideas are in part his, but also partly a summary of some deist work published in his time.[8] There is only one true religion,

6. The root of the misunderstanding was in the very notion Leibniz formed about the Church. He distinguished the "invisible" and "visible" Churches. The invisible Church includes all souls of good will. It has only one dogma, to love God above all things and consequently to prefer him to everything else. It is the "temple of God." The visible Church takes on an external form, has an organized body and a hierarchy, and its leader is in Rome; it is the "temple of men." In short, it leads to the authentic Church, which is the invisible one, to the City of God. On four occasions Bossuet rose up against this doctrine and rejected the religious rationalism it implied. Cf. Foucher de Careil, V.339–40.

7. London, 1696.

8. *Parallèle entre la raison originale ou la loi de la nature, le paganisme ou la corruption de la loi de la nature, la loi de Moïse ou le paganisme reformé, et le Christianisme ou la loi de la nature rétablie*, commented upon in Baruzi, *Leibniz*, 486–92. "No piece of writing can inform

that of "holy reason," which is God's voice, and which, contrary to what Rousseau will teach, the author of nature has put in human hearts "as an infallible oracle." Of course, this oracle is universal. Religions based on authority depend on a book, and they would be lost if the book were lost. Reason can never be completely lost: "So, Reason is the origin of a universal, perfect religion that can rightly be called the law of nature." This law of nature "is spread throughout all peoples, always the same and eternal." But let us not imagine that our philosopher renounces Christianity here. Quite the contrary, this religion of reason is genuine Christianity. Indeed, what was the Christian religion originally but liberation from pagan superstition and Jewish ritualism? Far from wanting to add new rites to old ones, Christianity was "an institution intended to rectify ethics, give us correct ideas about divinity, and consequently to uproot superstitious opinions and practices." We would return to Christianity simply by returning to reason.

If this were Leibniz's complete thought on this subject, it would be correct to say, as indeed has been said about him: "Union does not mean unity. Leibniz sought practical unification of Christians separated dogmatically rather than dogmatic unity."[9] This amounts to saying that he had despaired of solving the problem, because he himself saw clearly that nothing separates souls more deeply than dogmatic divisions, and if every society worthy of the name is a union of souls, how are we to unite in practice what we leave dogmatically separated? This is far from having been his deepest thinking. Leibniz never despaired of uniting souls in one single dogmatic truth. He too had his "authentic Christianity," less

us more certainly about Leibniz's personal faith" (486). Baruzi already underlined the expression "the law of nature is the Catholic religion" (488). The passage has been published by Gaston Grua, *Gottfried Wilhelm Freiherr von Leibniz: Textes inédits* (Paris: Presses Universitaires de France, 1948) [reprinted in New York: Garland, 1985], 1:46. The interpretation of this piece is much more nuanced in Grua (1:46n174). It is self-evident that if this text represents the definitive personal thinking of Leibniz, as Baruzi thinks, nothing else is needed to establish that Leibniz thoroughly naturalized Christianity.

9. Baruzi, *Leibniz*, 58.

simplistic than Toland's and profound in a different way, more genuinely religious as well, and consequently more Christian, but which being at bottom only a philosophical specter of the Gospel, could engender only a spectral Christianity.

Nothing demonstrates this more clearly than a valuable text that has just been revealed to us: *Specimen Demonstrationum Catholicarum seu Apologia Fidei ex Ratione*.[10] To reconstruct an apology for faith, we must recur to reason, but how does Leibniz understand that? Admirably informed as always, Leibniz knows everything about the traditional methods of Christian apologetics, and he approves them. Miracles, martyrs, and constant tradition of the Church are all true and excellent, but let us not forget an even stronger argument that we all have in front of us. There is certainly a reason that God has permitted a progressively closer alliance between philosophical reason and faith, which, at the point when Leibniz wrote, had just accomplished an admirable harmony of Christianity and philosophical truth: *Consensus admirabilis religionis nostrae et philosophiae verae*. Of course, this true philosophy is that of Leibniz. It is particularly not that of Descartes, which Leibniz combated for many reasons, but quite specifically because, insofar as the error of Descartes's philosophy made it unacceptable, it risked sowing disunity among minds, rendering the Christian Republic's unity impossible. This is not a historical inference. Leibniz says it himself when he justifies the plan of his apology. He writes these pages "*ne quid [Ecclesia] Respublica Christiana ... a philosophia nova detrimentum capiat*."[11] His hesitation between *Church* and *Christian Republic* is significant. They are the same things for him, but whatever name we give it, the new society will certainly achieve its unity by finding its common truth in Leibniz's own philosophy.

We should see no trace of personal vanity in this. Leibniz is no

10. Grua, *Textes inédits*, 1:27–30.
11. Ibid., 1:27.

more than the scholar whose understanding is the first to bow before its own discovery. Moreover he speaks from experience. He himself began by being a Cartesian. As long as he was a Cartesian, the incompatibility of the new science with the Christian faith was only too evident to him. But in the measure in which he formed his own philosophy, he observed with surprise that Descartes's new philosophy was false wherever it was opposed to religion. "I found myself," he wrote in the same place, "in the position of a man who, after wandering for a long time in a forest, suddenly finds he has emerged into open ground and sees that, against all expectation, he has returned to the exact point where he entered the forest."[12] From there comes Leibniz's insistence on the necessity of recurring to certain metaphysics of forms and "energies" beyond Descartes's mechanism in order to justify the confused but sometimes correct views of Aristotle by deepening them. This is also the true standpoint from which we may capture the meaning of works considered well known, such as the *Monadology* and the *Discourse on Metaphysics*. By defining the principles of universal philosophical truth, they lay foundations of the new Christendom.

Nothing is odder than Leibniz's universe. Composed of individuals, each of which is an irreducible unity, a "monad" that has neither doors nor windows to communicate with others, Leibniz still forms an admirable system where each individual expresses all the others in its fashion and arranges with them in the unity of the whole. Here we return to the Holy City of Cecrops of which

12. Leibniz's opposition is philosophical in the first place, but his animosity against Descartes is explained by the fear of seeing Descartes's success jeopardize the religious organization of the world by preaching a false philosophy. See these writings in Carl Immanuel Gerhardt, *Die philosophischen Schriften von G. W. Leibniz*, 7 vols. (Berlin: Weidman, 1875–90), 4:274–406 [A partial reproduction in book form is *Philosophischen Schriften / Gottfried Wilhelm Leibniz* (Frankfurt am Main: Suhrkamp, 1996)]. A connection developed between this opposition and Leibniz's desire to employ the Jesuits with a view to his own goals. See the remarkable passage in Baruzi, *Leibniz*, 66: "I remember that I made a plan once to show how an order like theirs (and indeed I see nothing more appropriate) could do a very great service to humankind . . . At the same time, I added the plan for a new philosophy that would have absolutely obliterated that of Descartes," and so forth.

Epictetus spoke, a physical world that can be called an unconscious society, which needs only to become self-aware, to know itself, and to will itself in order to become a social body worthy of the name. This miracle is the work of God, supreme and perfect legislator, whose wisdom and power harmonize the monads among themselves and makes them behave as if they communicated, without their really communicating. If we transposed this metaphysics in terms of contemporary politics, we would say that the world of the monads unites maximal individualism to maximal socialism: there, things are all together, and there, each is all alone.

That explains the enormous importance of the concept of law in Leibniz's doctrine. The laws of God unite the monads and harmonize them in such an admirable way that each of them has only to develop the sequence of its states spontaneously to agree with all the others, or rather to find itself spontaneously in agreement with them. The ascendant hierarchy of beings from the simple monads up to souls, which are monads capable of perception, and then on up to minds (*mentes*, *Geister*), leads us from the level of nature that is only nature to that of society. Minds are not simply "mirrors" of the universe like souls, "but rather images of divinity itself or of the very Author of Nature, capable of knowing the system of the universe and of imitating in some measure through an architectonic sampling, since each mind is a little divinity in its department" (*Monadology* §83).

Accordingly, Leibniz's universe is at the same time a City of gods and a City of God. Like the creator, the philosopher, in whom the expression of the universe attains the highest point it can attain in the human mind, has the art of making the maximum perfection fit into the least possible volume and of achieving it with the most perfect simplicity of means. In the *Monadology* Leibniz, like God in the universe, resolves a problem of maximum and minimum. Aware through intellectual knowledge of the laws of the whole of which he is part, the philosopher passes from the order of nature to the social order. Knowing the perfection of the author of nature, he embraces his laws with loving acceptance that raises him from the order of nature to the order of grace. Thus, the authentic City of God is born and gradually established, in which, according to the explicit words of *Monadology* §88, universal harmony "makes things lead to grace by the very paths of nature." A more thorough naturalization of grace has not been seen, nor consequently more complete substitution of metaphysics for religion. Leibniz establishes a new City of God on the ruins of grace. In St. Augustine the City of God draws being, movement, and life from grace. Here we are no longer dealing with Catholicism or Protestantism. Luther and Calvin would have detested this universe even more than some of our Scholastics, who themselves would have diminished the role of nature. For the reformers hope to accede to grace, not through nature or even with it, but against it. We do not imagine Luther writing a treatise on the harmony of the laws of nature and grace. Here we are closer than ever to what we called, with Carl L. Becker, *The Heavenly City of the Eighteenth-Century Philosophers*. The complete secularization of the City of God is now accomplished. The only divinity that still dominates the City is the one that the revolutionary rites would soon celebrate: the goddess of Reason.

This should not be forgotten when reading the last articles of the *Discourse on Metaphysics*, whose language, so Christian, is so empty of Christian substance. The City of God is made up of those who believe in him and love him. It is "the most perfect city or republic, just as the city of the universe composed of all minds together," under the supreme authority of the "Monarch of minds." These are important truths, almost unknown to ancient philosophers, says Leibniz, but which Jesus Christ revealed to us in a simple, familiar language that all can understand. What does Jesus' preaching of the "Kingdom of the Heavens" announce but "this perfect republic of minds that merits the label of *City of God*?" The same idea reappears in the fourth letter to Arnauld where Leibniz speaks of "the universal republic whose monarch is God," and again in the fifth letter, where we all appear as citizens of this city, "composed of so many little gods under the great God. Because created minds can be said not to differ from God except by way of less to more, of finite to infinite." Again, in the sixth letter he refers to "the republic of the universe whose monarch is God." The whole doctrine is summed up in *The New System of the Nature and Communication of Substances* §16:

> Since every mind is like a separate world, sufficient unto itself, independent of any other creature, embracing the infinite, expressing the universe, it is as lasting, as subsistent, and as absolute as the universe of creatures itself. Thus, we must judge that it must always be represented in the fashion most likely to contribute to the perfection of all the minds that achieve their moral union in the City of God.

In Leibniz's mind this is the social and political ideal recommended by the *Discourse on Metaphysics* (1685). Leibniz diplomatically sends a simple summary of it to the great Arnauld, a prudent summary, on which Leibniz counts to mollify Arnauld and get the remainder by him. But Arnauld smells a trap. In two years of correspondence Leibniz does not succeed in persuading Arnauld that his doctrine does not destroy free choice. It would have been more difficult still to prove to this Jansenist that the doctrine does not exclude grace. Yet it is on the totally naturalistic doctrine that our philosopher counts in order to unite souls in the City of God. The common bond of his Christian religion is to be a completely de-Christianized deism.

Nothing would discourage Leibniz. Incapable of convincing Arnauld, he was equally unable to convert Bossuet to his Catholicism of reason. The bishop of Meaux's point of view was simple: have we ever heard of a Catholic who thought himself free to accept or reject the decision of the Council of Trent?[13] Failing in the

13. See Baruzi, *Leibniz*, 328–32, on the authority of ecumenical councils.

terrain of the visible Church, whose leader is in Rome, Leibniz turns to the invisible Church, of which the Reformed Church is in some way the seed, while awaiting its spread to humanity. The true City of God will be the city of persons of good will to whom peace on earth is already promised. Really, it might just as well be called humanity, with no reservations, all the more strange in that it is always the same. Since the sixteenth century, all the prophets of universal society have counted on the Jesuits to found it. All but Auguste Comte excluded the Turks. In fact, Leibniz means Muslims. Why? The strange thing is that this is because they are not Christians. The Turks have always been the enemy of Christ. Completely alien to the doctrine of spirit and truth preached by the Gospel, their religion is in fact politics, and their kingdom is of this world. The Turks want to rule and nothing else.[14]

The situation becomes more and more impossible before our eyes. To enter the promised land of the universal society, it is not necessary to be truly Christian in the sense in which the visible Church understands it, but one must remains Christian enough to at least be able to be Leibnizian. The *Discourse on Metaphysics* is the Gospel of the new Christian Republic.[15] As Leibniz, like Roger Bacon in the thirteenth century, does not hope to convert the Turks,

14. See ibid., 5–45, on the plans to conquer Egypt. See also 106–76 on Russia and the possible role of Peter the Great.

15. It is necessary to read Leibniz with the blinders that Bertrand Russell habitually wears to fail to see this evidence. In 1907 Jean Baruzi was already completely right to ask Russell by what right he considered the *Monadology* "a kind of fantastic fairy tale, coherent perhaps but totally arbitrary." Bertrand Russell, *A Critical Exposition of the Philosophy of Leibniz* (London: George Allen and Unwin, 1937), xiii. By what right, Baruzi asks, can one consider totally arbitrary a work that Leibniz himself never declared to be such? Certainly, but that is not what is really strange. By what right does Russell set aside the *Monadology* and substitute the *Discourse on Metaphysics* as expressing the very essence of Leibniz's system? The doctrine is exactly the *Monadology*'s doctrine. The *Discourse* advances by the same paths toward the same religious conclusion. In any case, if there is a point where the two works are indiscernible, it is certainly the spirit that inspires them. Unfortunately, Russell is not the only one who commits this error, nor is Leibniz the only victim. What professor of the history of philosophy has not taught Malebranche without his theology and Auguste Comte without his religion?

it will be necessary simply to suppress them. Crusades ought to serve for that, and the crime of Louis XIV is not having understood it. Instead of attacking Egypt and destroying the Turks, he went to wage war against a Christian country like Holland, thus losing once and for all time the opportunity to permanently guarantee the liberation of the Christian world. Wars between Christians are not only impious; they are politically stupid, because he who masters Egypt will be the generalissimo of Christendom.[16] While waiting, in the likeness of the poet Prudentius admiring God's plans for the Roman Empire, Leibniz sees in Europe the nucleus of the future universal society. Manifestly, that is the intention of providence, because insofar as Europe had allowed itself to be guided by the light of Christ, it certainly received the mission of enlightening the universe. Leibniz says that China, which is "the France of the East," will join Europe. Its beliefs about God, the soul, and the future life bring it so close to Christian beliefs that it will certainly be successfully integrated. Along with that, our philosopher does not lose interest in military force to guarantee that his program will be carried out. Every Aristotle has his Philip of Macedon. After counting on Louis XIV until the war with Holland, Leibniz turns to Charles XII of Sweden, who ends no better. But then with remarkable political flair, Leibniz lets his imagination roam around Muscovy. Leibniz is almost alone in taking seriously the young monarch who visited Europe incognito, whom today more than ever his country calls Peter the Great. Like so many after her, Leibniz's Europe wears a mantle that is too big. Geographically speaking, Europe is shipwrecked in China before the fact. Spiritually speaking, Leibniz's Europe appeals to a truth so weak that it destroys the unity of the Church on which she intends to base her own unity. If the *Discourse on Metaphysics* is not even the bond of Europe, it is still less that of the City of God.

Once again it only remains for us to accompany a noble dream-

16. Foucher de Careil, *Oeuvres*, 4:347–49.

er and his dreams to the common grave of dead illusions. That is more than Leibniz's contemporaries did. "I arrived in Hanover during November 1716," writes his friend John Ker of Kersland, "the day that the renowned Leibniz died, which caused me unspeakable grief. What grieves me even more deeply was how little the Hanoverians honored him after death, because he was buried rather like a highway robber than like a man who had been the glory of his homeland."[17] This, it must be said, is the fate of all pacifiers. They cannot wish to erase conflicts, without drawing all of them upon themselves. Leibniz died without having convinced anyone, exposed to the general distrust of those he wanted to unite, but his illusions sought out another body in order to survive in it. We will see under what form these illusions finally believed they had found that body one hundred years later.

17. Quoted by Baruzi, *Leibniz*, 508n2. Those familiar with Baruzi's book in all its aspects and who have grasped its unity will not be surprised to learn that in their deepest inspiration, Leibniz's efforts on behalf of religious union in spirit and beyond the letter of dogmas have Baruzi's complete sympathy. "What does it matter," Baruzi writes, " if this *faith* hardly resembles traditional faith? All theological concepts are found anew in Leibniz without losing anything of their essence" (498). This is the whole problem. "Theological concepts" are not faith, but if they are separated from it, they do not even remain theological; they become philosophical. Therefore, we would write to the contrary: all the theological concepts lose their essence at the very moment when they are separated from the substance of faith. This is precisely why so-called rational faith, swept along from its birth in the perpetual flux of philosophy, was incapable of being the foundation of the religious unity of the world.

NINE

The City of Scientists

THE WORK of Auguste Comte defies all classification. No simple formula can sum up its many facets, and the history of its influence makes it fairly obvious that it contained the seeds of several possible systems in the realms of science, philosophy, politics, and religion. Still, the particular angle under which we are to view it certainly remains one of the most legitimate, and perhaps the one that lets us discover what the doctrine's inner goal was from the start, which became more and more evident over time. For us, Comte is an incomparable witness and, if we may say so, a perfect experiment. He wants to constitute a universal society founded on the acceptance of a truth common to all humans. Because he recognized no such truth other than that of science, he used science as a basis to build his edifice. From that moment, the enterprise's internal logic dominated it. For science to become a social bond, it had to make itself philosophy and then religion.

The general nature of the problem becomes clearer, if, as we should, we link Comte's work to that of his precursor and teacher, Henry de Rouvroy, the count of Saint-Simon, born in Paris on October 17, 1760, and deceased in 1825. Like Comte, Saint-Simon is a world unto himself, and the diversity of his work is such that it has been given the most varied interpretations.[1] For some, Saint-

1. This curious personality has been judged in very different ways. Fortunately, we need not take a position about his mental health, because whether certain traits are considered normal or pathological, they have the same significance and meaning for us. For example, he believed or claimed he was Charlemagne's descendant. Better yet, his "ancestor" Charlemagne appeared to him and said, "'From the beginning of the world, no family has enjoyed the honor of producing a hero and a philosopher of the first rank. This

Simon is one of Positivism's messiahs: pride, tenacity, faith in his mission, an intense and sometimes morbid excitement, all indicate his quasi-mystical prophetic passion. For others, Saint-Simon appears to be a thoughtful social reformer, not at all mystical, who only prophesied to win public attention, moreover with a wink to his intelligent listeners. So much for the man and the doctrine. From one point of view Saint-Simon is an implacable critic of any establishment and an adversary of all theology, who substitutes science for revelation everywhere, and in the last analysis the protagonist of a social reform based on industrial production, who announces the era of organizers along with the "cybernetics" of our contemporaries. But also, he is the prophet of "New Christianity" who begins by declaring: *I believe in God*. He is the leader of what has been called "the Saint-Simonian religion." Ultimately, he considered himself to be God's spokesman to human beings.

The truth certainly seems to be that he was all that at the same time, not by chance and chaotically, but in one breath. With his first work, the *Letters of a Resident of Geneva* (1803), Saint-Simon announces his intention to put genius back in the place it ought to occupy in the city. That would be the first place, because men of genius alone are creators and, consequently, the true producers. "More honor to the Alexanders! Long live the Archimedes!" He addresses his project for reform directly to humanity. Its spirit is clearly defined in his second letter: all existing religions are abolished, but a new one is immediately organized. Newton sits beside God. The council that represents God on earth is called the "Council of Newton." This council will create others, each of

honor was reserved for my house. My son, your successes as a philosopher will equal the successes I won as a solider and political leader.' And he disappeared." So far, so good. What interests us is not finding out whether our reformer really descended from Charlemagne, nor whether he believed in the vision or made it up. The important thing is that if he invented an ancestor, he chose the founder of medieval Christendom. Regarding Saint-Simon and the formation of his most illustrious disciple, in preference to any other study, one must consult a work that is admirable from every point of view: Henri Gouhier, *La Jeunesse d'Auguste Comte*, 3 vols. (Paris: J. Vrin, 1933, 1936, 1941).

which will build a mausoleum for Newton, surrounded by schools, laboratories, and workshops, in short all of the institutions necessary for the scientific organization of human society. But let us not hesitate to say that the social reformer considers himself to be a religious leader at the same time. "It is God who has spoken to me," he calmly declares in his second *Letter of a Resident of Geneva*. "Would a man have been able to invent a religion superior to all religions that have existed?"[2] After that, we cannot be shocked that his work has been given such different interpretations. All of them are true. Saint-Simon is a messiah who was to be buried in Newton's tomb. At the same time, he is the author of the introduction to *Nineteenth-Century Scientific Work*,[3] of the *Work on Universal Gravitation*, and of *the Treatise on the Reorganization of*

2. Saint-Simon, *Lettres d'un habitant de Genève à ses contemporains* (1803), in *Oeuvres choisies* (Brussels: Fr. Van Meenen, 1859), 1:40, beginning of the third letter. Only a revelation could "give humanity the means to force each of its members to follow the precept of loving their neighbor" (1:41). God told him first of all: "Rome will renounce its pretension to be the center of my Church. The Pope's cardinals, bishops, and priests will cease to speak in my name" and so forth (1:32). The Council of Newton, which must direct humanity, "will divide it into four sections that will be called English, French, German, and Italian" (1:33). [Translator: At some point the four divisions become five, with the addition of the Spanish. See below.] "After their death, the faithful will be treated as they have merited during their lives" (1:34). See 1:36 on worship. Regarding future Crusades: "Learn that Europeans are the children of Abel. Learn that Asia and Africa are inhabited by Cain's posterity. See how bloodthirsty Africans are. Notice the indolence of Asians . . . Europeans will unite their forces. They will deliver their Greek brothers from the Turks. The founder of the religion will be the supreme leader of the armies of the faithful. These armies will submit the children of Cain to religion" and so forth (1:38–39). Abel and Cain remain the ancestors of the two Cities as in St. Augustine.

3. Saint-Simon, *Introduction aux travaux scientifiques du dix-neuvième siècle* (1808). This new Roger Bacon found his Clement IV in Napoleon I. "The emperor is the scientific leader of humanity" (*Oeuvres choisies*, 1:61). "I wait for the leader of the activities of the human mind, the great Napoleon, to speak" (1:226). "The Emperor would need a scientific second-in-command capable of understanding his projects and of furthering their execution. He would need a second Descartes" (1:236). Following the rule, Saint-Simon has little liking for Protestants (1:249–50) and gives greatest importance to Charlemagne, organizer of European society. "He made religion the bond of the federation. Luther brought turmoil to the federation" (1:254). On the other hand, Saint-Simon does not seem to have imagined converting the Jesuits (1:251) and will end by vowing their extermination (*Le nouveau Christianisme*, in ibid., 3:330–37).

European Society or On the Necessity and Means of Gathering the European Peoples into a Single Political Body While Preserving the National Independence of Each.[4] Had he found this problem's correct solution, it would be immensely useful to us today. His solution is simple. It is a new Christianity of science. Each learned society should send one or several deputies to Rome with the power and mission of electing a pope, and immediately upon election the pope should make a proclamation whose text Saint-Simon had prepared, as if he saw himself assured of election.[5] It will then remain only for him to condemn other religions as heretical, and thus assure the triumph of the new Christianity,[6] that is to say of his own Christianity, against Catholicism, Lutheranism, and even Judaism. The truth of Christianity is unquestionable. More than 1,800 years ago, Christianity founded an ethics once and for all, without anyone thereafter having been able to find another foundation. In that, it is divine. Christianity is destined to become the sole universal religion, because its ethics is the most general of all. To be universal, the ethics must be one, and the ethics of Christianity is one, because it rests upon a single principle: "Men should behave as brothers toward others." In short, the new expression of the principle of Christianity includes the whole system of social organization: science, fine arts, industry, and religious feeling.[7]

4. Saint-Simon, *De la réorganisation de la société européenne ou de la necessité et des moyens de rassembler les peuples de l'Europe en un seul corps politique en conservant à chacun son indépendance nationale* (1814). There we find the famous phrase: "The philosophy of the last century was revolutionary. That of the nineteenth century must be organizational" (2:256).

5. Saint-Simon, *Travail sur la gravitation universelle* (1813), conclusion. It is unfortunate that Saint-Simon only wrote a few lines of this papal proclamation (2:249).

6. This is the title of his 1825 work, *Le nouveau Christianisme*. In it Saint-Simon condemns Catholicism, Lutheranism, and Judaism as heretical. Heretical against what? Against true Christianity, which is his own: "I accuse the Pope and his Church of heresy" (3:331); "I accuse the Lutherans" (3:346).

7. "Yes, I believe in God" (ibid., 3:321). Regarding the single principle of Christianity, see 3:322. It remains for it to be generalized and extended to the whole earth; see 3:326–27, 369, 378–79.

Saint-Simon's career is like a sketch of that of Auguste Comte, who begins it anew by perfecting it. Comte had everything necessary to make a success of Saint-Simon's undertaking, if that had been possible: science, outstanding philosophical talent, a sense of organization, and the gift of authority. Like Mohammed, he had no doubt that his work inaugurated a new era in the history of humanity. His *Positivist Calendar for Any Year*, which started with 1789, the year of the revolution and beginning of the great crisis of the West, merits the subtitle Comte himself added: *Practical Picture of the Human Preparation Especially Destined for the Last Transition of the Western Republic Established since Charlemagne by the Free Connection of the Five Advanced Peoples, French, Italians, Spanish, British, and Germans*. The illustrious names that adorn this calendar's months and days are so many reminders of a collective effort as old as Western civilization itself to prepare the advent of a humanity finally united in the knowledge and love of the same truths. All the now familiar themes are there, each in the place that corresponds to it in this order. Charlemagne and medieval Christianity once more provide the pattern for a European republic that offers itself as the seed from which humanity will be born. On the third of the month Dante of the year 66 (Tuesday, July 18, 1854), Comte signed the catalogue of his Positivist Library in 150 volumes. The list of contents of the fourth section, *Synthesis*, in thirty volumes ends with the synthesis of syntheses, the *Positivist Catechism*, but its first four volumes are Aristotle's *Politics* and *Ethics*, the complete Bible, the Koran, and Augustine's *The City of God*. Comte's intellectual evolution recapitulates the historical evolution of the problem. With the simplicity of a blueprint it sets out the abstract conditions of its solution.

Nowadays we hardly ever read the little book where Comte expresses his fundamental intentions with the utmost clarity. Its title alone is a program: *Positivist Catechism or Brief Exposition of the Universal Religion in Thirteen Systematic Conversations between a Woman and* a *Priest of Humanity*. Philosophers do not utilize the literary genre of the catechism frequently, but it becomes necessary when one sets out to found a religion. This was Comte's intent. Published in 1852, the *Catechism* addresses the new religion's simple faithful, as in August 1855 the *Appeal to Conservatives* strives to rally leaders to it. In both instances we are dealing with an atheistic religion, founded and propagated as such by an atheist. In short, this is a religion that, in conformity with the word's very etymology, is no more than a social bond whose only function is to connect.[8]

Like Augustine, whose task Comte starts anew, Comte distinguishes the levels of social reality: *domus*, *urbs*, *orbis*, which he calls *family*, *fatherland*, and *humanity*. At the origin of everything is the family, the elementary domestic society whose social bond is love. It is the most intimate and most perfect society of all, but also the most restricted. Broader, but less intimately united, political societies are superposed upon families. Their principle is the necessity of collective action in view of the common good of their members, and the particular rule that governs this kind of social group is the level of material predominance that stems from this association. In truth, this level includes no theoretical limit. Why would the political body unnecessarily restrict the limits of a power upon which the happiness of its members depends? In fact, the political society naturally tends to grow in a progressive extension based on force with an inclination toward tyranny. By its very nature, it tends to extend itself universally by increasing its strength indefinitely, but Comte's personal notion, which is very acute and totally correct, is that this is an error, because the undertaking is contradictory in its principle. On the one hand, there is a tendency toward a universal society. On the other hand, each particular political body tends itself to become this universal society by im-

8. Auguste Comte, *Catéchisme positiviste, ou sommaire exposition de la religion universelle*, apostolic edition of the Positivist Apostolate (Paris, 1891). This is the year 133 after the Great Crisis, that is to say, the 1789 French Revolution.

posing itself on others by force, as if the resulting material domination and tyranny could be genuine *social* bonds. Both simple and profound, this view of Comte eliminates all past or future attempts to found a universal society on force. An empire does not deserve the label of society.

How can the problem be resolved? It has already been resolved in the past, or at least the principle of its solution has already been found, although its application has never been put into effect. The Middle Ages understood very well that a society of political societies cannot be a political society itself. It can only be a religious society. Therefore, the Middle Ages also understood that a society worthy of the name rests upon common acceptance of a single truth, the only bond capable of linking its members organically. Thus, the fact is that the only means of going beyond political society is to enter into a religious society. Here we are not dealing with an artifice or a palliative to cover up a difficulty. Nor is the issue to recur to some new metaphysics to replace an absent religion. Henceforth, the very essence of religion will be to become a "sociolatry" and to make itself accepted as the only possible social bond. At least in this capacity, it will be absolutely necessary. Humanity will be a religion or it will not be.

Of all the avatars of the City of God, this last one was the least anticipated. Yet it is deduced with geometrical rigor from the data of the problem, as Comte understands them. The issue is not to return to the Middle Ages, which is an irretrievably abolished past. The famous law of the three stages teaches that in its linear, progressive development, the positive spirit successively goes beyond the theological and metaphysical states of thought, and that normally it goes beyond them not to return again. The medieval City of God was tied to the belief in the existence of a God who was the first and last cause of humans. Accordingly, the problem was simple: one God, one truth, one love, and one society, which was none other than the City of God. What happened afterward was simply that this God ceased to exist in the mind of humans. It was not necessary to make him die, but simply that the natural development of the positive spirit made God pass from the state of real being to that of metaphysical principle, before eliminating him completely in benefit of scientific explanation. God was not killed, but left behind. He progressively fell into disuse. The proof of this is furnished by the so-called Course of Positive Philosophy, the sum of general philosophical conclusions founded on science, which will henceforth replace the theology of the Middle Ages and the metaphysics of the seventeenth century in the human mind. No more God or theology, and consequently no more religion or universal society. Such would seem to be Comte's conclusion. The dazzling boldness of his undertaking, even if doomed to failure, is measured by the completely opposite conclusion that he deduces from these premises. Comte wants to pursue the end without the means. Desiring a universal society without God, he concludes that the time has come to inaugurate an atheistic religion to construct the future universal society upon it. Nothing says this more clearly than the *System of Positive Politics*.[9] Whatever we may think of the content that its inventor assigns it, the concept of "positive faith," which is a "demonstrable faith" substituted by Comte for the idea of "theological faith," marvelously illustrates the internal dialectical necessity that controls the solution of the problem. A rigorous proportional analogy imposes itself, if one wishes to construct the City of Man in contrast to the City of God.[10]

If the word could be purged of all pejorative connotations, we would say that Comte's Humanity parodies St. Augustine's City of

9. Auguste Comte, *Système de politique positive*, 2:305. "Positivism today comes to take up again the immense task [namely, that of the Middle Ages] of building, with a suitable doctrine and in a favorable situation, so as to finally determine the definitive formation of the authentic Universal Church. Although this social domain must initially be limited to Western peoples and to those who derive from them, its faith is real enough and complete enough to be equally suited to all parts of the human planet."

10. *Auguste Comte conservateur* (Paris: H. LeSoudier, 1898), 254; this is an extract from his last work, 1851–57.

God. According to the bishop of Hippo, a city was a collection of rational beings united by common love of the same truth and the same good. Comte also places "love as principle" at the origin of the universal society of tomorrow. He is convinced of it: "No human coalition can persist for long if it does not become essentially voluntary." In St. Augustine's Christian City, supernatural faith provides the object of this love. Therefore, we will henceforth have natural faith that includes activity as well as intelligence and feeling to furnish the common truth from which Humanity must live. Only "positive faith that really embraces all human existence will sufficiently link different earthly cities" while waiting the development of the new Church.[11] Positivism will succeed where Christianity could only fail. Positivism too has dogma, but it is demonstrable dogma no less certain than science from which it takes its content. Consequently, this dogma is directly universalizable, or rather it is universal with complete legitimacy. It too disposes of spiritual power, but it is legitimate spiritual power, as the dogma on which it rests is necessary in the eyes of reason. It too can have a priesthood, because just as priests formerly possessed the theological truth of faith, so henceforth Positivist philosophers will possess the doctrinal truth that will make them the guides and leaders of Humanity. Let us add that the new priesthood will not commit the errors of the old priesthood in the area of political and social authority. Respecting the strict distinction between the spiritual and temporal better than was done in the past, the positive priesthood will not govern. It will formulate, teach, and maintain the rules according to which political society will be governed, without needing anything to guarantee its authority other than the spontaneous influence exercised by the doctrine's evidence upon minds and hearts. Understood thus, "spiritual power" will be the prerogative of two groups inseparably united in constant cooperation: first the sages

11. Comte, *Système de politique positive* (Paris: Carilian-Goeury and Victor Dalmont, 1825), 2:306.

or, if we prefer, priests, who possess Positivism's theoretical truth and consequently form its "intellectual power"; second, women enlightened by the priests and exercising the "moral power" that will be justly assigned them. A third social power will be added to these two spiritual powers, the material power in the hands of the mighty and the rich, which will constitute temporal power properly so-called. Thus, force will belong to temporal power. Reason and affection will belong to the spiritual power, although the Positivist society will unite all constructive forces required to build a society worthy of the name in a complete synthesis.

It is hardly necessary to underline the relations of analogy and sometimes parallelisms between medieval Christianity and Positivist Humanity. Comte himself frequently indicated them, not only to pay a debt that he did not dream of repudiating, but also and especially because his Positivism regarded itself as the sole legitimate heir to the past and, therefore, also the sole qualified founder of the future. As Comte himself understood the Middle Ages, they became "the Catholic preparation" of the Positivist era in his mind. Propagation of the Christian faith and worship of the Christian God had only prepared the time when "the true Great Being will worthily occupy the whole human planet."[12] The *Great*

12. Ibid., 2:363. Comte's religion is far from being a simple transposition of Catholicism. Comte does not spare criticism against Catholicism when he thinks that Catholicism deserves it. However, the Catholic Church is certainly what the Positivist Church claims to succeed. The Great Being itself, or Humanity, is a true eternal City, which consists more of the dead than the living, and which includes the future as well as the past. Comte goes so far in this direction that in his doctrine the present can only be conceived in function of the past and of the future (Comte, *Système*, 2:364–65). In the same sense, see: "Positivism limits itself to systematically constructing what the theologian had always established spontaneously" (4:381). "Man becomes uneasy, and Humanity leads him" (2:455). Furthermore, to be convinced of the place Comte himself expected to occupy in history, it suffices to reread his letter of February 28, 1852, to Senator Vieillard: "Next, it is necessary to observe that the new philosophy, which directly reorganizes modern ideas, could fulfill its normal office by leading to the founding of the only religion also capable of reorganizing the corresponding sentiments, the supreme mover of real existence. In a word, the career of St. Paul had to succeed that of Aristotle under pain of ultimately aborting the incomparable mission that I had initially dared to take on." Comte, preface to *Système de politique positive*, 2:xxxi.

Being means the substitute for God in Positivist religion, namely Humanity.

Is Comte living a dream? In his mind it is not a dream. Positivist dogma already exists: it is Comte's philosophy. The priesthood is already represented by the disciples that Comte has won, however few they may be. The high priest of Humanity is completely indicated. He has not been elected. He can be none other than its founder and prophet, he who, after being Aristotle in the first half of his career, has been able to become St. Paul in the second half. The new Church is thus a *de facto* reality, but its leader does not intend to neglect the lessons contained in the history of the old one.

The Church had a pope. Humanity will have a high priest, and, just as there is the collection of Peter's Pence in the Church of our day, Comte foresees the need for a Positivist subsidy. In these matters the high priest of Humanity takes the long view, but he rightly anticipates that there will be considerable expenses. If the sixty thousand gold francs he requests seem to be a generous allowance, let us take note that he already sees himself surrounded by seven "national superiors, that is to say, bishops, without speaking of a hundred thousand priests, vicars, and aspirants, not to mention seminarians," to whose recruitment he looks forward.[13] Like several of his predecessors, Comte dreams of converting the Jesuits. Nothing is more natural. What interest can the Society of Jesus, the Church's most potent support, have in basing itself upon now outmoded dogma? On the contrary, if it replaces its medieval theology by Positivist dogma, it will serve itself by serving the religion of Humanity. The new pope does not intend to waste the spiritual forces that sprang from the religious genius of St. Ignatius Loyola.[14]

13. There are three priestly ranks: aspirants, age twenty-eight, vicars or substitutes, age thirty-five, and priests, age forty-two (Comte, *Catéchisme positive*, 268). A priest ought to earn 12,000 gold francs, "plus the compensations for the diocesan circuit" (270). Each "philosophical presbytery consists of seven priests and three vicars" (270). Marriage is obligatory for priests.

14. *Auguste Comte Conservateur*, 256: "In the Instructions that you desire in this

This new ecclesiastical hierarchy will possess doctrinal authority. Its head will be able to speak with the force given his words by the certainty of expressing demonstrated truths. A dogma is most justified when it no longer rests on faith but on knowledge. There is no freedom of thought in mathematics. Why then would the new Church tolerate rebellion against the truth? As Comte reproduces Campanella in his appeal to the Jesuits, he renews Campanella in his denunciation of Protestants, those dissidents by vocation, whose essential opposition to all dogmatism is a constant threat to the doctrinal unity without which any social unity worthy of the name is impossible. The new dogmatism of Positivist reason claims all the prerogatives of dogmatism of the Christian faith to which it is heir. From the opening of the preface that Comte wrote for his *Positivist Catechism*, the new pope has no scruple in exercising his right to exclude from the new Church heretics, schismatics, and generally speaking all rebels whatsoever, whose dissidence threatens the unity of Humanity. Even the punishments are foreseen, classified, and ordered hierarchically, from domestic reproof for private faults on up to public reprimand and, if necessary, temporary or permanent "social excommunication" for the more serious public offenses. The Positivist religion does not hesitate in the face of a system of prohibitions.[15]

---

regard, I recommend to you special contact with the Jesuits who, from every point of view, are the best instruments and defenders of Catholicism. They must be spontaneously purged in New York of the vices that the hope of dominating inspires in them at Paris. Among Catholics they are the ones best able to appreciate Positivism's talent for the reconstruction of the spiritual power vainly attempted by the founder of Jesuitism." Moreover, that is why, just as Comte de-Christianizes Catholicism, he de-Jesuitizes the Jesuits. He calls them *Ignatians*, which "delivers them from a name as vicious in itself as it is generally discredited." Inversely, *Protestantism* is a synonym of *anarchy* (259).

15. Indeed, here Comte reproduces the excommunication already pronounced October 19, 1851, after a summary of five hours, at the close of his third *Cours philosophique sur l'histoire générale de l'Humanité*. Here is the text: "In the name of the past and of the future, the theoretical and practical servants of Humanity come to assume worthily the general supervision of earthly affairs in order to construct finally the true moral, intellectual, and material providence by irrevocably excluding from political supremacy all the different slaves of God, Catholics, Protestants, and deists, as being simultaneously both backward

This is to say that by making itself rational, the faith guarantees us the right to exercise totalitarian authority. Henceforth no order of social life will escape the priesthood's influence, because the priesthood will furnish art as it will furnish science. There was great religious art in the Middle Ages. In a society where the spiritual power controls all intellectual production, whose monopoly it possesses *de facto*, all art and all literature will be religious from now on. To be brief, let us say that once the life of each human is put at the service of the Great Being, it will be entirely devoted to its worship. As Positivist religion has its calendar and its saints, it has private worship, with morning, noon, and evening prayer.[16] It has the sacraments, and not just seven but nine.

A short time after birth, *presentation* informs Humanity of its future member's arrival into the world. At the age of fourteen comes *initiation* into the service of Humanity. At twenty-one *admission* to serve Humanity is observed. At the age of twenty-eight *destination* marks the choice of a career. Around thirty there is *marriage*, a commitment that is irrevocable and indissoluble, even after the spouse's demise.[17] At forty-two *maturity* is celebrated, marking the moment at which the servant of Humanity attains the fullness of his or her social development. *Retirement* at sixty-three is the moment when a human freely renounces his practical activity and thereafter only expects an advisory role. The next to last

---

and disruptive" (Comte, *Catéchisme positiviste*, 1). The expression "slaves of God" makes it clear that in spite of everything, there is a component shared by Comte's Positivism and the dialectical materialism that descends from Feuerbach. This is human rebellion against God. It is not just atheism but antitheism.

16. Comte, *Système de politique positive*, 4:114–18; see 4:120–21 on "sociolatry," as well as Comte, *Catèchisme positiviste*, 107–11.

17. Comte seriously examined the problem of mixed marriages. While awaiting the general triumph of the new religion, he provisionally authorizes marriages between Positivists, on the one hand, and monotheists, polytheists, or even fetishists, on the other. Of course, mixed marriage is only permitted "to any Positivist liberated enough from earlier religions to participate passively in any of their ceremonies without any deceitful adherence" (Comte, *Système de politique positive*, 4:408–10). The conversion of a spouse to Positivism is an outcome that can always be hoped for.

sacrament is *transformation*, to replace the horrible ceremony of Catholic funerals, as if Comte did not perceived that he is drawing from the Church's *vita mutatur non tollitur* the very protest that he raises against it. In the course of this ceremony, to console those close to the deceased, they are made to hope for the deceased person's solemn *incorporation* into Humanity. This is the object of the final sacrament, administered seven years after death of someone worthy of it.[18]

Propagation of the positive path poses problems even for the religion of Humanity, but Comte has some notion of what its future will be. He knows that time works for him. The necessary development of the positive spirit, which reaches maturity in the works of Humanity's first high priest, guarantees the undertaking's future success. Sooner or later, but rather sooner, if institutions are organized with a view to favoring Positivism's progress, Positivism will conquer the government of societies as it conquered those of nature, and the new religion will spread in proportion to the progress of the positive spirit in the world. The nucleus of the future society already exists, and that is what we saw described by the subtitle of the *Positivist Calendar*. It is the Western Republic that includes France, Italy, Spain, England, and Germany. Comte is aware of the existence of the United States, where he had even thought of going in his youth, but he was not able to find a distinct spiritual existence for the United States. Benjamin Franklin, the modern Socrates, has Comte's complete admiration, but Franklin is a European. As for Russia, whose "noble Tsar" Comte respects, it inspires Comte with more fear than confidence. Comte dreads a new political universalism from that quarter, whose capital would be St. Petersburg. We can only say that it suffices to read Moscow instead of St. Petersburg for Comte to have been completely right.

18. See Comte, *Catéchisme positiviste*, 111–21, for his sacramental system of the religion of Humanity. See 124 on the future temples to the Great Being, all oriented toward Paris. For the plan of the grand temple of humanity with its system of schools and scientific collections, see 394–96.

As every political society needs a capital, what will be the capital of Humanity? The answer is a matter of history. After he poses the problem, Comte falls back into the rut traced through the centuries that every historian of Western civilization naturally follows. In his turn, and no doubt quite spontaneously, Comte takes up the old medieval theme *de translatione studii*. First there was Athens, then Rome, from which civilization was transferred to Paris. It has been there since the Middle Ages. Therefore, *de facto*, Paris is the capital of the Western Republic. At least for the present it is the capital, but even at present, this fact involves a serious difficulty in Comte's view. At the same time that Paris is the seat of the Western Republic's spiritual power, it is the political capital of France. We know that Comte insists on a strict distinction of spiritual and temporal powers. He does not care to see the high priest of Humanity threatened in his spiritual independence by the chief of State's political power. He will have none of that! If Paris must choose between remaining the capital of France and becoming the Rome of the Western Republic, Comte does not doubt for an instant that the choice is obvious. So, behold him decentralizing France and cutting it into seventeen provinces. To use his own language, Comte submits France to "political decomposition" needed for "religious reorganization." How could Paris hesitate between remaining the political capital of France and becoming the religious capital of Humanity? Still, even this was not to be the final state of the project. As Comte grew old, he shut himself up more and more in the logic of his dream, at the same time one of the most unreal and the most lucid that a philosopher has ever conceived. Humanity, in which he already lives and that equals the ends of the earth in his mind, could not have a city indefinitely for its capital as western as the present capital of France. Thus Comte foresees the future transfer of the capital from Paris to Constantinople.[19] In his imagination he already sees the earth covered by

19. Through a calculation that recalls the computations of Christian theologians

Positivist temples surrounded by cloisters where the future priests of Humanity are peacefully initiated into the principles of the new religion, preparing themselves for their task as spiritual directors of the world. However, the first and best disciples of Comte were disturbed by a spiritual evolution that led them so far from the positive science from which it had started. Émile Littré, John Stuart Mill, and still others, one after another deserted a cause that they no longer recognized as theirs. Indeed, Comte speaks henceforth of something other than the philosophical synthesis of the science that he had initially promised and procured for them. He has just achieved the final metamorphosis of the City of God into an Earthly City where man is at the same time god and priest, and where he adores himself in the manner that reason demands.

This time the experiment has been carried out with such perfect rigor that it can be considered conclusive. If the universal society, born of religion, returns to religion in Auguste Comte's Positivism, it is because between Augustine and Comte everything else has been tried in turn and tried in vain. There is no longer a Positivist Church, and its founder's dream died with him. Neither the Aristotelian Scholasticism offered by Dante nor the metaphysical theology of Campanella, nor Leibniz's theological metaphysics, nor Comte's scientific philosophy provided the universal society with the bond that the Christian wisdom of faith had immediately offered it from the time of Augustine. It remains for us to draw a lesson from this experience that is already twenty centuries old. It may be, and this would not be the only case, that in seeking a universal society only by the ways of which humans without God dispose, our contemporaries desire a Christian end without desiring the Christian means. The lesson would be simple, therefore: unless we resign ourselves once more to the false unity of some empire founded on force or of a pseudo-society without a common

---

about the ages of the world, Comte "presumes that this final revolution will take place in seven centuries" (*Catéchisme positiviste*, 398).

bond of minds and hearts, it is necessary either to renounce the ideal of a universal society or to seek again the common bond in Christian faith. There can be a City of Man, and it will not be made without politicians, jurists, scholars, and philosophers, but still less will it be made without the Church and theologians.

TEN

The Church and Universal Society

THE ELEMENTS of this problem, whose evolution over time we have followed, are neither numerous nor difficult to recognize, but because they are constantly mixed up with the elements of different problems, it would be useful to classify them. In the first place, this whole account supposes that the Augustinian definition of a people is true, and even the only true definition, at least in its meaning, whatever terms are used to express it. To admit the truth of the definition does not imply that all the human groups that we call peoples satisfy the requirements of this definition. Very few humans are united by their common love of really identical goods, but they form a people only in the measure in which they are. The mineral, vegetable, or animal kingdoms are only metaphors. Society properly speaking only begins with reason, and consequently with humans. Physical force is certainly a bond, but it is not a social bond. There is a society only where the harmony of minds and hearts binds the individuals and persons together. Accordingly, those for whom harmony is the bond form a people.

This history further supposes that Christianity has revealed the idea of a religious society founded on faith in Jesus Christ, open to humans of every race and every country, provided only that they live from faith. St. Augustine names this people the City of God, whose laborer in time and in this world is the Church of Christ. This City of God, which includes the dead and those who are yet to be born as well as the living, exactly satisfies the definition of a people, because it is born of a common love for a common good known identically thanks to the perfect unity of faith.

In this sense, the problem of the City of God is mixed up in practice for us with the problem of the Church, whose peculiar function is to lead humans to the kingdom of Christ, which is the kingdom of heaven. No citizen of this City of God belongs to the Earthly City, which is its antithesis, but all belong to some temporal city. Accordingly, each human has a dual allegiance, if we may speak this way.[1] The fact that one is natural and the other supernatural does not eliminate the problem, because, by including a Christian people within the temporal sphere, the Church does not eliminate time. It creates a people in time whose temporal behavior is that of a Christian people. The practices common to peoples by the fact that they are Christians constitute Christian civilization. The collection of peoples united by their love of Christian civilization's common good constitutes Christendom.

One of the most curious aspects of the problem is that, up to the present, it has remained on the fringes, so to speak, of theology strictly understood. It is not a classical question, similar to those we are sure of finding in any commentary on the *Sentences* or in a summa of theology, questions whose placement in such works can even be predicted accurately. St. Bonaventure, St. Thomas Aquinas, Duns Scotus, and William of Ockham all have a definite doctrine about the relations of temporal and spiritual powers or about empire and papacy. However, our problem, that of the City of God on its pilgrimage through time with its possible consequences for the organization of the earth, the political unification of the

1. The comment holds indifferently for all humans, because those who do not belong to the City of God by that very fact are citizens of the *Civitas Terrena*, whose impact upon the temporal sphere is no less visible and no less powerful than that of the Heavenly City. That has never been clearer than it is today. Marxism is the most sustained effort the world has ever known to establish the perfect coincidence of the temporal city and the Earthly City. It actively prepares the reign of the Anti-Christ. The Church's jurisdiction over the temporal realm has precisely the goal of preventing him from putting it at the service of the Earthly City and, instead, has the goal of putting it at the service of the City of God. St. Thomas's doctrine in *De Regimine Principum*, regarding the hierarchical subordination of the temporal to the Church, defines its basis with perfect clarity: it is a subordination of means to end.

globe, and the advent of a temporal era of justice and peace, generally remain in the background of Christian speculation, although we see it burst forth in the work of rare visionaries like Roger Bacon and Dante.

Yet it is certainly tied to another problem whose central place within theology cannot be ignored, that of faith and its propagation among humans. Insofar as it is theological, this problem escapes the philosopher's competence and even more the historian's. The only thing the latter can do is to observe the way in which it is posed. This is the huge theological problem of apologetics, and it is not simple. Reduced to its essential elements, it comes down to knowing how a truth of faith can be universalized, a truth that essentially transcends the power of demonstrative reason. On the one hand, God has given to his apostles and to their successors the mission to teach all nations. On the other hand, this teaching with which they are charged is faith in the Son of God and hope of his kingdom, by promising them, furthermore, that he will be with them in their labors until the consummation of time. The task has lasted twenty centuries, and those who preach the Gospel are faced with the same difficulties. It is good, right, and necessary to accumulate reasons for believing. It is possible to demonstrate that humans ought to believe the word of God. It is possible to show what the word of God is, and that what it teaches is either rationally true or rationally possible. Certain theologians like Anselm and Duns Scotus claim to be able to give necessary demonstrations of its possibility. However, ultimately, faith is not naturally transmittable by simple rational demonstrations. It does not stem from a simple assent to evidence of intellectual knowledge, but from consent in which the will takes part, and this is precisely why the problem is posed of finding how to universalize it.

First let us be sure of this point. If there is a theologian whose confidence in reason is beyond doubt, it is certainly St. Thomas Aquinas. His *Summa Contra Gentiles* I.6 contains an exposition of the motives that lead to reason's acceptance of truths that exceed it. Christianity does not conquer by force of arms like Islam. It does not seduce men with the promise of pleasure. It summons them to a concept of the world and love of invisible things for which it asks them to renounce everything that human consent ordinarily involves and even, if necessary, to suffer persecution for the truth. In short, Christianity would have had all odds against it, if God had not supported the preaching of it by miraculous deeds that surpass the natural means of which humans dispose. By this proof that it was God who spoke, God proves at the same time that it is reasonable to believe in the truth of his word, even when the evidence of this truth escapes natural reason. If we add to that a miracle still more surprising than the cure of the sick or resurrection of the dead—the divine infusion of the gifts of the Holy Spirit instantly filling simple, uneducated minds with eloquence and wisdom—we understand how an innumerable multitude of the ignorant and the learned has embraced the Christian religion. Still, assent based on a miracle is itself a miracle. It is even, St. Thomas says, the greatest miracle, this sight of mortal minds giving their assent to the Christian faith whose teaching exceeds the grasp of the human understanding, restrains carnal pleasures, and teaches us to despise the visible things of the world in order to aspire to the invisible: *quibus animos mortalium assentire et maximum miraculum est et manifestum divinae inspirationis opus*. This whole development is a commentary on Hebrews 2:3. It is in perfect harmony with the constant teaching of St. Thomas on the nature of faith: *fides non habet inquisitionem rationis naturalis demonstrantis id quod creditur.*[2] Lastly, the development simply takes up what has been the Church's perennial teaching since St. Paul: *fides est non apparentium* (Heb 11:1). Moreover, this is why faith is religiously meritorious. There is no merit in recognizing what can be demonstrated.

This nature of faith is at the root of our problem. It imposes

2. *Summa Theologiae* II-II, q. 2, a. 1, ad 1.

the literally superhuman task on the laborers of the City of God of obtaining from human understanding the acceptance of a truth that is not naturally demonstrable. Not only is faith not transmissible by way of simple rational demonstration, but also, precisely as faith, it does not even involve search: *non habet inquisitionem rationis naturalis demonstrantis id quod creditur*. Faith is not search but peace in adherence to the word of God. The great Scholastics were not misled on this. All their effort of intellection moved within faith and mystery that none among them wanted to empty. Their theology was search, but a search that would have had no object without the peace of faith. This is why to defend and propagate faith by theology seemed to them to be the only possible way of constructing a city common to all humanity, the only universal society about which they had a clear idea was neither the Republic of believers, nor of Christendom, but of the Church. Their position is still sound today, and it remains the only one that is clear as well as true. The Church is the earthly Jerusalem that prepares, within time, the achievement of the heavenly Jerusalem. It is the perfect society that forms Christians precisely as Christians, in short, the only society whose very essence is to be Christian. If other types of societies exist that claim the title of "Christian," they all presuppose the Church, which does not presuppose any of them herself. She is the integral Christian society, sufficient unto herself and complete by definition.

From that it follows that any project of a Christian Republic, extending the boundaries of the Church to the temporal realm, postulates the prior existence and acknowledgement of the Church. We say *of the Church* and not *of a church*, because if this society desires to be universal and if it desires to be one, it must be an extension into the temporal realm of one and the same church from which it takes its unity.

Even that is not enough. To take its unity from the Church, every society that invokes the Church must accept its religious jurisdiction and with greater reason its moral jurisdiction, that is to say, a jurisdiction extended to the wider temporal order in the measure that problems of morality are posed there. These are not the only problems posed there, but they are posed in every order: in regard to the political and social order whose tranquility is called *peace*; in regard to war, which can be just or unjust, but which never escapes the rules of law and ethics; in regard to governments and their subjects, none of whom is above the laws of God nor above the duties that these laws impose on them. Whether this jurisdiction is called direct or indirect hardly matters at bottom provided that it is acknowledged in some terms and in the spirit in which St. Thomas Aquinas defines it: in spiritual matters, it is better to obey the pope; in temporal matters it is better to obey the prince, but better still the pope, who occupies the summit of the two orders.[3] The sense of these words is clear. The spiritual realm is not subject to the temporal realm. The prince, who has authority in the temporal realm, has none in the spiritual realm. But temporal is subject to the spiritual. The pope, who has authority in the spiritual realm, therefore also has authority in the temporal realm in any measure in which the latter falls under the spiritual. The formula is simple and it suffices to apply it to see that it involves a precise meaning. The pope is not the temporal sovereign of any of the people of the earth, but has sovereign authority of the manner in which all people conduct their politics.[4] As vicar of Christ the

3. *In II Sententiarum*, d. 44, exposition of the text, ad 4.

4. Innumerable misunderstandings continually spring up on this point, as the elements at issue are complex. On the one hand, the pope is not king, president, or prime minister of any particular people. Insofar as the politics of a people is a collection of temporal means utilized with a view to temporal goods, the pope "does not do politics." But this does not mean that he "is not concerned with politics," a manifestly false proposition (recall Leo XIII and his policy of rallying in France) and furthermore absurd. This does not even mean that the pope's action upon politics is only indirect. It is absolutely direct and immediate, but it is of a different order. The pope exercises a direct action on politics, like grace on nature and faith on reason. And as this action upon the temporal order can only be exercised in the temporal order, politics of the Church must exist, conducted in the world by the Church in the person of the Supreme Pontiff, effectively acting as

king, the pope judges all peoples in Christ's name and in virtue of Christ's authority.

It is easy to foresee what reaction awaits words like these. Before fighting with phantasms, this answer should be understood in function of the problem whose historical elements we have already studied. Even if the Church had the power, it would not desire to recur to it to suppress other religions; *non violentia* says St. Thomas (*Summa Contra Gentiles* I.6). Preaching by arms does not befit the Prince of Peace. Likewise the Church does not dream of imposing her jurisdiction upon the temporal order by violence or trickery. The Church lacks the means for that, and if it had them, they would in no way serve the Church's ends.[5] We are deal-

---

sovereign. What maintains the distinction of orders is not that the Church's jurisdiction is "indirect." It is that it directly bears upon the temporal order with a view to a non-temporal end, and that it intervenes in the politics of peoples with a view to results that are *specifically* different from those that the peoples themselves immediately envisage with what they call *politics*. This is why the means of its political action are different. The Church's effective power in the world ultimately rests on the extension and depth of faith.

5. It seems inappropriate to us to describe the Church's authority over the temporal order as "indirect." Moreover, it is not necessary to safeguard the distinction of the temporal and the spiritual, which is the distinction between nature and grace viewed in one of its particular aspects. Grace does not suppress nature. Revelation does not suppress reason. The Church does not suppress the State. The pope does not dispossess Caesar: grace restores and perfects nature in all orders, precisely because it is not nature itself. It does not grant *esse*, it confers *bene esse*. That is why, even if it is the people who are Caesar, the pope has the right of direct government over it. But the pope does not govern like Caesar. To take Pascal's expression, "that is a different and higher order." This is precisely the cause of the visible exasperation that the different candidates for the world empire feel toward the Church. The political and temporal effects of Rome's jurisdiction stem from a cause that, precisely because it is neither political nor temporal, escapes them. They possess weapons of physical force that can ravage Christianity and vex the Church. Ultimately, they have no power against faith. For faith also is of a different, higher order. Without introducing a definition whose intention is healthy but whose basis is doubtful, we understand thus that religion circulates throughout all of politics and regulates it from within without being mixed up with it. "Subjiciens ei principatus et postestates," we read on Good Friday in the Mass of the Pre-Sanctified. What the Church prays for is the same as what she desires. The issue is not to grant unto Caesar what is Caesar's, but to understand that what is Caesar's belongs first to God. No simple formula suffices to define this point. Recently, it was said: the State is not an instrument at the Church's service, and inversely. This thinking is probably healthy, but the expression lets the reality it attempts to express escape on all sides. The State is an instrument in the service of the Church's

ing with something different. Here we address those who are more numerous than is thought and who would like to construct the universal society whose concept the Church has revealed to the world, without accepting the uniqueness of the Church or acknowledging its jurisdiction. Nothing obliges them to desire such a society, but if they want it, and do so rightly as an end that is desirable in itself, they must also will the means. It is neither violence nor intolerance to insist that it is simply contradictory to will an end without willing the means.

Yet this is what happens in our times. In October 1933, in Philadelphia, at the closing session of the Sixth Catholic Congress of the Episcopal Church, Bishop William T. Manning of New York forcefully declared:

> Men's minds are open to the ideal of the One, Catholic, and Universal Church as witnessing to the Unity of Humanity. No religion that is sectarian, or provincial, or local, or merely individualistic, can now satisfy either the hearts or the imagination of men.... It is the ideal of the world-wide Catholic Church, the Divine Society of which Christ is the Head and One Cornerstone, which alone is great enough to meet the visions and longings of the present time.

---

religious goods. Whether the State itself admits that, this is what it is for the Church. Inversely, it is absolutely true that the Church is not an instrument in the service of the State; but it is no less true that because the Church itself serves a higher goal than that of the State, the State needs the Church, which makes it better, even if the Church does not do the State a "service." This is why the Church's religious jurisdiction, without changing nature at all, has direct political impacts. It cannot be exercised over the temporal order without having such impacts. For the same reason, there are no grounds for hope that those who deny the existence of the supernatural and religious order would accept that the Church's religious authority over the temporal order is not *essentially* political. Since for them everything is essentially political, the jurisdiction exercised by the pope is political by definition. For example, if the pope forbids voting for Communists, every Communist will see political intervention in a religious decision whose direct impact on politics is obvious. The Communist will be mistaken in fact as well as in principle. An error that is unavoidable as long as a false perspective lasts is still an error. We have already said that the truth seems to be that the Church never *does* politics, but that it occupies itself with politics always and rightly. The Church has direct religious authority over politics by reason of its moral and religious implication, that is to say, according to the traditional formula, insofar as politics involves faith and morality directly or indirectly.

Who among us would not approve such words?[6] Except that these words must not be separated from the commentary. There is no question at all, a spokesman of the same Church declared immediately, of reunion with Rome under the pope's authority. "There can be no complete reunion with Rome," said Bishop George Craig Stewart of Chicago, "until Rome surrenders its postulate, which is that unless you are in communion with Rome, you are not a Catholic." In short, the first condition required for a universal religious society to be possible is that the only Church that is one should first renounce its being by abdicating its unity.

We are not dealing with a dialectical refutation here, and we hope this will be perceived. Its effectiveness would be middling, as usual. It is useless to desire to make a response to one's interlocutor to which the interlocutor himself would have no response, because there is always a response. The only important thing is to search with the interlocutor for an answer to his own question. Without a Christian truth, there could be neither a Christian Church nor a Christian society. Without a truth that is one, there could not be a Church that is one or a Christian society that is genuinely one. In the *de facto* discussion in which we are situated, mutual tolerance of Churches is an excellent thing, but it would be better that there should be no opportunity to exercise it. In any case tolerance cannot pass for union, still less for unity. We cannot want jurisdiction without wanting one jurisdiction and accepting authority. "The imperative duty of Protestantism," says a Protes-

6. We take these texts from the *New York Times* (October 27, 1933): "Dr. Manning Says One Church Is Needed." [Translator: The complete text of Bishop Manning's talk, "The Future of the Kingdom," which was delivered on October 26, 1933, is available at anglicanhistory.org/usa/wtmanning/future1933.html.] "We are not going to bring politics into religion," continues Bishop Manning, "but we are going to bring religion into politics and into the whole of life. It is for us to show that membership in the Holy, Catholic Church is a matter not only of theology and theory but of life and service." Certainly, but how will we get a "catholic" church if there is no agreement about theology and theory? The Congress's office and two bishops were not mistaken in declaring the next day, according to the same newspaper, that the movement's goal was not "reunion with Rome under the Pope's spiritual authority." There might have been uncertainty about that.

tant, "is world peace. If it will not tolerate such a jurisdiction as Hildebrand's, which is certainly the case, then in God's name, let it suggest a more efficient jurisdiction of its own."[7] Yes, but if Protestantism is incapable of suggesting one, let it renounce achieving the spiritual and temporal unity of the world, or else, for the love of heaven, let it accept Hildebrand's jurisdiction.

Therefore, if a lesson emerges about the history of the City of God and the avatars it has assumed during the course of the centuries, it is, first of all, that it cannot be metamorphosized. But it is also that every attempt to usurp its title and goal can bring misfortune to the human societies that claim to realize it on earth. What is common to these attempts is the substitution of a human bond for the bond of faith, like philosophy or science. This occurs in the hope that that human bond will be universalized more easily than faith and that thereby the birth of a universal society will be facilitated. The operation regularly results in failure. It is important to know and say this in a time when so many generous spirits strive to give meaning to notions as important as those of *Europe* or *Humanity*. Nothing is more legitimate than the ideal whose name each of them bears, but these are temporal projects, which is to say they are not exclusively material but conceived with a view to guaranteeing that humans have more happiness in this life and, first of all, have peace, which is the condition for everything else. This time we are certainly dealing with peace as the world gives it, or at least which we might wish the world knew better how to give.

Whatever its form may be some day, Europe can never be more than a geographic, economic, political, and social reality even if the peoples who composed Europe should be as fruitful in spiritual accomplishments in the future as they were in the past. Even more fruitful if possible, and above all, let us hope, happier, though it would be imprudent to burden its notion with mystical

7. S. Parkes Cadman, *Christianity and the State* (New York: Macmillan, 1924), 327. See particularly chap. 9, "The Challenge to Protestantism."

sense that nothing destines it to contain. We know what Europe is when we know its structures and political frontiers. It will always be dangerous to hold up this real Europe as a sort of temporal Church, creator and possessor of a kind of universal truth that alone can unify humans. The peoples of Europe have been powerful transformers and multipliers of spiritual goods that they have received from everywhere, from ancient Chaldea and fabled Egypt to Palestine, things that cannot belong to them as their own because they are universal by right. What is true in America is also true in Europe, in whatever order of truth we deal with. What is beautiful in Europe is also beautiful in America, whatever the art we are dealing with. It would be lamentable that the birth of Europe should be the occasion of a new nationalism of things of the spirit, a little broader spatially, but no more intelligent than the old one. It would be still more lamentable that we should be satisfied by the new myth of the "European Person," with which we are threatened, without having much idea how to define that person other than, as is proposed without irony, by the dual contrast to the Russian Person and the American Person. The more firmly we want a political Europe the more it is important not to make it into a spiritual chimera.[8] We must be resigned in advance: the European Person will be one among all others, without spiritual privileges and who is worth exactly what he is. In good as in evil, everything done in Europe will be similarly European.

Needless to say, Europe itself can only be born as one of the world's countries among others. The confused aspiration of our contemporaries toward "one world," so strongly expounded by Wendell Wilkie in his book, is a sure sign that the earth is in labor

8. In desperation, it has recently been proposed to define the European as the person of contradiction, symbolized by the broken cross. The symbol is imported from Asia. Still, let us acknowledge that this definition is irrefutable. How can we make it clear that any notion whatsoever of European is false, if the more contradictory it is, the more applicable it is? Unfortunately, it is impossible to verify that whose very inconsistency removes it from refutation.

to give birth to its unity. This birth will not be accomplished without pains. It would not be wise to multiply the pains unrestrainedly by involving ourselves ahead of time in deadend streets. The worst error would be to imagine Europe or even Humanity as a perfection of the concept of universal Church or as the authentic City of God. Whatever the manner in which they are organized and united, temporal societies always form a society that is only temporal itself, more vast but the same in nature. Nothing is more certain than that this society has spiritual bonds and that certain of the bonds have universal value. Science, art, letters, law, philosophy, and even so much technology, which we would like to hope will become less and less pernicious and more and more human, are so many forces that by their spiritual nature and their universal scope continually unite humans more and more closely. But the size of a society does not change its essence. To be other than an agglomeration of peoples more or less empirically prevented from doing each other mutual harm, a society must live upon one truth. To become *one* people itself, it must achieve the definition posited by St. Augustine: a collection of human beings sharing in the love of one and the same good.[9]

9. Without much hope of avoiding confusions that are inevitable in any case, we will still express the wish that we not be taken to deny things that we do not affirm and that we do not have to affirm, because they are not pertinent to our subject. We have not undertaken to show in what temporal conditions a European or human society is possible, but to underline its Christian condition, which, if rejected or forgotten, makes that society impossible. Far from minimizing the importance of juridical, political, economic, industrial, and financial techniques, we judge that they are primary necessities. This is still truer of the unifying force of temporal universalization of natural truth in every order. On the contrary, we have often lamented seeing the urgent task of their technical organization sacrificed to their subtle exploitation by old or new nationalisms that utilize them with a view to their own goals or to chimeras whose pursuit leads away from the authentic goal. If the body were prepared first, it would certainly find its soul. Yet ultimately, the religious condition remains necessary for the success of the undertaking. In any case, the undertaking will surely never be complete. By the very fact that it is a harmony and therefore entails consent, a people can refuse to belong to it. Even beyond those who reject the undertaking, it does not authentically integrate those who only enter it passively: stones of the city that are not living rock. But, the temporal city will be precisely universalized all the more surely and will become all the more genuinely "a people," in the measure in

What will this good be? If the history of the avatars of the notion of City of God since the Middle Ages has meaning, it signifies that outside the universalism of faith, a universalism of reason capable of replacing faith has not been found. As paradoxical as it may be, the result of the experiment is clear: even where reason divides, faith unites. Is it even a paradox? With no exceptions, the theologians teach that the truth of the word of God is more certain and more infallible than even the best-established certainties of natural reason. If we are alert here, what presents itself as a *de facto* paradox at the empirical level of history appears as a *de jure* truth on the transcendent level of theology. It is not surprising but necessary that when reasons touch upon the highest intelligible things, whose knowledge is the ultimate goal of human beings, then perfect, stable harmony depends on a supernatural light that unites them. Therefore, it is no longer surprising but necessary that the harmony of human beings in the love of the temporal human common good, insofar as natural reason permits us to know and attain it, never engenders more than a society that is certainly real but lives in a provisional order and is endowed with imperfect unity. In the measure in which, as we hope, the human society of tomorrow is achievable, it not only must not take itself to be a Church but must accept from the Church the perfect unity toward which it tends and that it is incapable of giving itself.

Should we forget that, behold the procession of ancient answers that already returns before our eyes, twenty times tried, twenty times refuted by the facts, and yet always the same. We are offered a universal empire as in the time of Alexander the Great, Napoleon, or still others that we knew afterward. It is not completely certain that empires are totally harmful or even useless. Several of them have contributed their share in lessening the

---

which it is more completely ordered to the end of the Church, which is the City of God. It can be feared that the temporal city rejects this. In this case it will continue to be sought in vain throughout false orders and false unities. In short, it will continue to tend to be without ever coming to exist.

earth's political fragmentation, even if at the cost of great suffering, and nothing proves that their time has past. Except that if it is rather difficult to foresee the choice of destiny, we know better how the adventure will turn out once began. Even James Burnham, who recently proposed an "American World Empire," that is to say a "world federation created and directed by the United States," clearly sees, on the one hand, that the "Russian World Federation" is likewise an open possibility, and on the other hand that even a world empire as generously minded as that of the Americans and which at the start would only be "a people's protective association" could degenerate into a tyrannical despotism on the part of the initially protecting nation. Whether we are dealing with a simple possibility, as is the case here, or with an absolute certainty, as is the case of the Russian empire, the result ultimately would remain the same. There would be an empire, that is to say submission to power, not a union of hearts and therefore a society.[10] The last known attempt to define a truth common to all humans and to make love of it as the bond of a genuine society was made by

10. After reflecting for a long time, it did not seem evident to us that Marxism was part of the history of our problem. Insofar as Marx's universal society is the City of Man erected against the City of God, its universal society not only adds nothing to Comte's atheism but also, upon analysis, reveals itself to be incomparably poorer in content. Assuredly, Marx's universal society is another sign of the times, and as such the idea is worthy of study, but it would add nothing to what we already know. Furthermore, and above all, Marx's dialectical materialism is completely foreign, in fact as in principle, to the great tradition of a spiritual society founded solely on the acknowledgment of one and the same truth by humans communicating in the same love. Persuaded, following Condorcet, that the progress of humanity is ultimately inevitable, Marx, however, does not see its cause in optimistic Enlightenment philosophy, but in the efficacy of necessary economic laws. Our blunders may delay the effects of those laws, but they cannot ultimately prevent them. It is no longer spirit that leads but matter. Whether we admit Marx's doctrine or not, his own Marxism ends on the vision of humanity bound by finally conscious submission to the same determinism, less different from the Stoic acceptance of the cosmos than is believed; none of those whom we have examined, from Augustine to Comte, would call that a society. Comte held that Positivism was the only effective antidote to Communism. Let us add that from Lenin to Stalin, Marxism has only slipped down the slope of political imperialism. At the date on which we write these lines, the candidates to the universal empire are found in Moscow.

Auguste Comte.[11] This does not prove that Comte's attempt must remain the last, but because the truth to which he appeals is that of positive science, it is difficult to imagine that natural reason could henceforth propose a bond whose universality was more strictly natural. What makes Comtism a definitive experiment is that in order to extract a social bond for it, its author previously had to organize the objective truths of science in function of a subjective principle. Positivism's founder explicitly demonstrated that what is called *absolute* or *pure Positivism* today is impossible. He thereby demonstrated that the science of things cannot be the unifying truth of humans or the bond of their society.

Accordingly, it remains that in the measure in which the temporal society of humans will occur, it will never be achieved except as an image of the perfect, supernatural society that is the City of God. Through St. Augustine, the Church first proposed to human beings the ideal of a society of the children of God, united to him and among themselves by the bonds of faith, hope, and charity. Indeed, they told themselves, it is the only society worthy of the name, but we are going to make it ourselves on this earth with a view to humans and by their own means. We know the result.

11. We say: a society founded on the same love for the same truth. This is a point that must be understood, because recent writings signed by philosophers take as admitted that the Church and Marxism are "totalitarianisms" of the same kind. There is no substance to that for the simple reason that the Church's end differs from that of the State, as well as its means, as we have said. Nothing makes this more apparent than their respective attitude on the subject of doctrinal truth. The truth of Christianity makes and maintains the Church whereas for the time that the States and parties last, they make and maintain the truth of the doctrine that they use. Precisely because they appeal to temporal truths the artifact explodes in plain view. Nowhere is this more visible than in the case of Marxism, become Leninism and then Stalinism, which still claims to be the same "scientific" truth to which *The Communist Manifesto* appealed more than one hundred years ago. If it is the same truth, we are in the presence of a unique phenomenon in the history of modern times: a "scientific" system that is a hundred years old and yet still true. The concept of religious dogma has meaning, and it is because it is religious. By being eternal, it is unchangeably imposed upon the faithful who serve it. The very concept of scientific dogma is absurd, and that is why, instead of serving it, its faithful must impose it in order to be served by it. The Party is not right because its doctrine is true. The doctrine is true because the Party is always right.

Moreover, St. Augustine foresaw it. It is called *Babel* or *confusion*. It is the typical case of those ideas of which G. K. Chesterton said the world is full: Christian ideas gone mad. Their family is numerous but clearly recognizable: it is the family of divine goals that humans try to appropriate for their selfish benefit when they come to believe they have invented the goals themselves. The succession of metamorphoses of the City of God has no other meaning. It is the history of an obstinate effort to make a temporal city of this eternal city, by substituting for faith any conceivable natural bond as the unifying force of this society.

Does it follow that the Church works against the City of Men? Quite the opposite. Those who work against the City of Men are the ones who make its concept contradictory and its birth impossible by encouraging it to take itself as a substitute for the Church. Gradually, everything has to be put to work to build it, including the great spiritual forces whose very universality qualifies them for this task: science, art, law, and ethics. We cannot doubt that a human society of whatever type may be born at the end of their efforts, but it will be all the more worthy of the name of society insofar as it is better ordered toward the perfect society that it cannot be, and in view of which its own end is itself only a means. Christians are engaged as humans and citizens in the task of assuring their temporal cities' common good, but they find themselves charged as Christians with the still higher responsibility making Christianity inform the temporal order more generally, wherever they are and in all the areas in which it is given them to act. To use a centuries-old term, it is about these areas that we request the theologians to tell us whether it is suitable or not to designate them by the name of *Christendom*.

By whatever name this Christian people is designated, it is the same as what the *Letter to Diognetus* and *The City of God* already described as spread throughout the world in the manner in which the soul is everywhere co-present to the body it animates. It has no other being than that of the Church, and it can only expect it under the Church's guidance. Being outside time itself, the Church's truth can be expressed in a multitude of tongues and animate various temporal institutions that succeed each other in time and are spread about in space. That is why, even if this Christian people changes its appearance in the course of the centuries, because it inhabits different temporalities successively, it remains one in time, as it is one in space, because it lives off the one unchanging life of the Church.

This part of the City of God, sojourning in time, is also the leaven of the temporal city that seeks to be born, whose idea is the Heavenly City. Outside the Christian people, and in some manner on its fringe, which is its area of irradiation and influence, we find the temporal society that has not yet been born of the Word and of the spirit, but that the mere presence of the Church slowly summons and persuades to reform itself in her image. Thus, a kind of diffuse civilization is born around the Church, observable in the course of history. If we may speak in these terms, it constitutes the pagan civilization's catechumenate for the title of Christian civilization. Also, by the Christian elements it already has, even if it fights against them or ignores them, it is the hope and preparation of a temporal society that must appeal to a principle that transcends humans in order to unite all humans. That is nothing other than God known by faith. The Christian believes in the City of God, and the very hope he has of it is a certainty. Human beings have the right to hope in the Human City, but this hope is not a certainty. The only thing that the historian could do to help them is to place before their eyes, along with the genuine object of their hope, the cause of their repeated failures to make it a reality, and the means at their disposition to succeed in that. What the historian cannot do is to make humans want what they need to want in order to attain the end they themselves desire. We cannot even know if they will ever want it. When the historian judges by the past, as is naturally his tendency, he rather feels some uneasiness, but whatever must be the temporal future of humans, one thing at least is sure. If the earth's temporal unity is possible, it will not be enough that humans should fervently desire their city in order for that city to arrive at last, along with the earthly peace that they await from it. Its birth is not necessary, and in any case it will not take place sooner or later, depending on what they do or do not do. If it does come, it will be their work. Tomorrow, in a century, or in ten centuries, perhaps humans will still say that the means proposed to them is unacceptable, but then as now that will only be another way for them to say that they do not genuinely want the end. The end is what commands. The City of Man can only be built in the shadow of the cross, as a suburb of the City of God.

SELECTED BIBLIOGRAPHY

Translator's note: I have compiled this bibliography from Gilson's notes. Included in square brackets are some subsequent editions of books, cited to facilitate further study, as well as full citation information where this was missing from Gilson's text.

Amabali, Luigi. *Fra Tommaso Campanella, la sua congiura, i suoi processi e la sua pazzia*. 3 vols. Naples: Morano, 1882; reprinted in New York: Burt Franklin, 1971.

Ambrose. *De Fide, De Incarnatione, and Epistolae*. In Patrologiae Cursus Completus: Series Latina, ed Migne, 16.

Aquinas, Thomas. *De Regimine Principum*. [*De Regno sive De Regimine Principum ad Regem Cypri*, in *Opuscula Omnia nec non Opera Minora*, vol. 1: *Opuscula Philosophica*. Paris: Lethielleux, 1949.]

———. *In Decem Libros Ethicorum Aristotelis ad Nichomachum Expositio*. [Edited by Angelo M. Pirotta, OP. Turin: Marietti, 1934.]

———. *In II Sententiarum*. [*Scriptum super Libros Sententiarum Magistri Petri Lombardi*. Edited by Pierre Mandonnet, OP. Paris, Lethielleux, 1929.]

———. *Summa contra Gentiles*. [Turin: Marietti, 1927.]

———. *Summa Theologica*. [Turin: Marietti, 1891.]

Aristotle. *Politics*. [In *The Complete Works of Aristotle*, edited by Jonathan Barnes. 2 vols. Princeton, N.J.: Princeton University Press, 1984.]

Augustine. *De Civitate Dei*. In Patrologiae Cursus Completus: Series Latina, ed. Migne, 41. [Translated by William Babcock as *City of God*. 2 vols. Hyde Park, N.Y.: New City Press, 2012–13.]

———. *De Genesi ad Litteram* and *De Vera Religione*. In Patrologiae Cursus Completus: Series Latina, ed. Migne, 34.

———. *Ennarationes in Psalmos*. In Patrologiae Cursus Completus: Series Latina, ed. Migne, 36–37. [A selection of Augustine's commentaries on the psalms is found in Nicene and Post-Nicene Fathers, series 1, ed. Schaff, vol. 8.]

———. Letter 136 and Letter 138. In Patrologiae Cursus Completus: Series Latina, ed. Migne, 33. [In Nicene and Post-Nicene Fathers, series 1, ed. Schaff, vol. 1.]

———. *Retractationes*. In Patrologiae Cursus Completus: Series Latina, ed. Migne, 32.

Bacon, Roger. *Compendium Philosophiae*. In *Opera Quaedam Hactenus Ineditata*, edited by John Sherrin Brewer. London: Longman, Green, Longman and Roberts, 1859.

———. *Opus Majus*. Edited by John Henry Bridges. Oxford: Clarendon Press, 1897.

———. *Opus Tertium*. In *Opera Quaedam Hactenus Inedita*, edited by John Sherrin Brewer. London: Longman, Green, Longman and Roberts, 1859.

Barker, Ernest. *Church, State, and Study*. London, Methuen, 1930. [Reprinted in Westport, Conn.: Greenwood Press, 1974.]

———. *Greek Political Theory: Plato and His Predecessors*. London: Methuen, 1917.

Baruzi, Jean. *Leibniz et l'organisation religieuse de la terre*. Paris: F. Alcan, 1907.

Baynes, Norman. "Constantine the Great and the Christian Church." Raleigh Lecture. *Proceedings of the British Academy* 15 (1929).

Becker, Carl L. *The Heavenly City of the Eighteenth-Century Philosophers*. New Haven, Conn.: Yale University Press, 1932.

Bible. See *La Sainte Bible (version A. Crampon)*.

Blanchet, Léon. *Campanella*. Paris: F. Alcan, 1920. [Reprinted in New York: Burt Franklin, 1971; Whitefish, Mont.: Kessinger, 2010.]

Boehmer, Heinrich. *Kirche und Staat in England und in der Normandie im XI und XII Jahrhundert*. Leipzig: Dieterich, 1899.

Boissier, Gaston. *La fin du paganisme. Étude sur les dernières luttes religieuses en Occident au quatrième siècle*, vol. 2. Paris: Hachette, 1894. [Reprinted in New York: G. Olms, 1987.]

———. *La religion romaine d'Auguste aux Antonins*. Paris: Hachette, 1874.

Bohnenstadt, Elisabeth. "Kirche und Reich im Schrifttum des Nikolaus von Cues." In *Cusanus-Studien*, acts of the sessions of the Academy of Science, Philosophy and History section, XXX-1, Heidelberg, 1939.

Bonaventure. *Quaestiones Disputatae de Perfectione Evangelica*, vol. V in *Opera Omnia*. Quaracchi: Ex Typographia Colegii Sancti Bonaventurae, 1882–1902. [Translated into English as *Quaestiones Disputatae de Perfectione Evangelica* by Thomas Reist and Robert J. Karris. St. Bonaventure, N.Y.: Franciscan Institute Publications, 2008.]

Brooke, Zachary Nugent. *The English Church and the Papacy from the Conquest to the Reign of John*. Cambridge: Cambridge University Press, 1931.

Cadman, S. Parkes. *Christianity and the State*. New York: Macmillan, 1924.

Campanella, Tommaso, OP. *Atheismus Triumphatus, seu Reductio ad Religionem per Scientiarum Veritates*. Rome: Apud Haeredem Bartholomaei Zannetti, 1631.

———. *Città del Sole*. Critical edition with introduction and notes by Giuseppe Paladino. Naples, 1920.

———. *Civitas Solis, Poetica idea reipublicae philosophicae*. Utrecht, 1643.

———. *De Sensu Rerum et Magia*. 1637. [Also Frankfurt: Apud Egenolphum Emmelium, 1620.]

———. *Discorsi ai principi de Italia*. 1595. [See *Discurso ai principi d'Italia ed altri scritti filosofici*. Edited by Luigi Firpo. Turin: Chiantore, 1945.]

———. *Il governo ecclesiastico*. 1595.

———. *Monarchia di Spagna*. 1620. [See *De Monarchia Hispanica*. Amstelodami: Apud Ludovicum Elseverium, 1640.]

———. *Monarchia Messiae*. 1635.

———. *Monarchie delle nazioni*. Aesii: Apud Gregorium Arnazzinum, 1633.

———. *Quod Reminiscetur et Convertitur ad Dominum Universi Fines Terrae* (Psalm 21), vol. 1. Edited by Romanus Amerio. Padua: Cedam, 1939 (written 1615–18).

———. *Realis Philosophiae Epilogisticae Partes Quatuor* (includes *Civitas Solis, Appendix Politiae, Idea Reipublicae Philosophicae*). Frankfurt, 1623.

Carlyle, A. J. "St. Augustine and the City of God." In F. J. C. Hearnshaw, *The Social and Political Ideas of Some Great Medieval Thinkers*, 42–51. London: G. G. Harraph, 1923.

Carlyle, Robert Warrand, and Alexander James Carlyle. *History of Medieval Political Theory in the West*. London: W. Blackwood and Sons, 1903. [New York: Barnes and Noble, 1964.]

Carton, Raoul. *L'Expérience mystique de l'illumination intérieure chez Roger Bacon*. Paris: J. Vrin, 1924.

Carusi, Enrico. "Nuovi documenti sui processi di Tommasso Campanella." In *Giornale critico della filosofia italiana* VIII (1927), fasc. 5, doc. 72, of May 22, 1621.

Causse, Antonin. *Israel et la vision de l'humanité*. Strasbourg: Librairie Istra, 1924.

Cicero. *Pro Quinto Ligurio*. [*Pro Milone*. Translated by N. H. Watts. Loeb Classical Library 252. Cambridge, Mass.: Harvard University Press, 1979.]

Combès, Gustave. *La doctrine politique de saint Augustin*. Paris: Plon, 1927.

Comte, Auguste. *Auguste Comte méconnu, Auguste Comte conservateur*. Extract from his last work, 1851–57. Paris: LeSoudier, 1898. [*Appel aux conservateurs*, Paris: V. Dalmont, 1855.]

———. *Catéchisme positiviste, ou sommaire exposition de la religion universelle*. Apostolic edition of the Positivist Apostolate. Paris, 1891. [First edition, Paris: Chez l'auteur, 1852; second edition, Paris: Leroux, 1874. *Positivist Catechism*, translated by Richard Congreve. London, J. Chapman, 1858; third edition, London: Kegan Paul, Trench, Trübner, 1891.]

———. *Système de politique positive*. 4 vols. Vol. 1, Paris: L. Matthias, Carilian-

Goeury, Victor Dalmont, 1851; vols. 2–4, Paris: Carilian-Goeury and Victor Dalmont, 1852–54. [*System of Positive Polity*. London, Longmans, Green, 1875–77; vol. 1, translated by John Henry Bridges; vol. 2, translated by Frederic Harrison; vol. 3, translated by Edward Spencer Beesly et al.; vol. 4, translated by Richard Congreve.]

Cruce, Emeric. *Le nouveau Cynée ou Discours des occasiones et moyens d'establir une paix génèrale & la liberté du commerce par tout le monde*. Paris: Jacques Villery, 1623. [*The New Cyneas of Emeric Cruce*. Translated by Thomas Willing Balch. Philadelphia: Allen, Lane, and Scott, 1909.]

Dante Alighieri. *De Monarchia*. Text of Edward Moore, edited by William Henry Vincent Reade. Oxford: Clarendon Press, 1916. [I have quoted from the translation of Aurelia Henry, *The De Monarchia of Dante Alighieri*. Boston/Cambridge: Houghton Mifflin/Riverside Press, 1904.]

Dawson, Christopher. *The Making of Europe*. London: Macmillan, 1932.

Delbos, Victor. *La philosophie pratique de Kant*. Paris: F. Alcan, 1905.

Drouet, Joseph. *L'abbé de Saint-Pierre.* Paris: Champion, 1912.

Duhem, Pierre. *Un fragment inédit de l'Opus Tertium*. Quaracchi: Ex Typographia Collegii S. Bonaventurae, 1909.

Foucher de Careil, Louis-Alexandre. *Oeuvres de Leibniz, publiées pour la première fois d'après les manuscrits originaux*. 7 vols. Paris, 1859–75. See especially *Observation sur le Projet d'une Paix Perpétuelle de M. L'abbé de Sainte-Pierre.*

Fustel de Coulanges, Numa Denis. *La Cité Antique.* Twenty-eighth edition. Paris: Hachette, 1924.

Gandillac, Maurice de. *La philosophie de Nicolas de Cues*. Paris: Aubier-Montaigne, 1941.

———. "Preface." In Nicholas of Cusa, *Oeuvres choisies de Nicolas de Cues*. Paris: Aubier-Montaigne, 1942.

Gerard of Rouen, Bishop (attributed). *De Consecratione Pontificum et Regum.* In *Libelli de Lite*, 3:663. [*Libelli de Lite Imperatorum et Pontificum Saeculis XI et XII Conscripti*. Monumenta Germaniae Historica. 3 vols. Hanover: Impensis Bibliopoli Hahniani, 1891–97.]

Gilson, Étienne. *Dante et la philosophie*. Paris: J. Vrin, 1939. [*Dante the Philosopher*. Translated by David Moore. New York: Sheed and Ward, 1949. Reissued as *Dante and Philosophy*. New York: Harper and Row, 1963; reprinted in Gloucester, Mass.: P. Smith, 1968.]

———. *L'esprit de la philosophie médiévale*. Paris: J. Vrin, 1932 [*The Spirit of Medieval Philosophy*. Translated by A. C. H. Downes. London: Sheed and Ward, 1936.]

Gouhier, Henri. *La Jeunesse d'Auguste Comte*. 3 vols. Paris: J. Vrin, 1933, 1936, 1941.

Goumy, Édouard. *Étude sur la vie et les écrits de l'Abbé de Saint-Pierre*. Paris: Hachette, 1859.

Grua, Gaston. *Gottfried Wilhelm Freiherr von Leibniz. Textes inédits*. Paris: Presses Universitaires de France, 1948. [Reprinted in New York: Garland, 1985.]

Harnack, Adolf von. *Mission und Ausbreitung des Christentums*. Third edition. Leipzig: J. C. Hinrichs, 1915.

Haubst, Rudolf. "Johannes von Segovia im Gespräch mit Nikolaus von Kues und Jean Germain über die Göttliche Dreieinigkeit und ihre Verkündigung vor den Mohammedanern." *Münchener Theologisches Zeitschrift* 2 (1951): 115–29.

Kant, Immanuel. *Projet de paix perpétuelle*. Translated by Jean Gibelin. Paris: J. Vrin, 1948. [*Perpetual Peace and Other Essays on Politics, History, and Morals*. Edited by Ted Humphries. Indianapolis, Ind.: Hackett, 1982.]

Labriolle, Pierre de. *La réaction paiênne. Essai sur la polémique antichrétienne du Ier au VIe siècle*. Paris: L'artisan du livre, 1934.

La Sainte Bible (version A. Crampon). Edited and revised by members of the Society of Jesus with the cooperation of professors of Saint Sulpice. Paris: Desclé, 1905; Rome: Tournai, 1939.

Leclercq, Henri. "Église et État." In *Dictionnaire d'archéologie et de liturgie*, edited by Fernand Cabrol and Henri Leclercq, 10:2255–2556. Paris: Delouzey et Ané, 1907–53.

Leibniz, Gottfried Wilhelm. *Die philosophische Schriften von G. W. Leibniz*. Edited by Carl Immanuel Gerhardt. 7 vols. Berlin: Weidman, 1875–90. [A partial reproduction in book form is *Philosophische Schriften / Gottfried Wilhelm Leibniz*, Frankfurt am Main: Suhrkamp, 1996.]

Les Français à la Recherche d'une Société des Nations. Paris: Bibliothèque de la Civilisation française, 1920.

Lods, Adolphe. *Israël des origines au milieu du VIIIe siècle*. Paris: Renaissance du livre, 1932. [Reprinted in Paris: A. Michel, 1969. See *Israel from Its Beginnings to the Middle of the Eighth Century*. Translated by S. H. Hooke. London: Routledge and Kegan Paul, 1948.]

Marcus Aurelius. *Meditations*. [*Marcus Aurelius and His Times*. New York: Walter J. Black, 1945.]

Mesnard, Pierre. *L'essor de la philosophie politique au XVIe siècle*. Paris: Boivin, 1936.

Mommsen, Theodore. "St. Augustine and the Christian Idea of Progress." *Journal of the History of Ideas* 12 (1951): 346–74.

Nicholas of Cusa. *De Concordantia Catholica*. 1433. [In *Opera Omnia*. Leipzig: F. Meiner, 1932.]

———. *De Docta Ignorantia*. [*On Learned Ignorance*. In *Complete Philosophical and Theological Treatises of Nicholas of Cusa*, translated by Jasper Hospers. Minneapolis, Minn.: A. J. Banning Press, 2001.]

———. *De Pace Fidei*. 1454.

Nourisson, Jean Félix. *La philosophie de Saint Augustin*. Paris: Didier, 1869.

Piganiol, André. *Essai sur les origines de Rome.* Paris: E. de Boccard, 1917.

Plutarch. *De Alexandri Magni Fortuna sive Virtute*. In *Plutarchi Caeronensis Scripta Moralia Graece et Latine*, edited by Jean-Frédéric Dübner. Paris: Firmin-Didot, 1839–41.

Postel, Guillaume. *Alcorani seu Legis Mahometi et Evangelistarum Concordiae Liber.* 1543.

———. *Cosmographiae Disciplinae Compendium*. Basel, 1561.

———. *Les très merveilleuses victories des femmes du Nouveau Monde et comme elles doivent à tout le monde par raison commander et meme à ceux qui auront la monarchie du monde civile*. 1553.

———. *Quatuor Librorum de Orbis Terrae Concordia Primus*. Basel, 1544.

Prudentius. *Contra Symmachum II.* [*Contra Orationem Symmachi*. Translated by H. J. Thompson. Loeb Classical Library 398. Cambridge, Mass.: Harvard University Press, 1979.]

Rolbiecki, John Joseph. *The Political Philosophy of Dante Alighieri*. Washington, D.C.: The Catholic University of America Press, 1921.

Rousseau, Jean-Jacques. *Émile*. In *Oeuvres*, vol. 5.

———. *Extract du projet pour de paix de monsieur l'abbé de Saint-Pierre*. In *Oeuvres*, 6:397–439. [*A Lasting Peace through the Federation of Europe*. New York: Herman and Stephens, 1955.]

———. "Judgement sur la Polysynodie." In *Oeuvres*, 6:440–55.

———. *Oeuvres complètes de J. J. Rousseau*. Paris: Baudouin, 1826.

Rupp, Jean. *L'idée de chrétienté dans la pensée pontificale des origines à Innocent III*. Paris: Les Presses Modernes, 1939.

Russell, Bertrand. *A Critical Exposition of the Philosophy of Leibniz*. Second edition. London: George Allen and Unwin, 1937.

Saint-Pierre, l'Abbé de (Charles-Irénée de Castel de Saint-Pierre). *Discours sur la polysynodie*. London (really Paris): Jacob Tonsson, 1718.

———. *Mémoire pour rendre la paix perpetuelle en Europe*. Cologne: Jaques [sic] la Pacifique, 1712.

———. *Mémoire sur la réparation des chemins*. Paris, 1708. Reedited as *Mémoire sur la police des chemins*, 1715.

———. *Projet pour rendre la paix perpétuelle en Europe*. 2 vols. Utrecht: Schouten, 1713.

Saint-Simon, Count of (Claude Henri de Rouvroy). *De la réorganisation de la société européenne ou de la necessité et des moyens de rassembler les peuples de l'Europe en un seul corps politique en conservant à chacun son indépendance nationale*. In *Oeuvres choisies*, vol. 2. [Paris: A. Egron, 1814.]

———. *Introduction aux travaux scientifiques du dix-neuvième siècle*. In *Oeuvres choisies*, vol. 1. [Paris: J. L. Scherff, 1807.]

———. *Le nouveau Christianisme, dialogue entre un conservateur et un novateur*. In *Oeuvres choisies*, vol. 3. [Paris: Bossange père, 1825.]

———. *Lettres d'un habitant de Genève à ses contemporains*. In *Oeuvres choisies*, vol. 1. [*Lettres* reprinted in Paris: Félix Alcan, 1925.]

———. *Oeuvres choisies*. 3 vols. Brussels: Fr. Van Meenen, 1859. [Reprinted in New York: Olms, 1973.]

———. *Travail sur la gravitation universelle*. In *Oeuvres choisies*, vol. 2. [Paris, 1813.]

Sallust. *Catalina*. [*The War with Cataline*. Translated by J. C. Folfe. Loeb Classical Library 116. Cambridge, Mass.: Harvard University Press, 2013.]

Scharpff, Franz Anton. *Des Cardinals und Bischofs Nicholaus von Cusa wichtigste Schriften*. Freiburg im Briesgau: Herder, 1862.

Schilling, Otto. *Die Staats- und Soziallehre des hl. Augustinus*. Freiburg im Breisgau: Herder, 1910.

Scholz, Heinrich. *Glaube und Unglaube in der Weltgeschichte. Ein Kommentar zu Augustinus' De Civitate Dei, mit einem Exkurs: Fruitio Dei, ein Beitrag zur Geschichte der Theologie in der Mystik*. Leipzig: J. C. Hinrichs, 1911.

Seneca. *Ad Marciam*, *De Tranquillitate Animi*, and *Consolatio ad Helviam Matrem*. [In *Moral Essays*, vol. 2, translated by John W. Basore. Loeb Classical Library 254. Cambridge, Mass.: Harvard University Press, 1965.]

Strabo. *Strabonis Geographica: Graece cum versione refecta*. Edited by C. Müller and F. Dübner. Paris: Firmin Didot, 1853.

Sully, Duke of (Maximilien de Béthune). *Mémoires de sages et royalles oeconomies d'Estat domestiques, politiques et militares de Henry le Grand*. Amstelredam (Rouen): A. de Clearetimelee et G. de Pistariste, 1649. [*Memoires of the Duke of Sully*. Revised edition. London: H. G. Bain, 1856.]

Tarn, W. W. "Alexander and the Unity of Mankind." *Proceedings of the British Academy* 19, n.d.; published separately in London: Milford, 1933.

Tertullian. *Apologeticum*. [In *Minucius Felix*, translated by T. R. Glover. Loeb Classical Library 250. Cambridge, Mass.: Harvard University Press, 1940.]

Toland, John. *Christianity not Mysterious*. London: 1696; reproduced New York, Garland, 1978.

Ueberweg, Friedrich. *Grundriss der Geschichte der Philosophie*, vol. 3. Twelfth edition. Berlin: Verlag E. S. Mittler und Sohn, 1924. [Basel: B. Schwabe, 1983.]

Vansteenberge, Edmond. *Le cardinal Nicolas de Cues (1401–1465). L'action, la pensée*. Paris: H. Champion, 1920. [Reprinted in Frankfurt: Minerva GmbH, 1963; Geneva: Statkine Reprints, 1974.]

Wilamowitz-Möllendorf, Ulrich von, and B. Niese. *Staat und Gesellschaft der Griechen und Römer*. Berlin: B. G. Teubner, 1910.

INDEX OF NAMES

GENERAL INDEX